RADICAL ARTIFICE

RADICAL ARTIFICE

Writing Poetry in the Age of Media

Marjorie Perloff

The University of Chicago Press · Chicago and London

Marjorie Perloff, the Sadie Dernham Patek Professor of Humanities at Stanford University, is the author of seven books, including *The Futurist Moment: Avant-Garde, Avant Guerre, and the Language of Rupture*, also published by the University of Chicago Press.

The University of Chicago Press, Chicago 60637
The University of Chicago Press, Ltd., London
© 1991 by The University of Chicago
All rights reserved. Published 1991
Printed in the United States of America

00 99 98 97 96 95 94 93 92 91   5 4 3 2 1

ISBN 0-226-65733-7 (cloth)

Library of Congress Cataloging-in-Publication Data

Perloff, Marjorie.
    Radical artifice : writing poetry in the age of media / Marjorie Perloff.
        p.   cm.
    Includes bibliographical references and index.
    1. American poetry—20th century—History and criticism—Theory, etc.   2. Experimental poetry, American—History and criticism.   3. Mass media and literature—United States. 4. Avant-garde (Aesthetics)—United States.   5. Experimental poetry—Authorship.   6. Radicalism in literature.   7. Poetics.   I. Title.
PS325.P38   1991
811'.5409—dc20   91-14057

For Alexandra Perloff-Giles

Contents

Illustrations

Spring Quarter 1988. In my English 362 graduate seminar on the inter-
face of postmodern poetry and theory (Poetheory or Theorypo for short),
the students were reading John Cage, Robert Smithson, Roland Barthes's
Empire of Signs, Charles Bernstein's *Content's Dream*, Susan Howe's *My
Emily Dickinson*, Jacques Derrida's *Postcard*, Steve McCaffery's *North
of Intention* and *Panopticon*, Lyn Hejinian's *Writing Is an Aid to Mem-
ory*. The texts discussed sometimes seemed hopelessly opaque, and one
day a student who had recently come to the United States from Yugo-
slavia asked in exasperation, "Why can't they write like Kafka?"

Why, indeed? What the student meant, of course, was that Kafka, no
matter how difficult his meanings, how subtle his network of refer-
ences, how ambiguous his tone, wrote prose whose syntax is perfectly
lucid. "Someone must have been telling lies about Joseph K., for with-
out having done anything wrong he was arrested one fine morning."
Whatever mysteries and complexities are contained in that opening
sentence of *The Trial*, there is no doubt that the subject of the passive
verb construction "was arrested" is the pronoun "he" or that the adjec-
tive "fine" modifies the noun "morning." But what do we do with this
sentence from Diane Ward's "Never without One": "Dark windows in
which a list followed by facts in us erupt chilling comparing"? The
words are familiar enough, even ordinary, but what goes with what
and why?

Our first response to such "sentences," especially when there is a
whole paragraph or page of them, is that we are the victims of some
kind of scam. There are, so the common wisdom goes, a bunch of man-
darin poets around (from the Objectivists and Concrete poets to the so-
called Language school, with the well-known figure of John Ashbery
squarely at the center) who have some sort of murky relationship to
Deconstruction and write meaningless and pretentious trash that they
pass off as literature. Or to put it less pejoratively, the demand for a
natural or *transparent* poetry (Pound's famous "direct treatment of the
thing"), a demand that was the cornerstone of modernism, has given
way, for reasons unclear, to the *artifice* one associates, not with a robust
modernism, but with the nineteenth-century fin-de-siècle. For reasons
unclear, a significant body of poetry (or what claims to be poetry) has
been produced that is unnaturally *difficult*—eccentric in its syntax, ob-
scure in its language, and mathematical rather than musical in its form.

Why can't they write like Kafka? Or at least like Robert Lowell or, in

our own time, Seamus Heaney? Perhaps, what I shall call here the po-
etry of *radical artifice* will just disappear. Perhaps, but in the mean-
time, it keeps turning up like a virus: in England, in the work of Tom
Raworth, Jeremy Prynne, and Allen Fisher; in France, in the *Oulipo*
group around Georges Perec and among such related poet-intellectuals
as Emmanuel Hocquard, Claude Royet-Journaud, Jacques Roubaud,
and Anne-Marie Albiach; in the Soviet Union, in the "conceptual"
poetry of Arkadii Dragomoschenko, Alexei Parshchikov, and Dmitry
Prigov; in Spain, in the publications of the Zasterle Press and journals
like *Pagina;* and, perhaps most interestingly, in Canada, where the
Concrete poetry movement of the fifties and sixties and the emergence
of sound-text poetry and performance work have generated, often with-
out direct connection to its U.S. counterparts, the very rich and vital
experimentalism in evidence in such journals as *Raddle Moon, Writ-
ing, Rampike,* and *Tessera.* And there are parallels in such Australian
publications as *Scripsi* and *Meanjin.* If the turn away from the "natural
look" is some sort of academic plot (Derrideans/Foucaultians and Lan-
guage poets unite!), it certainly has an odd international base.

Why, in any case, the rapprochement between poetry and theory?
Perhaps it is time to drop the labels and consider what it is that is hap-
pening to poetic writing in the late twentieth century. The central
fact—and this is why the situation in Australia or Spain or, for that
matter, in Japan is so similar to our own—is that we now live in an
electronic culture. This is, of course, a truism but we have yet to under-
stand the interplay between lyric poetry, generally regarded as the most
conservative, the most intransigent of the "high" arts, and the elec-
tronic media.

Postmodernism, we are regularly told, represents the breakdown of
the paradigm of the "great divide" (Andreas Huyssen's term) between
high art and mass culture, a paradigm that modernist critics, for ex-
ample those of the Frankfurt school, had accepted as axiomatic. No
longer, in the words of Rosalind Krauss, do we accept the "sublimation
model," according to which "the function of art is to sublimate or trans-
form experience, raising it from ordinary to extraordinary, from com-
monplace to unique, from low to high; with the special genius of the
artist being that he or she has the gifts to perform this function" (*Oc-
tober* 56 [Spring 1991]: 3).

But alternate models have generally proved more effective in dealing
with popular culture than with work that makes claims to being "art."
The new Madonna film, the TV sitcom, the deodorant ad, the graffiti—
these are now being scrutinized with a care once lavished on the poetry
of Donne or the fiction of Flaubert. But the small-press poetry collec-

tion, the artist's book, the video-poem, the "new music" composition—despite all the talk of "desublimation" models and high/low crossovers, these forms continue to elude us. Jasper Johns's encaustic paintings of the American flag, for example, obviously have some relation to color photographs of the "real" flag, fluttering in the breeze on suburban flag-poles, but the difference between the two is finally more striking than their similarity and we call the former, not the latter, "art."

What I want to suggest here is that, even as the "great divide" between "high" and "low" breaks down, the discourses of art and the mass media are not merely exchangeable; rather, theirs is a relationship of enormous variation and complexity. Even Krauss, in the passage cited, is interested in "retaining the notion of an interface between art and mass culture as the issue in question, and thus is not completely dissolving the category of art altogether" (5). At the same time—and this remains the more common tendency, at least so far as poetry is concerned—we must avoid the impasse of the Englit or Creative Writing classroom, where the literary text too often continues to be treated as an object detachable from its context, as if a "poem" could exist in the United States today that has not been shaped by the electronic culture that has produced it. There is today no landscape uncontaminated by sound bytes or computer blips, no mountain peak or lonely valley beyond the reach of the cellular phone and the microcassette player. Increasingly, then, the poet's arena is the electronic world—the world of the *Donahue Show* and MTV, of *People* magazine and the *National Enquirer*, of Internet and MCI mail relayed around the world by modem, as in the case of the new journal ⟨*Postmodern Culture*⟩, which publishes fiction, literary and cultural criticism via electronic mail.

Kafka, as I told my Yugoslavian student in what was of course a preliminary and flip answer to her very good question, didn't have television. In this book I want to examine the poetic experiments of those who do, beginning with the figure of an older poet who is not usually considered a poet at all but a composer, a performance artist, a conceptual artist, an inventor—a polymath, let us say, who, as he approaches his eightieth birthday, is almost as controversial as he was forty years ago. That poet is John Cage and this book is written, so to speak, under his sign even though his work is discussed only intermittently. The importance of Cage for postmodern poetics cannot be overestimated, for it was Cage who understood, at least as early as the fifties, that from now on poetry would have to position itself, not vis-à-vis the landscape or the city or this or that political event, but in relation to the media that, like it or not, occupy an increasingly large part of our verbal, visual, and acoustic space.

"Poetry," said Wallace Stevens, "is the scholar's art." Precisely be-
cause poetry seems on the face of it the most remote of the various liter-
ary genres that we read "against" media discourse, it should be an
interesting test case of what Cage has defined as the aesthetic of "inter-
penetration and nonobstruction," the "situation of decentering" where
"each thing is at the center." Asked by an interviewer how he tolerates
the incessant traffic noise below his fourth-floor window in lower Man-
hattan, Cage responded, "At first I thought I couldn't sleep through it.
Then I found a way of transposing the sounds into images so that they
entered into my dreams without waking me up." Of such transpositions,
we might say, the poetry of late twentieth-century America is made.

Acknowledgments

Chapters 1–4 of *Radical Artifice* were delivered in March 1990 as the Ward-Phillips Lectures at Notre Dame University. I owe a great debt to the members of the Notre Dame English Department who provided me, not only with superb hospitality, during a week's stay, but also with very useful feedback: let me single out Jacqueline Brogan, Joseph Buttigieg, Steven Fredman, and John Matthias, and, for negative criticism that put me on my mettle, Jim Collins. My greatest Notre Dame debt is to Gerald Bruns, whose intellectual rigor, theoretical brilliance, and understanding of poetry have been an inspiration to me for years.

I have also learned a great deal from colleagues at other universities that provided lecture invitations as well as constructive criticism: in particular, Neil Schmitz, Robert Creeley, and Robert Bertholf at SUNY-Buffalo, Alan Golding at the University of Louisville, Nina Auerbach, Stuart Curran, James Engel, and Alan Filreis at the University of Pennsylvania, Nancy Leonard and Lawrence Kramer at Bard College, Jessica Prinz at Ohio State University, Cheryl Lester and Janet Sharistanian at the University of Kansas, Stanley Stewart at the University of California-Riverside, W. J. T. Mitchell, Marie-Florine Bruneau, and Charles Krance at the University of Chicago, Renée Hubert at the University of California-Irvine, the poets Robert Gluck, Michael Davidson, Kathleen Fraser, Michael Palmer, and Steven Ratcliff at the San Francisco Poetry Center, where chapter 3 was delivered as the annual George Oppen Memorial Lecture in 1989.

Other debts are more personal. Charles Altieri, Charles Bernstein, Ronald Bush, Ulla Dydo, Fred Garber, Albert Gelpi, Daniel Herwitz, Susan Howe, Hank Lazer, Herbert Lindenberger, Karen MacCormack, Steve McCaffery, William McPheron, Douglas Messerli, Jann Pasler, Peter Quartermain, Claude Rawson, and Gregory Ulmer have read portions of the manuscript or discussed its issues with me. Martha Banta drew on her extensive knowledge of advertising and popular culture to help me locate materials for chapters 3 and 4. A special debt goes to Jerome McGann, Cary Nelson, Joan Retallack, and Robert von Hallberg for their very careful readings of the entire manuscript, at various stages, and their invaluable suggestions for change. But perhaps I learned the most from my very argumentative and skeptical Stanford graduate seminar, Thé Theory of Poetry / The Poetry of Theory, conducted in the spring of 1988.

Short portions of the following chapters, usually in quite different form, have been published, elsewhere: The section on Steve McCaffery's "Lag" in chapter 4, in *Contemporary Poetry Meets Modern Theory*, ed. Anthony Easthope and John Thompson (New York: Simon & Schuster; Brighton: Harvester, 1991); the section on John Cage's *Roaratorio* in chapter 5, in *Postmodern Genres*, ed. Marjorie Perloff (Norman: University of Oklahoma Press, 1989); the section on Lyn Hejinian's *My Life* in chapter 5 in *Denver Quarterly* 25, no. 4 (Spring 1991); a short version of the section on John Ashbery's "Business Personals" in chapter 6, in *Verse* 8, no. 1 (Spring 1991); the section on John Cage's *I–VI* in chapter 7, in *Parnassus* 16, no. 2 (1991). I am grateful to the editors of these books and journals for their early support and advice.

My editor at Chicago, Alan Thomas, with whom I was also fortunate to work on *The Futurist Moment*, is not just a fine editor: he is a superb and often sardonic reader, who won't let the author get away with anything. I am also grateful to have once again had the help of Jean Eckenfels with the manuscript.

As always, my family has participated actively in the project. I have drawn on Nancy Perloff's expertise in twentieth-century art and music movements and Carey Perloff's knowledge of the period's theatrical language, particularly that of Beckett and Pinter. Most of the reproductions in this book were made at the UCLA Medical Center photography lab, thanks to my husband, Joseph Perloff, who incidentally also tried to teach me about chaos theory.

This book is dedicated to my granddaughter Alexandra Perloff-Giles, who won't read it, at least not in the near future since she just celebrated her first birthday, but who will grow up to recognize the "new" textual world here described as quite simply the norm.

Stanford and Pacific Palisades, 1990

Marjorie Perloff

1   *Avant-Garde or Endgame?*

There is constant surprise at the new tricks language plays on us when we get
into a new field.
—Wittgenstein, *Lectures and Conversations* (1938) [1]

CompuServe—the electronic information service that allows anyone
who owns a computer with a modem and the requisite software to be-
come a member, thus gaining access to a Garden of Earthly Delights
that includes the Associated Press wire service, Standard & Poor's, a
shopping mall where one can buy Godiva chocolates, Crabtree & Eve-
lyn soaps, or Brooks Brothers suits, and the EAASY SABRE desk, which
provides flight information and makes airline reservations—has a
monthly magazine with feature articles like "Designs on Success,"
"New Vendors Flock to Forums," and "Fly the Frugal Skies." Lest *Compu-
Serve Magazine* be thought hopelessly crass, concerned with nothing
but consumerism, it also boasts a series of Credos, the first and most
important being the "Computing Services Credo," [2] which goes like this:

> For those who call out for advice,
> answers, even mere companionship,
> in a discomfiting computer world,
> we throw you the online rope that
> connects to the main. No man is
> an island unto himself. Herein the
> Control-G tolls for thee.

Here, lineated as a poem, with justified left and right margins and the
foreshortened last line centered below, is a rather remarkable variant of
a text most of us know, at least in part, not so much from its source,
John Donne's *Devotions upon Emergent Occasions* (1624), but proba-
bly from Ernest Hemingway's *For Whom the Bell Tolls* (the movie ver-
sion of which stars Gary Cooper and Ingrid Bergman), or, if not from
Hemingway, from the countless novels, TV shows, greeting cards, and
newspaper articles, in which the phrases "no man is an island," and
"for whom the bell tolls" are regularly recycled with portentous
urgency. What Donne actually wrote was this:

> No man is an *Iland*, intire of it selfe; every man is a peece of the *Conti-
> nent*, a part of the *maine*; if a *Clod* bee washed away by the *Sea*, *Europe*
> is the lesse, as well as if a *Promontorie* were, as well as if a *Mannor* of
> thy *friends* or of *thine owne* were; any mans *death* diminishes *me*, be-

1

cause I am involved in *Mankinde;* and therefore never send to know for
whom the *bell* tolls; It tolls for *thee*.[3]

"Every man is a peece of the *Continent*": in Computing Services Credo
terms, this means that in a "discomfiting computer world," all of us can
now hook into "the *maine*," that is, "the main" CompuServe center by
using a computer code or an 800 number, a number which has neatly
replaced the "*Mannor* of thy *friends*" as a source of "companionship."
In this strange new computer world, to be "involved in *Mankinde*"
means, not that one participates in the joys and griefs of others and in-
volves oneself in their lives (and hence deaths), but that one belongs to
the right program network, so that, in times of trouble, one can be
thrown "the online rope." Hence "No man is an island unto himself"
(note the pronoun shift from the original), not because Death is the
great leveler, but, on the contrary, because life, if we can call it that, is
available at the mere touch of the Control-G button, whence comes the
"advice" and "companionship" of a message on the computer screen. A
lifeline in the form of an "online rope," appropriately designated as a
"Control."

If *CompuServe Magazine* serves up bits and pieces of garbled John
Donne, our own poets and artists are now responding, consciously or
not, to these media messages—whether on video or FAX or in the print
media—which, try as we may to avoid them, now permeate our verbal
as well as our visual and acoustic space. As I write this, for example, I
am wondering whether to check the INBOX of my modem MCI-Mail sys-
tem to see if there are any messages from the editors of ⟨*Postmodern
Culture*⟩, the new electronic "international and interdisciplinary forum
for discussions of contemporary literature, theory, and culture," pub-
lished at North Carolina State University, on whose editorial board I
serve.[4] If there is such a message in the INBOX, I can then respond by
typing "pmc@ncsuvm.ncsu.edu," and use the CREATE command to
make my own message, which will be instantly relayed to North Caro-
lina, three thousand miles away from Los Angeles, where I live, as well
as three hours later. The ease and convenience of such speedy commu-
nication is breathtaking, and yet there is something quite terrifying
about electronic mail, whose appearance in standard screen format
makes even the telephone seem warm and sensuous, the repository of
what is, after all, a human voice, even if that voice is itself increasingly
pre-recorded, whether on the answering machine or in telephone adver-
tising campaigns.

The impact of electronic technology on our lives is now the object of
intense study, but what remains obscure is the role, if any, this technol-

ogy has in shaping the ostensibly private language of poetry. Current thinking is sharply divided on this question but few of the answers are optimistic. Perhaps the most common response to what has been called the digital revolution[5] has been simple rejection, the will, we might say, *not to change*, no matter how "different" the world out there seems to be. In recent years, for example, a movement has emerged that calls itself the New Formalism, or sometimes the New Narrative or Expansive poetry.[6] The main thrust of New Formalist poetics, as Frederick Feirstein and Frederick Turner explain in their Introduction to a collection of New Formalist manifestos, is to move "beyond the short free verse autobiographical lyric" of the present, returning poetry to meter (which is almost invariably equated with iambic pentameter) and narrative.[7] The "successful" narrative poem, writes Robert McDowell, should have "a beginning, a middle, and an end," its time frame should be "compressed," its characters should be "memorable" in being "consistent" ("an act must logically follow acts preceding it"), its locale specific and "identifiable," and its subject "compelling" (FF l05ʹ–6). E. A. Robinson, Robert Frost, Robinson Jeffers—these are New Formalist heroes, with the lofty Englit tradition (Milton to Wordsworth and Arnold) squarely behind these "robinets."

No doubt, the New Formalists do have a genuine grievance against the dominant lyric mode of the seventies and eighties, with its repetitive dwelling on delicate insight and "sensitive" response, its nostalgia for the "natural," and its excessive reliance on simulated speech and breath pause as determinants of line breaks and verse structure.[8] But the real issue is not whether to write in free verse or iambic pentameter, anymore than it is whether to foreground the lyric self or to have that self tell a "compelling" story. More properly put, the question would be: given the particular options (and nonoptions) of writing at the turn of the twenty-first century, what significant role can poetic language play? "The whole purpose of a lyric poem," writes Frederick Feirstein, "is to sing: to sing in a natural, not puffed up, way so that one can reach an audience" (FF xi). But what is a "natural" as opposed to a "puffed up" way of singing that will reach "an audience" accustomed to VCRs, FAX machines, Walkmans, laser printers, cellular phones, answering machines, computer games, and video terminals? And why should lyric be "natural" rather than artificial? Did Donne's lyric "sing" in a natural way? Or Pope's? What, for that matter, is natural about the heroic couplet or the Spenserian stanza? Or even Dickinson's four-line hymn stanza—is that natural?

"We . . . found we needed meter and sometimes rhyme," writes Feirstein, "to create the contrapuntal tensions in the verse that would match the tension in the action" (FF x). The norm here is by no means "natural," as Feirstein seems to think, but a specifically Romantic and Modernist one, coming down to us from Coleridge via I. A. Richards and Allen Tate. Indeed, despite their professed scorn for the dominant free-verse poetic of their immediate elders, the New Formalists, coming, as they do by and large, out of the very same writing programs and English departments, are given to statements like the following by Richard Moore: "It is now possible to become a Ph.D. in our literature and not have the foggiest notion of the few simple rules that Milton used in composing his lines" (FF 33). *Simple* rules? Milton, whose prosody is surely one of the most complex and difficult to characterize in English poetry? And in the same vein Dana Gioia asks, "Why . . . could a poet like Milton, an unquestioned master of the short, concentrated poem, also manage brilliant longer poems whereas our contemporaries cannot?" (FF 5). The answer, one might respond, is contained in the question, implying as it does that to "manage brilliant longer poems" is some sort of certifiable skill that poets "like Milton" (was there really any other poet like Milton?) have "mastered." Rather like the ability to fill out both the short and the long version of one's income tax form. Witness Gioia's own iambic pentameter:

> Turning the corner, we discovered it
> just as the old wrought-iron lamps went on—
> a quiet, tree-lined street, only one block long,
> resting between the noisy avenues. (FF 206)

It is hard to know what meter does for this prosaic account: the first two lines jog along, putting weight on syllables that require no foregrounding, whereas the third line, with its extra syllable and seven primary stresses, calls attention to the filler words "only one block long"—a bit of information which is largely redundant, the epiphany of light being exactly the same if the quiet and predictably tree-lined street were two blocks long.

Indeed—and this is one of the ironies of the current situation—a linguistic analysis would reveal that Dana Gioia's lineation is much closer to the model it purports to reject (say, the lyric of Richard Hugo) than it is to Wordsworth or Arnold or Frost. But this is not to say that the New Formalist critique of free verse is merely frivolous. What it tells us (and we will find surprisingly similar complaints lodged against standard free verse by the critique from the poetic left) is that the dominant modes of mid-century seem to be played out. Naked Poetry, Confessional Poetry, Open Form, Projective Verse—what could sound, in 1990, more tired? And the same holds true for comparable developments in the other arts: the happening, the body sculpture, the "live" performance piece in the white-walled art gallery, the *Learning from Las Vegas* slot-machine decor, and "ugly is beautiful" tract house which is really custom-built and costs millions—these paradoxically seem to belong to a time now more remote than the avant-garde of the 1910s and 1920s or, for that matter, more remote than the fin-de-siècle Vienna of Wittgenstein. What is it that has happened and where are we going? And what does our avant-garde—if that word still has meaning—look like?

I say "if" because the news that the avant-garde is dead is now widely circulated. In his influential *Theory of the Avant-Garde* (German edition, 1974; English translation, 1984), Peter Bürger defines the avant-garde as that specific movement in the early twentieth century which sought, not to develop, as had been the case in Impressionism or Cubism or Fauvism, a particular style, nor to attack prior schools of art, but to call into question the very role of "art" as an institution in a bourgeois society.[9] Whereas medieval and Renaissance art, so the argument goes, was subject to "collective performance" and "collective reception," the bourgeois art of the post-Enlightenment was largely produced by isolated individuals for other isolated individuals. Divorced from the "praxis of life," it became increasingly autonomous and elitist, culminating in the Aestheticism of the late nineteenth century. It is this autonomy, this institutionalization of capitalist art as "unassociated with the life praxis of men [*sic*]" that Dada and Surrealism challenged.[10]

When, for example—and this is Bürger's Exhibit A—Marcel Duchamp signs a mass-produced object (in this case an ordinary urinal) and sends it to an art exhibition bearing the title *Fountain by R. Mutt* (fig. 1.1), "he negates the category of individual production," thus mocking "all claims to individual creativity" (PB 51–52). And Bürger concludes:

> Duchamp's provocation not only unmasks the art market where the signature means more than the quality of the work; it radically questions the very principle of art in bourgeois society according to which the individual is considered the creator of the work of art. Duchamp's Ready-Mades are not works of art but manifestations. Not from the form-content totality of the individual object Duchamp signs can one infer the meaning, but only from the contrast between mass-produced object on the one hand and signature and art exhibit on the other. It is obvious that this kind of provocation cannot be repeated indefinitely. The provocation depends on what it turns against. (PB 52)

This analysis, which has been widely accepted,[11] raises some hard questions. First, it implies that Duchamp might have made the same point by turning any mass-produced object into a readymade, that the object chosen is entirely arbitrary. But to turn a urinal upside down and call it *Fountain* immediately produces a host of connotations, as does the "signature," *R. Mutt*, with its playful allusion to the "Mutt and Jeff" comic strip and its punning on *Armut* (in German, 'poverty'), *Mutti* ('Mama'), *Mut* ('courage'), or, more ingeniously, *ars mutt* ('art' in French + mongrel dog in American slang = mongrel art).[12]

Second, the shape of this "fountain" is equivocal: on the one hand, its now-classic abstract form relates it to any number of modernist sculptures; on the other, the relation of hole to whole, of straight line to curve, is itself sexually playful and hence semantically charged. What,

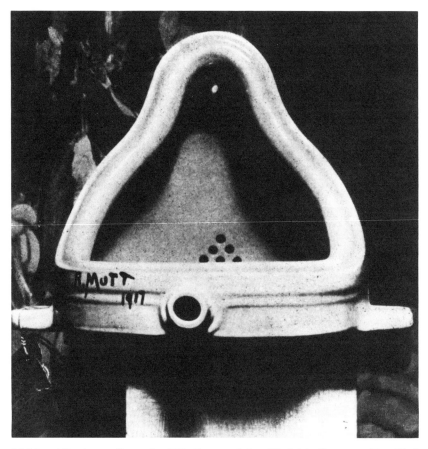

1.1 Marcel Duchamp, *Fountain*, 1917. Photograph by Alfred Stieglitz. From *The Blind Man*, No. 2 (New York, May 1917), p. 4. This was the only publicly known image of *Fountain* until World War II.

1.2 Marcel Duchamp, *Why Not Sneeze, Rose Sélavy?* 1964 (replica of 1921 original). Painted metal birdcage containing 151 white marble blocks, thermometer, and piece of cuttlebone: cage, 4 7/8 × 8 3/4 × 6 3/8 inches. Collection, Museum of Modern Art, New York. Gift of Gallerie Schwarz.

after all, is the relation of the male artist (Duchamp/R. Mutt) and of the urinal's original male function to this rounded organic shape, this highly suggestive female form called "fountain"?[13] Such sexual punning and double entendre regularly characterize Duchamp's readymades: witness the birdcage filled with sugar cubes (actually pieces of marble) called *Why Not Sneeze, Rose Sélavy?* (fig. 1.2), with its thermometer and phallic-shaped cuttlebone, or again, the famous *Bicycle Wheel* (fig. 1.3), with its dislocated transportation system, its equivocation between indoors and outdoors, stasis and movement, its metal rod's male "penetration" of the female "seat," and its invitation to the viewer to give the wheel a spin.

Ironically, of course, the Duchampian signature on the "indifferent" object, which Bürger takes to be a pure protest against the capitalist art

1.3 Marcel Duchamp, *Bicycle Wheel*, 1951 (third version, after lost original of 1913). Assemblage: metal wheel, 25 1/2 inches in diameter, mounted on painted wood stool, 23 3/4 inches high; overall 50 1/2 inches high. Sidney and Harriet Janis Collection, gift to the Museum of Modern Art, New York.

market, "where the signature means more than the quality of the work," has now become at least as prestigious as that of such "great" Modernists as Braque or Matisse. Absorption into the dominant museum culture testifies, so Bürger and like-minded critics have argued, to the inexorable commodification of artworks under capitalism. "The avant garde," writes Hal Foster, "helped to recycle the social discards of industrial capitalism back into its productive system, to mediate proletarian forms and subcultural styles (by the creation of new art, fashion, spectacles) in the interests not only of social control but also of commodity production."[14]

Given this premise, the so-called Neo-avant-garde is doomed from the start. Dada, Bürger argues, represents a moment of crisis that cannot be repeated: "Once the signed bottle drier has been accepted as an object that deserves a place in a museum, the provocation no longer provokes; it turns into its opposite. If an artist today signs a stove pipe and exhibits it, that artist certainly does not denounce the art market but adapts to it" (PB 52). And, accordingly, "The Neo-avant-garde, which stages for the second time the avant-gardiste break with tradition, becomes a manifestation that is void of sense and that permits the positing of any meaning whatever" (PB 61).

The thesis that the contemporary avant-garde is no more than a recycled version of Dada revolt, that it can do no more than spin, so to speak, its Duchampian wheels, returning again and again to the "scene of provocation" of the early century but devoid of that scene's inherently political motive, has become a commonplace of postmodern theorizing. "More and more," writes Hal Foster in "Against Pluralism," "art is directed by a cyclical mechanism akin to that which governs fashion, and the result is an ever-stylish neo-pop whose dimension is the popular past. An arrière-avant garde, such art functions in terms of returns and references rather than the utopian and anarchic transgressions of the avant garde" (REC 23). The notion of arrière-avant garde is picked up by Fredric Jameson, who argues that pastiche, which he defines as "blank parody," is the postmodern form par excellence because, "in a world in which stylistic innovation is no longer possible, all that is left is to imitate dead styles, to speak through the masks and with the voices of the styles in the imaginary museum."[15] And Andreas Huyssen observes: "The American postmodernist avant-garde . . . is not only the end game of avant-gardism. It also represents the fragmentation and decline of the avant-garde as a genuinely critical adversary culture."[16]

What then, asks Huyssen, is the relationship between avant-garde and postmodernism? Despite its "ultimate and perhaps inevitable failure," he posits, the avant-garde did aim "at developing an alternative relationship between high art and mass culture," a relationship that is now central. The "Great Divide," as Huyssen calls the Modernist "discourse which insists on the categorical distinction between high art and mass culture," breaks down: we now know that "not every work of art that does not conform to canonized notions of quality is therefore automatically a piece of Kitsch, and the working of Kitsch into art can indeed result in high-quality works" (AGD viii–ix). And throughout his book, Huyssen is at pains to be fair to such postmodern manifestations as Pop Art and especially to Andy Warhol, whom he takes very seriously.

Along the way, however, Huyssen is forced to admit that although the "postmodern sensibility of our time . . . raises the question of cultural tradition and conservation in the most fundamental way as an aesthetic and a political issue," it "doesn't always do it successfully, and often does it exploitatively" (AGD 216). How, then, does "art" respond "successfully" to popular culture and to what extent does popular culture successfully "contaminate" art? Huyssen calls for a "postmodernism of resistance, including resistance to that easy postmodernism of the 'anything goes' variety" (AGD 220), and he praises Pop Art for breaking through "the confines of the ivory tower in which art had been going around in circles in the 1950s" (AGD 142). Again, he refers to the new role of women "as a self-confident and creative force in the arts, in literature, film, and criticism," to ecology and the Green movements and to minority and Third World cultures as reconstituting the map of postmodernism and breaking down the dichotomy of high art/low art (AGD 220–21). But since the minority groups in question are hardly exemplars of mass culture, it is still not clear how that culture is to be incorporated into the new art. Indeed, by the end of the book, the focus has shifted from the great (high/low) divide in the arts to an emphasis on marginalization by the dominant culture as the key to postmodern art practices.

A similar case for oppressed groups is made by Fredric Jameson:

> The only authentic cultural production today has seemed to be that which can draw on the collective experience of marginal pockets of the social life of the world system: black literature and blues, British working-class rock, women's literature, gay literature, the *roman québécois*, the literature of the Third World; and this production is possible only to the degree to which these forms of collective life or collective solidarity have not yet been fully penetrated by the market and by the commodity system.[17]

Radical as this may sound, Jameson's invocation of the "marginal pockets of the social life of the world system" betrays a curiously Romantic nostalgia for a world elsewhere in which the authentic has "not yet" been destroyed or corrupted by the encroachment of first world imperialism and colonialism. But what if, as James Clifford has argued in a series of brilliant ethnographic studies, authenticity is itself no more than a relational term, a conscious "staging" in which a culture presents itself *in opposition* to external, often dominating alternatives"? As such, the "authentic" comes to be understood as a "constructed domain of truth," a "serious fiction."[18] Indeed "neither the experience nor the interpretive activity of the scientific researcher," in this case, the first world critic like Jameson, "can be considered innocent," criticism always being "a constructive negotiation involving at least two, and usually more, conscious, politically significant subjects" (PC 41). Thus, appealing as it may be to regard artistic practice—say, the *roman québécois* or "British working-class rock"—as the province of a still exotic other, the work itself betrays, however obliquely, its awareness of the global teleculture within which it negotiates. So at least James Clifford's amusing anecdote about the Trobriander medicine man presiding over magic rites and distributing betel nuts from his bright blue plastic Adidas bag (PC 148) would suggest. Then too, in the United States, minority status has itself become a kind of commodity, a salable quantity in the marketplace, provided it is judged sufficiently representative by the very dominant culture deplored in Jameson's brief. Subject matter, in this scheme of things, is all. At the same time, poets who question the official cultural space of "diversity," a space in which the dominant paradigms of representation remain quite intact, who believe that oppositionality has to do, not only with what a poem says, but with the formal, modal, and generic choices it makes—its use, say, of a nontraditional rhythmic base, a particular vernacular, or an incorporation of cited nonpoetic material—these poets continue to be relegated to the margins.

What this contradiction (between a literature *literally* marginalized, that is, excluded by the dominant culture and known to only a small and specialized readership, and a literature whose marginality is, so to speak, certified and institutionalized) might mean remains elusive in Jameson's version of postindustrial society, with its "blank irony," its "death of the subject," and its "disappearance of a sense of history" (AA 125). Endgame, fragmentation, decline, the "no longer possible"— the vocabulary of apocalypse adumbrated by Jameson now pervades the discussion of art practices. In their recent *Postmodern Scene* (rather

sensationally subtitled *Excremental Culture and Hyper-Aesthetics*),
Arthur Kroker and David Cook declare that "Ours is a *fin-de-millénium*
consciousness which, existing at the end of history in the twilight time
of ultramodernism (of technology) and hyper-primitivism (of public
moods), uncovers a great arc of disintegration and decay against the
background radiation of parody, kitsch, and burnout."[19]

This was published in 1986 (fourteen years to go, as doomsayers were
putting it), and within just a few years, words like "radiation" and
"burnout" were perceived as much less threatening in the face of those
even newer words, *glasnost* and *perestroika*. Indeed, with the dissolu-
tion of the Soviet empire and the half-century-old East-West balance of
power, the kind of eschatological discourse we meet in Kroker and Cook
may soon give way to a new wave of Futuristic speculation, a search for
aesthetic possibilities latent in what now appears to be an ongoing and
open-ended series of global transformations.

At the moment however, the "sense of an ending" remains a power-
ful myth, even for critics not given to apocalyptic utterance. In
The Philosophical Disenfranchisement of Art (1986), for example,
Arthur C. Danto argues that the lesson to be learned from Duchamp's
readymades, as from Andy Warhol's Campbell Soup cans, is that there
are no longer objects with perceptible aesthetic properties, that, on the
contrary, the claim that, say, Duchamp's *Fountain* is a "work of art"
turns attention away from the work to the nature of interpretation. "In-
terpretation," writes Danto, "is in effect the lever with which an object
is lifted out of the real world and into the art-world. . . . Only in rela-
tionship to an interpretation is a material object an artwork" (DA 39).
Hence in our "post-historical period of art" (DA 111), we are witnessing
"the end of art" (one of Danto's chapter titles). When, for example,
Duchamp exhibits an ordinary snow shovel (fig. 1.4), identical to any
number of such shovels acquired from the same factory and wholly de-
void of aesthetic value, his gesture forces the viewer to generate an in-
terpretation to account for the work's claim to be art. Thus, "Art ends
with the advent of its own philosophy" (DA 107).

It is interesting that Danto provides no reproduction of Duchamp's
snow shovel nor does he mention that this readymade (curiously de-
familiarized by its isolated position in a glass case and hence seen as we
never see shovels in real life, where they are either arranged in rows at
the hardware store or stuck in a closet or covered with dirt or snow) is
called *In Advance of the Broken Arm*, with its suggestion of bourgeois
caution—the purchase of a shiny new snow shovel to prevent sidewalk
accidents that cause broken arms, the need for every proper household
to have a shovel, the shovel as industrialized society's replacement of

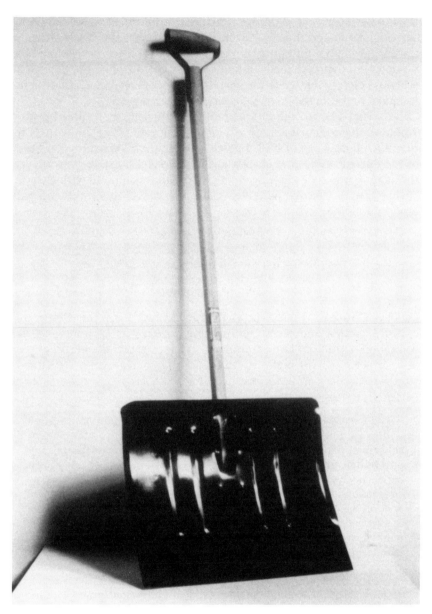

1.4 Marcel Duchamp, *In Advance of the Broken Arm*, 1915 (New York; original lost; 2d version, obtained by Duchamp for Katherine S. Dreir). Readymade: wood and galvanized-iron snow shovel, 47 3/4 inches high (121.3 cm). Inscribed on reverse of lower edge, in white paint: "IN ADVANCE OF THE BROKEN ARM MARCEL DUCHAMP (1915) *replica* 1945." Collection, Katherine S. Dreier, West Redding, Connecticut.

the human arm, and so on. By omitting this information, or rather, by denying the materiality (so to speak, the body) of the object in question, Danto's own interpretation is thus a self-fulfilling prophecy. Since we don't see the readymade or know its name (in Duchamp, the verbal is always closely related to the visual), art does indeed give way to "philosophy" and it is the critic who moves center stage.

But what about "the end of philosophy"? The "end of criticism"? Wouldn't these endgames have to follow "the end of art"? In conversation with John Cage in 1988, I posed the question: "What do you think of the current view that innovation is no longer possible, that indeed the avant-garde is dead?" Cage reflected a minute and said with a smile, "Even them?" A similar point was made by Marcel Broodthaers in a gallery publication:

> The aim of all art is commercial.
> My aim is equally commercial.
> The aim of criticism is just as commercial.
> Guardian of myself and of others,
> I do not know truly who to kick.[20]

Touché. Criticism is not somewhere outside and beyond the "great arc of disintegration and decay" within which we live: if art undergoes the commodification of "late capitalism," so, inevitably, does critical theory. Or perhaps, as I prefer to think, the parameters can be redefined. In a recent essay on postmodernism for the *Socialist Review*, Charles Bernstein writes:

> *We can act:* we are not trapped in the postmodern condition if we are willing to differentiate between works of art that suggest new ways of conceiving of our present world and those that seek rather to debunk any possibilities for meaning. To do this, one has to be able to distinguish between, on the one hand, a fragmentation that attempts to valorize the concept of a free-floating signifier unbounded to social significance . . . and, on the other, a fragmentation that reflects a conception of meaning as prevented by conventional narration and so uses disjunction as a method of tapping into other possibilities available within language. Failure to make such distinctions is similar to failing to distinguish between youth gangs, pacifist anarchists, Weatherpeople, anti-Sandinista contras, Salvadoran guerrillas, Islamic terrorists, or US state terrorists. Perhaps all of these groups are responding to the "same" stage of multinational capitalism. But the crucial point is that the *responses* cannot be understood as the same, unified as various interrelated "symptoms" of late capitalism. Nor are the "dominant" practices the exemplary ones that tell the "whole" story.[21]

Like Cage's and Broodthaers's, Bernstein's is a refusal, so to speak, on the part of the *maker* of art to provide its receptor with so many exempla of a theory already in place.[22] It is also a refusal to make easy generalizations: to take just one example, our penchant for the comparison of "profitable 'postmodern' artworld commodities to what were, in their own time, obscure and noncommercial 'modern' artworks," the comparison serving mainly to point up the telling symptoms of contemporary decline and fall.[23] Indeed, perhaps it would be more useful to work the other way around and to consider, more closely than we usually do, what really happens on the video screen, at the computer terminal, or in the advertising media, and then to see how poetic or art discourse positions itself vis-à-vis these powerful new environments. These are the questions I want to explore in the chapters that follow; for the present, let us consider some preliminaries.

II

Information theory provides us with a starting point. In a series of volumes beginning with *Hermes* (1968), for example, Michel Serres has studied the meaning and function of *noise*, the word being defined as "the set of those phenomena of interference that become obstacles to communication." "Obstacles" may be a misleading word here, Serres's point being that *noise* is not only incidental but *essential* to communication, whether at the level of writing (e.g., "waverings in the graphic forms, failures in the drawing, spelling errors, and so on"), of speech ("stammerings, mispronunciations, regional accents, dysphonias, and cacophonies"), or of the technical means of communication ("background noise, jamming, static, cut-offs, hyteresis, various interruptions").[24]

If, for example, a letter is written in careless or illegible script, there is interference in the reading process, which is to say that noise slows down communication. "The cacographer and the epigraphist" exchange roles, struggling as they do with noise as the common enemy: "*To hold a dialogue is to suppose a third man and to seek to exclude him.*" This third man, says Serres, is the *demon*, the "prosopopeia of noise" (H 67). Demon, because, with the exception of mathematics, "the kingdom of quasi-perfect communication," the "third man" is never successfully excluded. Indeed, in order for the "pure" discourse of mathematics to be possible, one must shut out the entire empiricist domain; "one must close one's eyes and cover one's ears to the song and the beauty of the sirens" (H 70).

Noise as unanticipated excess, as sirens' song—the phenomenon has always, of course, been with us. But given the complex electronic modes of communication that now exist, the possibility increases that what is received differs from what was sent.[25] The garbled or gratuitous FAX message is an obvious example. But Duchamp's "snow shovel" would be another—an example of an object whose reception depends largely on the noise that comes through the channel, on, for example, the information that its title is *In Advance of the Broken Arm*. In this sense, what the Russian Futurists called *ostranenie* ('making strange') increasingly becomes a function of the actual dissemination of the message, its sender not necessarily being equivalent to its original producer and its receiver hence playing a greatly enlarged role in the processing of the text.

This brings us to a consideration of the computer terminal itself. In an important recent essay, Richard A. Lanham points out that the use of the personal computer and its electronic display "is forcing a radical realignment of the alphabetic and graphic components of ordinary textual communication."[26] In the conventional printed book, after all, the written surface is, so Lanham reminds us, "not to be read aesthetically; that would only interfere with purely literate transparency." On the contrary, a page of print should stand to the thought conveyed "as a fine crystal goblet stands to the wine it contains" (RL 266). Such "unintermediated thought," such "unselfconscious transparency" has become, says Lanham, "a stylistic, one might almost say a cultural, ideal for Western civilization. The best style is the style not noticed; the best manners the most unobtrusive" (RL 266).

Enter pixeled ("pixels" are "picture elements," the dots which electronically paint the letters onto the computer screen) print, which calls the basic stylistic decorum of the "transparent" page into question. "Electronic typography is both creator-controlled and reader-controlled" (RL 266). I can, for example (especially with the MacIntosh) use a wide variety of Roman and Greek styles, redesign the shapes of the letters, make them brighter or dimmer, alter the alphabetic-graphic ratio of conventional literacy, alter the "normal" figure-ground relationships, and so on—all by touching a key. I can "transform" what is usually thought of as prose into what is usually thought of as poetry, simply by hitting the "indent" key and lineating the text. I can illuminate the text in various ways, use different colors, reformat it in italics or capitals, and so on. The textual surface has, in other words, become what Lanham calls "permanently bistable":

> We are always looking first AT [the text] and then THROUGH it, and this oscillation creates a different implied ideal of decorum, both stylistic

and behavioral. Look THROUGH a text and you are in the familiar world of the Newtonian Interlude, where facts were facts, the world just "out there," folks sincere central selves, and the best writing style dropped from the writer as "simply and directly as a stone falls to the ground," just as Thoreau counseled. Look AT a text, however, and we have deconstructed the Newtonian world into Pirandello's and yearn to "act naturally." We have always had ways of triggering this oscillation, but the old ways—printing prose consecutively and verse not, layering figures of sound and arrangement on the stylistic surface until it squeaked—were clumsy, slow, unchangeable, and above all author-controlled. . . . The difference is profound. . . . You return, by electronic ambages, to that Renaissance *sprezzatura* of rehearsed spontaneity which Newtonian science so unceremoniously set aside. (RL 267–69)

Lanham's analysis seems to me an excellent antidote to the more abstract—and generally gloomy—explanations of the fate of "literature" under "late" or "multinational" capitalism, or within "consumer culture." For one thing, it refuses to grant large-scale explanatory force to designations that, as even Fredric Jameson has recently remarked with respect to his own use of the term "late capitalism," have become identified "as leftist logo[s] which [are] ideologically and politically booby-trapped" (CLLC, xxi). For another, if we take the longer historical view and consider such earlier nontransparent page design as that of the medieval scribe, who inevitably elaborated on his alphabet design in the interest of visual beauty, we can see that, for better or worse, we are now at a moment when transparency—the typography that is "as transparent as a crystal goblet"[27]—can once again give way to what the Russian Futurists called "the word as such" (*slovo kak takovoe*).

Not only does the boundary between "verse" and "prose" break down but also the boundary between "creator" and "critic." For as I read X's text on the computer screen, I can, again with the flick of a finger, change it in any number of ways, reformat it to my liking, "improve it." Indeed, in the "interactive fiction" being written for the computer, the reader can choose the story's outcome, according to a series of possible moves. And in digitalized music programs, the distinction between time and space breaks down, the "composer" using the "Music Mouse" to make geometric motions that are then translated, by the computer, into sounds (see Lanham 274).

Such "digital equivalency," Lanham believes, "means that we can no longer pursue literary study by itself: the other arts will form part of literary study in an essential way" (RL 273). Indeed, "the personal computer itself constitutes the ultimate postmodern work of art. It introduces and focuses all the rhetorical themes advanced by the arts from Futurism onward. . . . The interactive audience which outrageous Futurist evenings forced upon Victorian conventions of passive silence finds its perfect fulfillment in the personal computer's radical enfranchisement of the perceiver. Cage's games of chance and Oldenburg's experiments in visual scaling become everyday routines in home computer graphics" (RL 279).

Such enthusiastic claims for the computer will strike many of us as excessively McLuhanesque, as too optimistic and uncritical of the culture within which and on which such technology operates. In what sense, after all, can such acquired behavior as computer formatting, largely conditioned as it is by the "hidden persuaders" of our culture, be considered "art"? What about the binary choices computer screen-prompts impose on the writer-reader, the necessity of always choosing between "yes" or "no," "up" or "down"? And, most disturbing, what about the gap between computer operation (a skill to be learned) and the internal computer system, which remains essentially inaccessible to the user? These are questions to which I shall return in later chapters. For the moment, however, I want to take up Lanham's very interesting suggestion that computer textuality transforms the way we *receive* as well as the way we create written texts and hence has important implications for the larger study of rhetoric.

Consider, for example, Lanham's discussion of *prose*, that little word taken for granted ever since Monsieur Jourdain was told (incorrectly, as it happens, since the short utterance units of speech are not its equivalent) that what he was speaking was prose. Lanham writes:

> So used are we to thinking black-and-white, continuous printed prose the norm of conceptual utterance, that it has taken a series of theoretical attacks and technological metamorphoses to make us see it for what it is: an act of extraordinary stylization, of remarkable, expressive self-denial. The lesson has been taught by theorists, from Marinetti to Burke and Derrida, and by personal computers which restore to the reader whole ranges of expressivity—graphics, fonts, typography, layout, color—which the prose stylist has abjured. Obviously these pressures will not *destroy* prose, but they may change its underlying decorum. And perhaps engender, at long last, a theory of prose style as radical artifice rather than native transparency. (RL 271)

This distinction between the prose of "radical artifice" and that of "native transparency" has been made by many of the poets I shall be discussing in subsequent chapters. Indeed, Lanham's proposals for a "returning rhetorical paideia" that might govern our study of electronic text, whether verbal, visual, or musical, are extremely useful in shifting attention away from content—the New Formalist prescription, say, that a poem tell a "good story," or the Foucaultian prescription that every narrative is a coded account of power struggle—to the larger formal and theoretical issues relating to poetry today. But since Lanham's concerns are avowedly pedagogical rather than more specifically aesthetic, some qualification may be in order.

The most cursory survey of contemporary poetics would show that, at least as far as what Charles Bernstein calls "official verse culture"[28] is concerned, technology, whether computer technology or the video, audio, and print media, remains, quite simply, the enemy, the locus of commodification and reification against which a "genuine" poetic discourse must react. In part, as I shall suggest in later chapters, the most interesting poetic and artistic compositions of our time do position themselves, consciously or unconsciously, against the languages of TV and advertising, but the dialectic between the two is highly mediated. It is by no means a case, as poets sometimes complain, of "competing" with television, of pitting the "authentic" individual self against an impersonal, exploitative other that commodifies the consciousness of the duped masses. For authenticity, as Jed Rasula has recently suggested, is itself a commodity, a product based on a now-specious "ideology of privacy" that adheres to the following principles:

> (1) it must demonstrate a restraint of the stimulations or aggressions that inhere in charged or intense language; (2) it must display fidelity to the poet's personal life; (3) this fidelity, this "being true to life" must affirm a certain sufficiency inherent in all of us; (4) it must be an innocuous artifact and in no way seek to challenge its status as private concern of a handful of consumers.[29]

The myth of "private concern" (e.g., "let me tell you what happened to me yesterday") runs headlong, so Rasula suggests, into the reality of non-privacy in our world. "It's no longer a matter of 'meeting the world half-way,'" he writes; "there's no such thing as privacy—privacy has been deleted. Leisure time is now archaic. What is now called leisure or free time is, instead, a differently calibrated sort of duty, the zone of bricolage in which we cut and snip and sort and paste our attentions, so we become prosthetic supplements to the total-body effect of the media, the coherent and pervasive final report that drifts along just out the door." Which is to say, that "instead of producing objects for the subject, ours is a system that produces subjects for the object" (JR 77).

Most contemporary writing that currently passes by the name of "poetry" belongs in this category which Rasula wittily calls PSI, for "Poetry Systems Incorporated, a subsidiary to data management systems" (JR 78). The business of this particular corporation is to produce the specialty item known as "the self," and it is readily available in popular magazines and at chain bookstores, its "corporate newsletter" being the *New York Times Book Review*. The "reader" for "PSI product" is, as is normal for TV, a digit, "a statistical guarantator of the precise scale of another kind of beast known as 'the audience.'" To this PSI-product audience, the "poem" is a form of instant uplift. Read one now and again and you'll participate in a ritual of "sensitivity" and "self-awareness." It is the mechanism of the poetry reading on campuses and in "poetry centers" across the United States.

At the same time, we are witnessing a poetic more consonant with the reading-writing mechanism of the new electronic "page." Like Serres and Lanham, Rasula places his emphasis on the writer *as reader*. "Normal channels," he suggests, "are the media of compliance. They are the means by which the unknown audience consents to captivity by testing positive to a numeracy syndrome, agreeing to a certain effacement in order to personally 'typify' some statistical groundswell" (JR 89). But when the audience—the reader—refuses "captivity" and demands a textuality that cannot be absorbed into or accommodated by the Mediaspeak or image field of "normal" telediscourse or digital display, a new interaction is produced, returning us, in Lanham's words "from a closed poetic to an open rhetoric."

III

Let us see how this might work in practice. The dominant poetic of the American sixties, a poetic, as I shall argue in subsequent chapters, of strenuous authenticity, the desire to present a self as natural, as organic, and as unmediated as possible, was likely to produce such "deep image" poems as the following by James Wright:

> *From a Bus Window in Central Ohio,*
> *Just before a Thunder Shower*
>
> Cribs loaded with roughage huddle together
> Before the north clouds.
> The wind tiptoes between poplars.
> The silver maple leaves squint
> Toward the ground.
> An old farmer, his scarlet face
> Apologetic with whiskey, swings back a barn door
> And calls a hundred black-and-white Holsteins
> From the clover field.[30]

Here the poem is conceived as an act of witnessing. The speaker-observer must capture the exact nuance of the moment, beginning with the long documentary title that tells us just where and when the recorded experience took place. A "Bus Window in Central Ohio, Just before a Thunder Shower"—a changeless place, as it were, in the heart of the nation (buses have been around for a long time), and a natural occurrence. The poem's images, presented directly in a series of simple declarative present-tense sentences, graphically convey that moment of strange quiet that precedes a storm, the moment when the corn cribs seem to "huddle together," the wind to "tiptoe between poplars," and, in an especially vivid metaphor, the "silver maple leaves [to] squint / Toward the ground." It is also the moment when the old farmer, perfectly attuned as he is to the elements despite his habitual but "apologetic" drinking, knows that it is time to call in the cows.

Such short imagistic poems depend for their effect on what Robert Lowell called "the grace of accuracy,"[31] a quality Wright had in abundance. No word is wasted: the perceiver's eye moves from the ground to the sky and back again, capturing for the reader the precise *frisson* that precedes the Ohio thunderstorm. The observer himself remains outside the picture frame ("bus window"), a seemingly impassive observer, even as everything that is seen and felt is filtered through his consciousness, defining a moment of ominous waiting, a foreboding of pain yet to come. Even the sound features—the slow trochaic rhythm, stressed diphthongs, and the alliteration and assonance (e.g., "The *si*lver ma*ple leav*es *squint*") emphasizing the integrity of the line, which is unpunctuated by caesurae—contribute to the sense that we are witnessing a "calm before the storm."

"Perfect" as such small "deep image" poems are, they are also oddly unambitious. As in the case of the Concrete Poetry to be discussed in chapter 4, their minimalism may be said to mask a certain fear—the fear, perhaps, of confronting more of "Central Ohio" than the phenomenology of impending thunderstorms, the reluctance, moreover, to relate nature to culture, to consider the implications of using what has become a fairly standard free-verse form (a set of short, irregular lines surrounded by white space) and a fixed subject position in a world that increasingly questions the validity of such conventions. In this respect, we might compare "From a Bus Window" to a poetic construct like John Cage's *Lecture on the Weather*, written more than a decade later for the Bicentennial of the United States and performed at irregular intervals since then.

In his headnote to "Preface to 'Lecture on the Weather'" (the only text available in print),[32] Cage explains that when the work was first commissioned by the Canadian Broadcasting Corporation, Richard Coulter suggested that it might be based on texts of Benjamin Franklin, but *Poor Richard's Almanac* did not strike Cage's fancy and he turned instead to his beloved Henry David Thoreau, specifically the *Essay on Civil Disobedience*, the *Journal*, and *Walden*.

In the Preface to the resulting *Lecture on the Weather*, Cage sketches in the background of the project:

> The first thing I thought of doing in relation to this work was to find an anthology of American aspirational thought and subject it to chance operations. I thought the resultant complex would help to change our present intellectual climate. I called up Dover and asked whether they published such an anthology. They didn't. I called a part of Columbia University concerned with American History and asked about aspirational thought. They knew nothing about it. I called the Information Desk of the New York Public Library at 42nd Street. The man who answered said: You may think I'm not serious but I am; if you're interested in aspiration, go to the Children's Library on 52nd Street. I did. I found that anthologies for children are written by adults: they are what adults think are good for children. The thickest one was edited by [Henry Steele] Commager (*Documents of American History*). It is a collection of legal judgments, presidential reports, congressional speeches. I began to realize that what is called balance between the branches of our government is not balance at all: all the branches of our government are occupied by lawyers.
>
> Of all professions the law is the least concerned with aspiration. It is concerned with precedent, not with discovery. (LW 3–4)

How to subvert this state of affairs, how to subordinate precedent to discovery, all the while paying homage to the qualities of American ingenuity, pragmatism, and good sense epitomized for Cage in the person of Thoreau—this is the problematic addressed in *Lecture on the Weather*, a media work that deconstructs the media, a "lecture" whose words cannot be heard, a choral composition whose "voices" are disembodied presences, a performance piece that anyone can perform but in which no one is in the spotlight.

To begin with, *Lecture on the Weather* is not a lecture at all, but an elaborate rule-generated collage-work:

> Subjecting Thoreau's writings to *I Ching* chance operations to obtain collage texts, I prepared parts for twelve speaker-vocalists (or -instrumentalists), stating my preference that they be American men who had become Canadian citizens. Along with these parts go recordings by Maryanne Amacher of breeze, rain, and finally thunder and in the last (thunder) section a film by Luis Frangella representing lightning by means of briefly projected negatives of Thoreau's drawings.[33]

Here, as so often in his "production notes," Cage assumes a casual air that his actual work belies. For one thing, the agreed-upon time-length for the spoken parts is rigidly fixed ("at least 22′45″ [5′ × 4′33″] and not more than 36′24″ [8′ × 4′33″])," the numerical reference being, of course, to Cage's famous early prepared piano piece *4′33″*. Again, the "entrance" of the taped sound events—breeze, rain, and thunder—is precisely timed, the breeze "to be faded in at the beginning," the rain "to be faded in after 11 or 12% of the total agreed-upon performance time-length has elapsed," and the thunder "to enter abruptly after 63 to 70% . . . has elapsed." Further directions indicate when the lights are to be lowered, when the "lightning" slides are to be projected, and inform the performers that the recording of thunder should "stop abruptly" before those of breeze and rain fade out, but that "this stop [should not] interrupt a thunderclap."

Thus, although the Thoreau texts themselves are chosen by chance operations, their actual collocation, together with sounds and visual images, is a strictly planned mathematical system. Since no single passage from Thoreau is repeated twice, and since each of the twelve text-sets must have the same length, the performance of the simultaneous reading is anything but random. The chance operation, in this context, is more properly understood as a form of constraint, a rule-generated process within which "weather conditions" occur.

Weather: "The condition of the atmosphere at a given place and time with respect to heat or cold, quantity of sunshine, presence or absence of rain, hail, thunder, fog, etc., violence or gentleness of the winds. Also the condition of the atmosphere regarded as subject to vicissitudes" (*OED*). Here is the key to Cage's composition, in which a strict rule-bound process is subjected to the "vicissitudes" of the "atmosphere at a given place and time." Specific events (whether the speaker-vocalists stand or sit and where they are located in relation to the audience, how or whether the audience is seated, whether the performance space is large or small, open or closed, etc.) inevitably differ from performance to performance. At the California Institute of the Arts (Valencia) performance in March 1984, the "theatre" was a large empty room with bare floorboards, rather like a gym, with a platform at one end, on which the twelve speaker-vocalists were placed, a projection screen behind them covering the whole wall. At the Strathmore Hall "Cagefest" in May 1989 (Rockville, Md.), on the other hand, the performance space was a much smaller conference room with french doors on one side and a fireplace on the other; the speaker-vocalists sat at a long table in front of the fireplace, facing the audience, which was quite conventionally seated in rows.

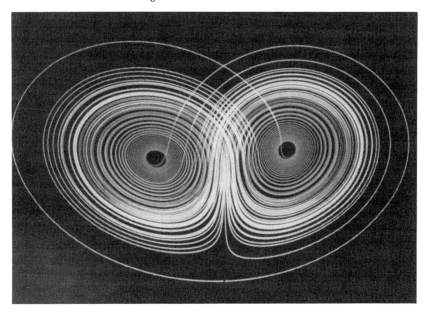

1.5 Heinz-Otto Peitgen, *The Lorenz Attractor*, in James Gleick, *Chaos: Making a New Science* (New York: Penguin, 1988), opposite p. 114.

No single version of *Lecture on the Weather*, whether live or video-taped, can thus claim the authority of representing the "real" Cage text, which therefore functions as a score-to-be-activated rather than as an art object to be replicated. Or, to put it in terms of chaos theory, which has many applications to Cage's work, the performance functions as a "strange attractor" or "unpredictable system," which "collapses to a point" at "a single instant in time," only to change, "ever so slightly" at the next instant (see fig. 1.5).[34]

But, as in the case of a "strange attractor," the loops and spirals of this particular structure stay within a finite space. No matter what the conditions of a given performance, the "lecture" opens with the recitation of the twelve vocalists, simultaneously reading twelve different sets of excerpts from Thoreau (from *Walden*, the *Essay on Civil Disobedience*, and the *Journal*),[35] while "weather" sounds (recordings of breeze, then rain, and, about two-thirds of the way through, thunder, the house gradually being darkened) begin to be heard, emanating from the walls or ceiling. The audience thus finds itself, not passively attending a lecture (indeed, the simultaneity of recited speech reflects, as

Cage has frequently remarked, our larger inability to listen to one another),[36] but participating in an environment. The performance, accordingly, is not *about* weather; it *is* weather.

At first, when one hears gentle breeze, birds chirping, and then light rain, one reminds oneself that this is, after all, mere sound effect, rather like a movie sound track; that the sound is not, in fact, "real." But as the rain becomes more insistent, as lightning flashes and thunderclaps begin to drown out the reading of Thoreau's text, a strange thing begins to happen—at least it did at the Cal Arts performance I attended. The audience, scattered around the room, some standing, some sitting on the floor, began to move closer and closer together. By the time the storm "broke," lightning flashes appearing on the large screen in the form of briefly projected negatives of drawings by Thoreau,[37] the audience had become something of a football huddle. Everyone wanted to join together and get out of the storm.

But because the "path" of this strange attractor is unpredictable, the communion I have described may be achieved in other ways. At the Strathmore Hall performance, for example, it happened (the "vicissitudes" of atmospheric conditions) that a torrential rain and thunderstorm took place just as the performance was beginning and, since the french doors were open to the outside, "this had," in the words of Joan Retallack, "the lovely effect of eradicating the distinction between 'inside' and 'outside'—the room, the performance, the concept of weather, as Cage presents it to us, including the 'weather' of coincidences, voices, ideas—all combining to cause the kind of storm that occurs in a particular . . . climate. That particular experience of that particular weather . . . in Rockville Md., May 5, 1989 at approximately 9 pm could only assume its particular and variable character with the kind of permeable boundaries—between the inside and outside of his pieces—that Cage structures into all of his work" (JR 6). Indeed, given the basic time-space constraints and the specific verbal, aural, and visual procedures designed by Cage for the *Lecture* (the "inside" of the piece), any number of other "weather conditions" (the "outside") are obviously possible.

Yet the multiplication of situations does not change the basic "shape" of the work. Toward the end of his Preface, Cage remarks, "More than anything else we need communion with everyone. Struggles for power have nothing to do with communion. Communion extends beyond borders: it is with one's enemies also. Thoreau said: 'The best communion men have is in silence'" (LW 5). This is the insight *Lecture on the Weather* enacts, whatever its specific performance conditions. Instead of lecturing us on communion, instead of defining community in terms of verbal images and metaphors, the piece gradually *transforms* a skeptical audience (an audience that cannot "hear" the words recited) into a community: by the end, when the storm is subsiding and patches of sunlight appear, we are all in it together.

Here, then, is a text peculiarly for the times. *Lecture on the Weather* is a verbal-visual-musical composition that relies on current technology for its execution. There is no complete written text, since the printed page cannot reproduce the simultaneous visual and sound features of the "lecture." The coordination of vocal elements, sound, and film image is achieved by elaborate computer calculations. Yet, so the "lecture" implies, the availability of such technology by no means implies that we are now slaves to automation and commodification, that we have come to the endgame of art. On the contrary, Cage is suggesting that even as the early New England settlers achieved a sense of community out of mutual deprivation, hardship, and want, two hundred years later, our own "deprivation" (the glut, for example, of "aspirational" writing as well as of media discourse) can be overcome, not by finding books in the library that will talk *about* community, but by finding ways to actually have it happen.

"An adequate theory of prose," Richard Lanham suggests, would reconceive prose style "as radical artifice rather than native transparency." That, too, is the paradox of *Lecture on the Weather*. Cage is too often misunderstood as the champion of the natural, the advocate of art as a "purposeless play" that is "simply a way of waking up to the very life we're living, which is so excellent once one gets one's mind and one's desires out of its way and lets it act of its own accord."[38] And in the "Preface to *Lecture on the Weather*," Cage cites Thoreau as saying, "Music is continuous; only listening is intermittent."

What Cage means by such statements is that the art construct must consistently tap into "life," must *use* what really happens in the external world as its materials, and that, vice versa, "life" is only "lived" when we perceive it as form and structure. But nothing is less *transparent* than a composition like *Lecture on the Weather*, in which the resources of such various media as film, soundtrack, pictogram, musical instrument, and of various genres like lecture, poem, journal, and drama are integrated by means of what Lanham calls "radical artifice." Indeed, the Duchamp readymade, which has had a profound influence on Cage's work and which Peter Bürger takes to be a kind of endpoint of avant-garde art (the "provocation" produced by the claim that an "ordinary" urinal could be construed as a work of art "cannot be repeated indefinitely," PB 52), here finds its antithetical match. Let me try to explain.

If the readymade is an "ordinary" industrial object, the "lecture on the weather" is a fabricated, simulated natural event. If the readymade turns a useful object (urinal, bicycle wheel, snow shovel, bottle rack) into an impersonal work of art, the "lecture" on weather turns the simulated event into one that behaves like a real one, causing the audience to take shelter from the cruel elements. Finally, if the readymade was appropriate to its modernist moment, a witty critique of "high art" pieties and prejudices in the early twentieth century, works like *Lecture on the Weather* are nothing if not appropriate to our moment, calling into question as they do our preoccupation with the lecture format— not only university lecture, of course, but any "address" A makes to B and C, whether on radio or TV, whether formal political address or the promotion of a new cosmetic product.

Whatever lectures we give or we attend, after all, none of us are likely to think of them as dangerous; on the contrary, the lecture is regarded as a little island of safety in a world of crowding, assault, and the unfriendly elements, like the tiptoeing hiss of the wind "between poplars" in Wright's weather poem. Accordingly, Cage created a lecture that would assault us with frightening noises and images, that would make us wish we were merely driving in freeway traffic. We might call it a case of defamiliarization, but defamiliarization of a sort the Russian Formalists, who disseminated the concept, would be hard put to recognize, the object of a work like *Lecture on the Weather* being, not to make the stone stony, but to stage an "event" that can change our environment and how we respond to it.

Such simulation is, of course, a case of marked artifice. Whereas Modernist poetics was overwhelmingly committed, at least in theory, to the "natural look," whether at the level of speech (Yeats's "natural words in the natural order"), the level of image (Pound's "the natural object is always the adequate symbol"), or the level of verse form ("free" verse being judged for the better part of the century as somehow more "natural" than meter and stanzaic structure), we are now witnessing a return to *artifice*, but a "radical artifice," to use Lanham's phrase, characterized by its opposition, not only to "the language really spoken by men" but also to what is loosely called Formalist (whether New or Old) verse, with its elaborate poetic diction and self-conscious return to "established" forms and genres. Artifice, in this sense, is less a matter of·ingenuity and manner, of elaboration and elegant subterfuge, than of the recognition that a poem or painting or performance text is a *made thing*—contrived, constructed, chosen—and that its reading is also a construction on the part of its audience. At its best, such construction empowers the audience by altering its perceptions of how things happen. Thus, even though a work like *Lecture on the Weather* is a collage of found texts—extracts from Thoreau, replicas of bird calls, recordings of thunder—its "weather" is charged with possibilities.

2   The Changing Face of Common Intercourse: Talk Poetry, Talk Show, and the Scene of Writing

. . . the natural words in the natural order is the formula.
—W. B. Yeats to Dorothy Wellesley[1]

. . . the natural object is always the adequate symbol.
—Ezra Pound, "A Retrospect"[2]

"Natural": the very word should be struck from the language.
—Charles Bernstein, "Stray Straws and Straw Men"[3]

In his famous lecture "The Music of Poetry" (1942), T. S. Eliot declares:

> there is one law of nature more powerful than any [other] . . . the law
> that poetry must not stray too far from the ordinary everyday language
> which we use and hear. Whether poetry is accentual or syllabic, rhymed
> or rhymeless, formal or free, it cannot afford to lose contact with the
> changing face of common intercourse.[4]

And a few pages later:

> So, while poetry attempts to convey something beyond what is conveyed
> in prose rhythms, it remains, all the same, *one person talking to an-
> other*. . . . Every revolution in poetry is apt to be, and sometimes to an-
> nounce itself to be, a *return to common speech*. This is the revolution
> which Wordsworth announced in his prefaces, and he was right: but
> the same revolution had been carried out a century before by Oldham,
> Waller, Denham, and Dryden; and the same revolution was due again
> something over a century later. . . . No poetry, of course, is ever exactly
> the same speech that the poet talks and hears: but it has to be in such a
> relation to the speech of his time that the listener or reader can say 'that
> is how I should talk if I could talk poetry.' (OPP 23–24; my italics)

Poetry as the simulation of natural speech: taken at face value,
Eliot's precept is, by his own account, in the straight line of Words-
worth; the poet, according to the 1800 "Preface to the *Lyrical Ballads*,"
is first and foremost "a man speaking to men."[5] Not that Eliot shares
Wordsworth's faith in the language of "low and rustic life" as that
which is most attuned to "the beautiful and permanent forms of na-
ture." "It is not the business of the poet," he writes, "to talk like *any*
class of society, but like himself—rather better, we hope, than any ac-

tual class."[6] "Common speech," in this context, means not the speech of the lower classes, but that which is *common* to everyone, that is, *natural* or everyday speech as we perceive it in our daily lives.

The criterion of "natural speech" was, in any case, to become a cornerstone of high modernist poetics.[7] "I have tried," writes Yeats to his father in 1913, "to make my work convincing with a speech so natural and dramatic that the hearer would feel the presence of a man thinking and feeling."[8] In a similar vein, Pound insists, in a 1915 letter to Harriet Monroe, that the language of poetry "must be a fine language, departing in no way from speech save by a heightened intensity. There must be no book words, no periphrases, no inversions. . . . nothing that you couldn't, in some circumstance, in the stress of some emotion, actually say."[9] From here it is just a step to the conviction that the speech act itself has poetic potential. "Poetry," as David Antin was to put it in the early seventies, is "made by a man up on his feet, talking."[10]

The identification of poetry with *manhood* is one I shall take up later; for the moment, consider the curious emphasis, in modernist discourse, on the role of poetry as purgative—a kind of cold shower. "The *norm* for a poet's language," observes Eliot, "is the way his contemporaries talk,"[11] provided, of course, that such talk—the language of the tribe, as Eliot, following Mallarmé, puts it—is *purified*, cleansed, given a well-deserved lift, the social function of poetry being, in Eliot's words, no less than "to affect the speech and the sensibility of the whole nation" (OPP 12). And Yeats describes his own process of self-modernization as an infusion of "cold light and tumbling clouds."[12]

Conversely, the declared enemy of modernism was said to be *artifice*, specifically the *artifice* of separating the *word* from the "natural object" to which it ostensibly refers. "We should write out our own thoughts," says Yeats in his autobiography, "in as nearly as possible the language we thought them in, as though in a letter to an intimate friend. We should not *disguise them in any way*" (Auto 102, my italics). Hence Eliot is critical of Valéry because "the words set free by [him] may tend to form a separate language. But the further the idiom, vocabulary, and syntax of poetry depart from those of prose, the more artificial the language of poetry will become" (PV xvi). For Eliot, *artificial* is a derogatory term because it implies that *words* can somehow be detached from *things*; as he puts it in his essay on Swinburne: "It is, in fact, the word that gives him the thrill, not the object. When you take to pieces any verse of Swinburne, you find always the object was not there—only the word."[13] And why would this be so bad? Because "Language in a healthy state presents the object, is so close to the object that the two are identified." Whereas in Swinburne: word and object "are identified . . . solely because the object has ceased to exist, because the meaning is merely the hallucination of meaning, because language, uprooted, has adapted itself to an independent life of atmospheric nourishment" (ESE 327).

The fear that the word will no longer adhere to the object haunts the poetics of modernism; it is a fear already latent, for that matter, in Wordsworth's "Preface." "Low and rustic life was generally chosen," explains Wordsworth in a famous passage, "because such men hourly communicate with the best objects from which the best part of language is originally derived; and because, from their rank in society and the sameness and narrow circle of their intercourse, being less under the influence of social vanity, they convey their feelings and notions in simple and unelaborated language" (WWP 869–70). From Coleridge on down, critics have insisted that this statement cannot be narrowly construed: in Coleridge's words in chapter 17 of the *Biographia Literaria*, "a rustic's language, purified from all provincialism and grossness, and so far reconstructed as to be made consistent with the rules of grammar (which are in essence no other than the laws of universal logic, applied to psychological materials) will not differ from the language of any other man of common-sense, however learned or refined he may be."[14] But from our perspective nearly two hundred years after the writing of the "Preface," the issue is less whether Wordsworth's language is that of the rustic or of Coleridge's broader category, the "man of common-sense," than that Wordsworth's preoccupation with "the language really spoken by men" can be seen as a kind of holding operation against the encroachments of an industrial mass society in which that language would undergo modes of mediation that would hardly involve communication "with the best objects from which the best part of language is originally derived." Indeed, a few pages further into the "Preface," Wordsworth refers somewhat bitterly to the "multitude of causes, unknown to former times, now acting with a combined force to blunt the discriminating powers of the mind. . . . The most effective of these causes are the great national events which are daily taking place, and the increasing accumulation of men in cities, where the uniformity of their occupations produces a craving for extraordinary incident, which the rapid communication of intelligence hourly gratifies" (WWP 872).

The hourly gratification of a "craving," on the part of the masses, "for extraordinary incident," a craving produced by the increasing "uniformity" of human occupation: here Wordsworth uncannily anticipates the problematic that now haunts some of our most original poetry. In Charles Bernstein's words in "Dysraphism:"

> Blinded by avenue and filled with
> adjacency. Arch or arched at. So there becomes bottles,
> hushed conductors, illustrated proclivities for puffed- /
> up benchmarks. Morose or comatose.[15]

A line like "Blinded by avenue and filled with / adjacency," for that matter, surely brings to mind Wordsworth's "The world is too much with us, late and soon, / Getting and spending we lay waste our powers." But what has happened to "the language really used by men"? To "the natural words in the natural order"? "In the room the women come and go / Talking of Michelangelo": there's a straightforward "normal" declarative sentence that anyone who has heard of Michelangelo can understand. Or again, "April is the cruellest month": a sentence that, if not quite plausible as a natural utterance, April conventionally being the month of spring rebirth, is certainly readily apprehended as a syntactic unit: subject nominative, copula, predicate nominative. But what sort of sentence is "Arch or arched at"? Is "Arch" a noun or a verb? If a verb, who is doing the arching? What does it mean to be "arched at?" And is the meaning of "Arch" the same as that of "arched"?

It may be that the fracture of language found in a poem like "Dysraphism" is merely perverse, the sort of willful and pretentious obscurantism Eliot warned about when he declared that poetry "cannot afford to lose contact with the changing face of common intercourse." Or is it possible that Eliot himself paid insufficient attention to the potential for *change* that "common intercourse" was inevitably undergoing? Despite the self-declared classicism of his later years,[16] there is no suggestion that Eliot ever abandoned his Romantic, indeed Rousseauistic faith in writing as the making present of a prior *natural* speech. In *Burnt Norton*, we read:

> Words strain,
> Crack and sometimes break, under the burden,
> Under the tension, slip, slide, perish,
> Decay with imprecision, will not stay in place,
> Will not stay still.[17]

The implication is that ideally, if the poet were equal to his task, words could and should represent the realities behind them, realities, so Eliot would have it, that belong to both poet and reader. Precision, in this context, means accuracy of transcription: the poet conveys, more precisely than can his nonpoetic counterpart, the meanings inherent in a particular set of experiences. Writing, by this argument, *makes present* what the poet wishes to *say*.

In the early twentieth century it still seemed possible to act on this doctrine. When Yeats visited peasant cottages in Galway and Sligo, gathering folk material that might find its way into the fabric of his poetry, when Eliot used the overheard speech of his cleaning woman—what he called "pure Ellen Kellond"[18]—as the basis for the Cockney monologue of Lil's malicious friend in "The Game of Chess," the working classes, whether rural or urban, still represented an exotic *other*, an other whose speech might be drawn into the poetic text in the interest of authenticity. Thus when Eliot produced a poem that contained the speech of a malicious low-class female gossip:

> But if Albert makes off, it won't be for lack of telling.
> You ought to be ashamed, I said, to look so antique.
> (And her only thirty-one).
> I can't help it, she said, pulling a long face,
> It's them pills I took, to bring it off, she said.
> (She's had five already, and nearly died of young George.)   (ECP 42)

such early readers of *The Waste Land* as F. R. Leavis and F. O. Matthiessen were quick to proclaim Eliot's triumph in capturing the *actual rhythms* of pub talk in 1920s London. And we continue to marvel at the vivid "realism" and precision of the Lil section, the brilliant juxtaposition of mock mimetic, as in the passage above, with the biblical rhythms of "HURRY UP PLEASE IT'S TIME" and the plaintive "Good night ladies," of Ophelia.

"Every revolution in poetry is apt to be, and sometimes to announce itself to be, a return to common speech." Eliot's dictum applies neatly to the self-declared revolution of the *New American Poetry*, as Donald Allen called his famous anthology of 1960. The work in question, says Allen in his Introduction, "has shown one common characteristic: a total rejection of all those qualities typical of academic verse"[19]—a reference, no doubt, to the traditional metrics, elaborate metaphor, and formal diction used by poets like Allen Tate, Howard Nemerov, or the early Robert Lowell. Allen's *New American Poetry* was soon followed by Stephen Berg and Robert Mezey's *Naked Poetry: Recent American Poetry in Open Forms* (1969), in whose Introduction the editors state, "We began with the firm conviction that the strongest and most alive poetry in America had abandoned or at least broken the grip of traditional meters and had set out, once again, into 'the wilderness of unopened life.'"[20]

The creation of this new "wilderness," of what Robert Duncan called the "opening of the field," as that opening was conceived by such diverse groups as the Projectivists and Beats, the San Francisco poets and "Deep Image" school, is by now a familiar story,[21] but I want to approach it here from a rather different angle, it being my own hunch that the very aggressiveness of the new demand for a free-verse and speech-based poetics testifies to a growing anxiety about the viability of the "natural style" in a world where nature is increasingly subject to the hitherto unimaginable operations of the various "quiet" revolutions of our time, especially that of the information revolution.

We might note, to begin with, that for the open-field poetics of the fifties, the speech base is no longer that of "common speech," as it was for Yeats and Eliot, and for Wordsworth before them, but the very personal utterance of the individual poet. Phrases like "finding one's voice" or "capturing the breath" now become prominent. In his famous manifesto "Projective Verse" (1950), Charles Olson sets himself apart from the "closed" or "print bred" verse of modernism and proclaims that "Verse now, 1950, if it is to go ahead, if it is to be of *essential* use, must, I take it, catch up and put into itself certain laws and possibilities of the breath, of the breathing of the man who writes." And a few pages later he declares that the requisites for the poetic line are:

> the HEAD, by way of the EAR, to the SYLLABLE
> the HEART, by way of the BREATH, to the LINE

Further "breath allows *all* the speech-force of language back in (speech is the 'solid' of verse, is the secret of a poem's energy)."[22]

Poetic speech is the making present, via the breath, of internal energy—not "common speech," the purview of such giant agencies as the OWI (Office of War Information), where Olson worked during the Second World War, but *this* speech, *my* speech. If "FORM" (according to Olson's second rule, which he took over from Robert Creeley) "IS NEVER MORE THAN THE EXTENSION OF CONTENT," the implicit corollary is that content is never more than the extension of the true voice of feeling.

As such, sixties poetics is largely consistent in its call for natural speech, direct utterance, and the line as breath unit. "Each line of *Howl*," explains Allen Ginsberg in 1959, "is a single breath unit. . . . it's a natural consequence, my own heightened conversation."[23] And two years later, "the mind must be trained, i.e., let loose, freed—to deal with itself as it actually is, and not to impose on itself, or its poetic artifacts, an arbitrarily preconceived pattern. . . . The only poetic tradition is the Voice out of the burning bush. The rest is trash, & will be consumed."[24] The stress on speech as vision is carried even further by Gary Snyder: "Breath is the outer world coming into one's body. . . . Breath is spirit, 'inspiration'. . . . Yet the muse remains a woman. Poetry is voice, and according to Indian tradition, voice *vak* (vox) is a

Goddess. . . . As Vak is wife to Brahma . . . so the voice, in everyone, is a mirror of his deepest self." [25]

The heroic stance of the male poet drawing inspiration from the female muse in the guise of goddess or Burning Bush constitutes what I take to be a kind of first stage alert in the face of the accelerated social and political change that characterizes the sixties. To put it another way: in a society where, as Arthur Kroker and David Cook put it, "class has disappeared into mass and mass has dissolved into the new black hole of the 'blip,'" [26] the poet's first response (and this is just as true of the women poets of the period) is likely to be what we might call the by-pass mode, that is, the desire to establish a direct line between self and spirit. "A partial definition of organic poetry," observed Denise Levertov in 1965, "might be that it is a method of apperception . . . based on an intuition of an order, a form beyond forms. . . . How does one go about such a poetry? I think it's like this: first there must be an experience, a sequence or constellation of perceptions of sufficient interest, felt by the poet intensely enough to demand of him [*sic*] their equivalence in words: he is *brought to speech.*" [27]

Brought to speech: this might be the epigraph—or perhaps the epitaph—of sixties poetry in America. [28] For by 1971 we find a poet like Robert Grenier writing:

> Why imitate "speech"? Various vehicle that American speech is in the different mouths of any of us, possessed of particular powers of colloquial usage, rhythmic pressure, etc., it is *only* such. *To me, all speeches say the same thing.* . . . I HATE SPEECH. [29]

And a few years later, Charles Bernstein observes that "There is no natural look or sound to a poem. Every element is intended, chosen. That is what makes a thing a poem" (CD 49).

II

Why is the natural now regarded with such suspicion? The reasons are many and complex, but we might begin by considering the role of the "common man" (or, increasingly, the "common woman") at our historical moment. "Think like a wise man," said Yeats, "but express our selves like the common people." But how *do* the common people, as distinct from others, express themselves in our late twentieth-century mass culture? As far as the media are concerned—and this is where most of us come into contact with representations of the people—class difference as determinant of language use has become insignificant.

True, soap operas and sitcoms now pay lip service to ethnic and racial diversity by including, say, a bit of the stereotypical ghettospeak of young blacks (e.g., Drusilla on CBS's *The Young and the Restless*), but such variations only serve to emphasize the television norm, which is that "real" people (as opposed to actors playing fictional roles), people like Dan Rather or Connie Chung or Barbara Walters or Tom Brokaw, slight differences in accent notwithstanding, use the same language, an up-to-date Standard American English, whose vocabulary, syntax, idiom, and even inflection are reassuringly uniform. Reassuring, in that viewers from Maine to Hawaii must be able to understand what is said on the CBS *Evening News* or on the *Today Show*.

No longer, in any case, is the hypothetical "common man" a presence to be memorably apprehended in the Scottish highlands like Wordsworth's Solitary Reaper or down at the village pub like Yeats's Old Tom, nor is the poet's contact with the exotic "common man" any longer likely to be the relationship with one's servants, as in the case of Eliot's Albert and Lil or, for that matter, Williams's Elsie, with "her great / ungainly hips and flopping breasts / addressed to cheap jewelry / and rich young men with fine eyes." Indeed, what Eliot called "the ordinary everyday language which we use and hear" has now entered an arena where "natural talk," filtered through the electronic media, packaged and processed, becomes the TV "talk show," *talk show* being an apt name for the transformation of speech into spectacle.

Poststructuralist theory (in this case most notably Derrida's "Writing before the Letter" in *Of Grammatology*) has of course been much preoccupied with this problem. Thanks to Derrida's elaborate dismantling of Western logocentrism, we now know—or do we?—that writing is by no means the natural representation of a prior speech, that indeed writing cannot be confined "to a secondary and instrumental function" as "translator of a full speech that was fully *present* (to itself, to its unsignified, to the other)."[30] But in accepting as axiomatic Derrida's argument *contra* the priority of speech, we sometimes forget that this argument too has its historical dimension. Surely, that is to say, it is not coincidence that the poststructuralist attack on "natural speech" as the embodiment of presence has come at a time when the available channels of speech communication have been so thoroughly mediated. As Michel de Certeau puts it in an essay called "The Jabbering of Social Life" (1980):

> Never has history talked so much or shown so much. Never, indeed, have the gods' ministers *made them speak* so continuously, in such detail and so injunctively as the producers of revelations and rules do today *in the name* of topicality. Our orthodoxy is made up of narrations of

"what's going on." . . . From morning till evening, unceasingly, streets and buildings are haunted by narratives. They articulate our existences by teaching us what they should be. They "cover the event," i.e., they *make* our legends. . . . Seized from the moment of awakening by the radio (the voice is the law), the listener walks all day through a forest of narrativities, journalistic, advertising and televised. . . . Our society has become a *narrated* society in a threefold sense: it is defined by *narratives* (the fables of our advertising and information), by *quotations* of them, and by their interminable *recitation.*[31]

Narratives, quotations, recitations: the contemporary speech overload can hardly help but have an impact on "the changing face of common intercourse." Consider—and this brings me finally to my chapter title—the modus operandi of a television show first aired in 1968 and still running strong: namely, the Donahue show. Phil Donahue now has quite a few competitors like Oprah Winfrey or Geraldo, but their programs are predictable variations of the model, the talk-show formula being almost identical whether the interviewer is male or female, black or white, East Coast or West Coast, and so on.

What sort of authentic speech do we hear and see expressed on *Donahue?* From Monday to Friday, five days a week, for a full hour, Phil Donahue, the all-American clean-cut average guy, performs what looks like a high-wire act as he leaps around the studio, recording the comments of his audience members on the topic of the day. Topics are almost always and reassuringly "everyday" and amenable to "normal speech"—for example, premarital and extramarital sex, masturbation, impotence, incest, rape, the rights of gay fathers and mothers, artificial insemination, surrogate motherhood, in-laws, day care, two-career couples, older man–younger woman marriages and the converse, alcoholism, drug abuse, AIDS education in the public schools—the list is all but endless. For each of these topics, Phil Donahue brings in a set of guest "experts"—experts falling into two categories: those who have "been there" and those who analyze "having been there."

Thus, in a "daring" program on incest, the "expert" (this actually happened!) is likely to be a woman whose father, a prison warden, forced her to commit incest with him. The father is also on the show as is the pitiful mother. These three principals are sure to be flanked by two "real" experts—in this case, two psychiatrists or therapists who have written about incest and who, as is invariably the case on talk shows, hold so-called opposite points of view on the issue. Or if the topic is drug abuse, the panelists are bound to include former abusers as well as, once again, the proverbial therapists. Significantly, no one seems to exist who is *currently* on drugs just as no one on the incest panel is currently having sexual relations with his or her child. The reason for this omission is simple: the media mechanism cannot permit the disruption that might take place if Donahue really permitted the natural words to occur in the natural order. Suppose, for example, that a few drunks were brought off the street and placed on the Donahue stage and suppose they promptly fell asleep or asked for a drink or started singing dirty songs, or threw empty bottles at members of the audience. Suppose, for that matter, that the talk-show guests just sat there and stared at the interviewer. How, in such a case, could the time frame contain its requisite plenitude?

"Every return in poetry," says Eliot, "is apt to be, and sometimes to announce itself to be, a return to common speech." Now let's look more closely at what "common speech" sounds like over the TV channel. To give a specific example: on Friday, 1 April 1988, the Donahue topic was "Couples who consider their marriage to be over but continue to live together." The author of a book on this subject was present as were three couples who were still living together, presumably "for the sake of the children," even though their practice was to invite their respective boyfriends or girlfriends over whenever they liked. As is usual on *Donahue*, a mock debate was in session, certain viewers expressing the opinion that such a sham marriage "is a big cop-out," others maintaining that, on the contrary, "In this day and age you don't have to lie about the way you really feel." One wife on the podium expressed the sentiment that "This way I still have both my guys near me . . . but I only sleep with one of them." This statement, like many other "outrageous" remarks, produced gales of laughter and applause from the audience. Evidently, they were amazed and delighted, if also a shade embarrassed, to see that a woman rather like themselves in appearance could have her cake and eat it too!

Along the way, the men and women who spoke both in favor of and against the living arrangement in question would begin with the clause "I think . . ." or "I believe . . ." or "It seems to me that. . . ." The constant reference to "I," coupled with a close-up shot of the speaker, would seem to suggest that the Death of the Subject, proclaimed in our more sophisticated intellectual circles, is vastly exaggerated. Here, acting as the home viewer's surrogates (7 to 7.5 million home viewers per day watch *Donahue*) [32] are people of all ages, both sexes, different races, and from all walks of life (with the proviso that they have applied to be guests on *Donahue* and have been screened as being "inappropriate"), who have *strong* opinions about personal feelings. Phil himself, moreover, seems to express strong feelings, speaking, as he does, from his location in the audience, not on the podium, taking phone calls, scoffing at what X says and baiting Y.

But if one listens carefully, these seemingly contradictory opinions are conveyed in a curiously consistent vocabulary. On *Donahue*, the seven virtues have been reduced to three: caring, compassionate, and candid. Given this three-*c* attitudinal profile as well as a big retrospective *R* for regret ("I now regret that I ever did such a thing!"), one can be forgiven—indeed admired—for almost anything. The gray-haired man on the screen actually committed incest with the unattractive young woman who is his daughter. But he now *regrets* it and, besides, she has managed to develop into a compassionate and caring young woman. And a woman candid enough to tell all about her ordeal in a new best-seller.

All these bits—or should we say bytes—of common speech, funnelled into Phil's eagerly waiting microphone, are perhaps best understood as what Jean Baudrillard has called *simulacra*—"models of a real without origin or reality: a hyperreal."[33] For if, so Baudrillard argues, "one agrees to define communication as an exchange, as a reciprocal space of a speech and a response, and thus of a *responsibility*," then television (or the media in general) is, by definition, that which "always prevents response."[34] Prevents it not because, as traditional Marxism would have it, our mass media are controlled by the consciousness industries of late capitalism, but because the media are themselves "the *effectors* of ideology" (RM 128). Indeed, once it is understood that "ideology does not exist in some place apart, as the discourse of the dominant class *before* it is channeled through the media," it follows that "all vague impulses to democratize content, subvert it, restore the 'transparency of the code,' control the information process, contrive a reversibility of circuits, or take power over media are hopeless—unless the monopoly of speech is broken; and one cannot break the monopoly of speech if one's goal is simply to distribute it equally to everyone" (RM 128–29).

It is precisely the "undifferentiation" of the audience that governs talk-show talk. The masses, as Steve McCaffery observes, become a "nebulous asocial abstraction, serialized into atomistic simulacrities (the 'privatism' of the family television receiving identical content as millions of other homes, *simulates* individuality)." Media narrative thus "absorbs communication as a model into its circuits."[35] We can, to take a concrete example, learn that Jim X "has chosen virginity" as a way of life; we even learn that Jim is a first-year medical student at Harvard; but our response to his situation is entirely constructed; there is no reciprocity between ourselves and the simulated "problem." Indeed, the next day more or less the same studio audience will respond just as favorably (or unfavorably) to John Y who is a sex addict. "Have a nice day," says Phil (or Oprah or Geraldo) at the end of the hour, smiling into the camera. But are "we" having a nice day? And who is to know whether we are or not?

The hyperreality of "the natural words in the natural order" is especially remarkable in the TV segments that cover national political campaigns. Consider, for example, the special broadcast in August 1987, in which the then-seven Democratic candidates were given the opportunity to make brief video segments about themselves and their families. Invariably, each segment opens with the smiling candidate, each in his neutral blue suit, flanked by wife, children, and a pet or two, against the backdrop of a "normal," "nice," but nondescript house. Invariably, the sun is shining and there are likely to be autumn leaves (but not too many!) underfoot. The candidate identifies family members by name and provides a "telling" detail here and there: for instance, "This is Johnny. He just passed his driving test." And then, dues to family values having been paid, the camera quickly removes the family and cuts to a close-up of the candidate's face.

The teenager's passing of the driving test is one that interests me, being the perfect synecdoche of the "language really used by men" as it appears on television. The candidate cannot tell "us"—the nameless and faceless—that his son is an athlete for that might offend those whose sons are *not* athletes or those who have no sons. But he can't say that his son is a bookish introvert either. He can't describe what kind of school the boy goes to without potential offense to someone out there. He can't describe the fights his son has with his daughter. Or his speeding ticket. Or his experimenting with speed. Indeed, the more we think about it, the more we realize that the candidate cannot say anything more specific about his son than that he is now legally driving a car. This is the level of abstraction to which the dream of a common language descends. Actual speech, no longer the exchange of "a man speaking to men," is emptied of all particularity of reference. The "real," as Steve McCaffery puts it, "is no longer the referent but the model absorbed" (NI 41).

III

What does all this have to do with the writing of poetry? The logical answer to this question is that poets are precisely those who, faced with the abstraction and emptying out of the mediaspeak I have been describing, strive to "reaffirm," in Louis Simpson's words, "the primacy of feeling," the conviction that "poetry is not a game played with words . . . it is in earnest." Indeed, "We need to speak again about common life . . . about offices and the people who work in them. About factories and the people who live in mean streets. . . . If we cannot bring these into poetry then something is missing—the life most people know." [36]

Simpson's view of the poet as sensitive other, giving voice to the "primacy of feeling," carries on what I have called the holding operation of the fifties and sixties, the poetic demand, if no longer for common speech, at least for *authentic speech*. To be a poet, at midcentury, was to "find one's own voice," to "bring to speech," as Denise Levertov put it, one's own experience. "Almost the whole problem of writing poetry," said Robert Lowell in 1961, "is to bring it back to what you really find." [37]

In Lowell's own case, this produced the remarkable poems of *Life Studies* and *For the Union Dead*, in which the simulation of voice—of a man actually speaking—is marked by what the poet himself was to call "the grace of accuracy":

> "I won't go with you. I want to stay with Grandpa!"
> That's how I threw cold water
> on my Mother and Father's
> watery martini pipe dreams at Sunday dinner.
> > ("My Last Afternoon with Uncle Devereux Winslow")

or

> All night the crib creaks;
> home from the healthy country to the sick city,
> my daughter in fever
> flounders in her chicken-colored sleeping bag.
> "Sorry," she mumbles like her dim-bulb father,
> > "sorry."
> > > ("During Fever")

or

> Nothing! No oil
> for the eye, nothing to pour
> on those waters or flames.
> I am tired. Everyone's tired of my turmoil.
> > ("Eye and Tooth") [38]

The "natural look" of these lines is, of course, cunningly contrived: the casual juxtaposition of "cold water" and "watery martini pipe dreams" introducing the central life-death theme of "My Last Afternoon," the ironic transference of the poet's anxiety to his baby daughter's "chicken-colored sleeping bag," the subtle water-fire tension and off-rhyme ("oil," "turmoil") of "Eye and Tooth," and so on. What seemed—and still seems—so memorable about these poems is the conjunction of careful artistry (the network of resonant images and metonymies) and an admirable candor—the willingness of the poet to write about his own "real" pain and to characterize himself self-deprecatingly as the baby's "dim-bulb father," to admit that "Everyone's tired of my turmoil."[39]

But the demands made on the "authentic" self were extremely difficult to sustain, even for a poet like Lowell, whose outsider status (a blueblood "Mayflower screwball" turned "fire-breathing C.O."-jailbird and mental patient) was a guarantee of an identity as representative as it was singular. Even in the case of such special selfhood, however, the tension between the "unique" consciousness and the increasingly indifferent external world could hardly be expressed without falling into the not entirely unrelated inflections of Donahue talk, with its similar accountings of coming "home . . . to the sick city," or the "martini pipe dreams" of one's relatives. "At their best," says Charles Altieri of Lowell's *Notebook* sonnets, "the poems include the reader in Lowell's charmed circle of those who, because of their despair, have developed the power to appreciate the limited joys and moments of shared feeling or clear insight that are all one can have."[40]

By the early seventies, such "moments of shared feeling" had too often shrunk into the wry anecdotalism of John Berryman's *Love and Fame:*

> Oh! I had my gyp *prepare* that tea.
> But she wasn't hungry or thirsty, she wanted to talk.
> She had not met an American before,
> to *talk* with; much less an American *poet.*
>
> I told her honestly I wasn't much of one yet but probably
>   would be.
> She preferred Racine to Shakespeare; I said I'd fix that
> & read her the King's cadenzas in *All's Well*
> about that jerk Bertram's father.[41]

This reminiscence of Berryman's Oxford exploits fulfills with a vengeance Eliot's criteria for a poetry that "must not stray too far from the ordinary everyday language which we use and hear." The exclamatory "Oh," the words italicized so as to simulate the girl's speech inflections, the "I said . . . she said" account, and the reference to the unattractive hero of *All's Well That End's Well* as "that jerk Bertram"—these are designed to create intimacy, informality, immediate presence. The problem—a problem Eliot tried to solve, at least in his earlier poetry, by attributing his "natural speech" to Prufrock or Lil or the Lady in *The Game of Chess*—was how to make *one's own* self a representative *self*, how to make what happens to that self matter, at a moment when the media were manufacturing and packaging "selves" by the hundreds and presenting them for our inspection. When, in the poem cited above, Berryman informs us that his girl's father is "an expert on sleep: praised, pioneered by Aldous Huxley. He lives by counselling in London," we are not far away from the mode of the *New Yorker* profile, e.g., "A prominent London psychiatrist whose mentor was Aldous Huxley, Jane Doe's father is an expert on sleep disorders."

At his best, in *The Dream Songs* and *Sonnets*, Berryman is of course much subtler and more interesting than this, but *Love and Fame* testifies to the increasing difficulties of placing the "self" in the "world" at a time when "sensitivity," "authenticity," and "being in touch with one's feelings" have been co-opted by the voices and faces on the video screen. "Were you very upset when you found out?" asks Geraldo of the man whose wife has just told the CBS audience that she has been a prostitute for years. "At first I was real upset," the man replies with a little smile, "but now I'm glad she has a job that she finds satisfying." "Upset," "glad," "satisfying"—what, one wonders, do these adjectives really mean given the context? And how does this talk-show exchange of feelings-designators affect the "finding" of one's "poetic voice"?

Asked by an interviewer whether he is trying to create a "language of revelation," Philip Levine replied:

> I don't know if I'm trying to create a language. I've never really thought about that. In a curious way, I'm not much interested in language. In my ideal poem, no words are noticed. You look through them into a vision of . . . just see the people, the place.[42]

Language, for the poetry that persists in its demand for authenticity, seems to be something of a distraction, interfering as it does with the direct communication between poet and reader; perhaps poetry can dispense with it altogether and go for the unmediated image. The resulting "transparency" is likely to look like this:

To Cipriano, in the Wind

> Where did your words go,
> Cipriano, spoken to me 38 years
> ago in the back of Peerless Cleaners,
> where raised on a little wooden platform
> you bowed to the hissing press
> and under the glaring bulb the scars

across your shoulders—"a gift
of my country"—gleamed like old wood.
"*Dignidad,*" you said into my boy's
wide eyes, "without is no riches."
And Ferrente, the dapper Sicilian
coatmaker, laughed. What could
a pants presser know of dignity?
That was the winter of '41, it
would take my brother off to war,
where you had come from, it would
bring great snowfalls, graying
in the streets, and the news of death
racing through the halls of my school.[43]

To say that the language of a poem like "To Cipriano" is "transparent," that the words are to be "looked through," is not, of course, quite accurate. We *see through* such language not because it is really "natural"—no one, after all, actually addresses a pants presser with the phrase, "Where did your words go, / Cipriano . . ."—but because the "natural look" has been carefully manufactured by a phraseology that insures a desired response on our part. "That was the winter of '41, it / would take my brother off to war"—oh yes, we know what that was all about. Indeed, Levine's celebrated *honesty,* the authenticity of his "spare" and "taut" idiom,[44] has to do less with what Yeats called "the presence of a man, thinking and feeling," than with the representations of such presence one meets in the world of *them*—the world of the politicians and media people the sensitive poet supposedly distrusts.[45] Cipriano, the pants presser, and Ferrente, "the dapper Sicilian / coatmaker," are true sentimental sitcom figures, even as the poet's "sensitive" memories of World War II have the inflections of a miniseries like *The Winds of War.* But then why should it be otherwise, the "common speech," as Levine receives it, always already bearing the imprint of the media circuits through which it is processed? As we read "To Cipriano," we can easily visualize the screen version, beginning with the shot of the teenage boy shyly chatting with the old pants presser "in the back of Peerless (get the irony?) Cleaners," and then cutting to scenes of Bataan, the allied troops liberating the Sicily Cipriano comes from, and so on.

"Where did your words go, / Cipriano?" asks the poet, a rhetorical question if ever there was one since he knows exactly, not only where crusty old "Cipriano's" words went but who put them in his mouth. Such poems—and they are legion—testify to the mounting pressure on the "authentic speech" model to be as graphic as possible, to make sure that "the scars / across your shoulders" illuminated by the "glaring bulb" are seen, even as we are to hear the "hissing press" punctuating such remarks as Cipriano's "*Dignidad* . . . without is no riches." Impercepti- bly, the norms have become those of the teleculture that "poetry" sup- posedly scorns. At the same time, the more radical poetries of the past few decades, whatever their particular differences, have come to recon- ceive the "opening of the field," not as an entrance into *authenticity*, but, on the contrary, as a turn toward *artifice*, toward poetry as making or praxis rather than poetry as impassioned speech, as self-expression.

"Artifice," says Charles Bernstein in a long verse essay called *Artifice of Absorption* (1987), "is a measure of a poem's / intractability to being read as the sum of its / devices & subject matters."[46] And further:

> To be absorbed in one's own immediate language practices
> & specialized lingo
> is to be confronted with the foreignness
> & unabsorbability of this plethora of
> *other* "available" material;
> the ideological strategy of mass entertainment,
> from bestsellers to TV to "common voice" poetry
> is to contradict this everpresent "other" reality through
> insulation into a fabricated "lowest" common
> denominator that, among its many guises, goes under
> the Romantic formula "irreducible human values." (AA 40)

The "plethora of *other* 'available' material" may prompt withdrawal into a world of one's own, where "natural" speech and authentic feeling still reign supreme. But once it is recognized that "the Romantic for- mula 'irreducible human values'" is itself "fabricated," withdrawal tends to give way to the urge to come to terms with the "unabsorbabil- ity" of other discourses.

The "artifice of absorption" takes, of course, many different forms, from, say, the gestural and playfully parodic lyric of John Ashbery, to the concrete or sound-text poem, to the *Oulipo* (rule-generated) work, to collage-text and performance,[47] and to the "antisyntactical" and "antireferential" lyric that goes by the name of Language poetry. All these are difficult poetries, difficult at least if one's norm is the "direct speech, direct feeling" model dominant in the sixties and early seven- ties. Confronted for the first time by the poetry of, say, Michael Palmer or Lyn Hejinian or Steve McCaffery, the reader is likely to lose patience. For instance with this:

> A cut of light
>   or a cutting
> grows of a whole night composed
> of day as well

the day the crystal's axes in a swarm drill
preciseness bristles of an emptiness sure
caught to tongue and left to lip
imitant blur
a night caught in such angles lit
                        (Clark Coolidge, *The Crystal Text*) [48]

"A cut of light": the first line looks reassuringly Romantic, but here what purports to be a sudden stab of insight is, so to speak, *denaturalized* by the proffered alternative: "A cut of light / or a cutting / [that] grows of a whole night." If the "cut" is more properly a plant cutting that takes a whole night to grow and if, further, the night is "composed / of day as well," the poem is describing, quite impersonally, how ideas, lodged deep within the mind, come to the surface of consciousness. Coolidge's structure is so tightly woven that we cannot extricate familiar syntactic units: "swarm," for example, may be a noun, indicating the place where the "crystal's axes" "drill." Or again, it may be an adjective signifying a particular kind of drill, a group drill within which preciseness bristles. To read this passage is to make connections, not via mimetic syntax, but via sound location: *cut, light, night, lit; crystal, drill-bristles; left to lip, lit,* etc. As such, constellations of meaning do begin to emerge: the poem opposes sharpness of focus ("A cut of light," "the crystal's axes," "preciseness bristles," "angles lit") to the "emptiness sure," the "imitant blur" of being inexpressive, "caught to tongue" (tongue-tied), "left to lip." It takes, evidently, a "whole night," a "night composed / of day as well," which is to say, perpetually, to get beyond that emptiness. But in the end we cannot be sure whether the "angles lit" illuminate the night or, conversely, whether they continue to be obstructed by the "night caught" in their beam. It is this sort of syntactic indeterminacy that prompted the perplexed graduate student from Yugoslavia to ask, in my poetry seminar at Stanford, "Why can't they write like Kafka?"

IV

Why *can't* they write like Kafka? Why is Kafka's extraordinary lucidity, the natural speech and "normal" syntax that paradoxically conveys the densest and most ambiguous meanings, no longer a viable model? There is no easy answer to these questions, but we might begin with the notion that whereas Kafka positioned himself vis-à-vis the discourses of law, of justice, of business, and of the bourgeois respectability and normalcy that characterized the Prague of his time and place, our own contact with these discourses tends to be always already mediated by a third voice, the voice of the media. Consequently, the poetic attempt to hold on to some measure of a unique and natural voice—what Charles Bernstein calls, with reference to Olson, "the *phallacy* of the heroic stance"[49]—with its masculinist allegory of language as the stride of a man and its idealization of voice as the locus of authority—is increasingly giving way to a poetry that, as Bernstein says of Ron Silliman, "emphasizes its medium as being constructed, rule governed, everywhere circumscribed by grammar & syntax, chosen vocabulary: designed, manipulated, picked, programmed, organized, & so an artifice, artifact—monadic, solipsistic, homemade, manufactured, mechanized, formulaic, willful" (CD 40–41). This catalog is purposely bombastic so as to emphasize what has become an article of faith for Language poetry: "Every phrase I write, every juxtaposition I make, is a manifestation of using a full-blown language: full of possibilities of meaning & impossibilities of meaning" (CD 46). And again, "there are no thoughts except through language, we are everywhere seeing through it, limited to it but not by it" (CD 49).

This is a long way from Levine's "In my ideal poem no words are noticed." The emphasis on the word rather than on the object behind it or the vision beyond it has had startling consequences. For one thing— and I shall turn to this difficult topic in my next chapter—the Image, conceived by modernist poetics as the "primary pigment" (Pound), the "objective correlative" (Eliot), the "vector" (Olson), begins to lose its authority as the poetic signature par excellence. For another, and this is my concern here, the new emphasis on the poetic medium as *constructed* and *rule-governed* calls into question the primacy of natural speech, spontaneous rhythms, and what Eliot called "common intercourse."

The case of Robert Creeley is instructive in this shift. Many readers who admired the Creeley of the fifties—a Creeley, so it seemed, still squarely in the Williams mode, became increasingly uneasy when Creeley published *Pieces* (1969) and *A Day Book* (1972). Thus M. L. Rosenthal, in what was to become a rather notorious review of the latter for *Parnassus*, complained that "there are too many passages . . . done either in telegraphese or in a comma-spiked, anti-idiomatic style that befuddles one's memory of the English tongue." For "few effects are as satisfying as the assimilation of natural speech into a powerful and melodic poem." Comparing Creeley's "The Edge" ("Place it, / make the space / of it") to its parent text, Williams's "Love Song" ("I lie here thinking of you"), Rosenthal remarks on Williams's "rich," "full-bodied," and "active imagery," imagery which "the Creeley poem echoes . . . but makes . . . almost static and reduces the emotion to an abstraction. Without Williams' phrasing—'yellow,' 'stain of love,' 'upon the world,' 'selvage'—it would have neither vigor nor concrete reference." [50]

But perhaps "natural speech," "active imagery," "vigor," and "concrete reference" are not what the Creeley of *Pieces* is after. Consider the opening section of "Again":

> One more day gone,
> done, found in
> the form of days.
>
> It began, it
> ended—was
> forward, backward,
>
> slow, fast a
> sun shone, clouds,
> high in the air I was
>
> for awhile with others,
> then came down
> on the ground again.
>
> No moon. A room in
> a hotel—to begin
> again. [51]

There is no use trying to read such a poem as a confessional lyric ("Here's what happened to me and how it made me feel . . ."). Creeley's is less a form of witnessing than of paragram, which is to say, following Leon S. Roudiez, that "its organization of words (and their denotations), grammar, and syntax is challenged by the infinite possibilities provided by letters or phonemes combining to form networks of signification not accessible through conventional reading habits" (quoted in McCaffery, NI 63). "The percolation of the word through the paragram," says Steve McCaffery, "contaminates the notion of an ideal, unitary meaning and thereby counters the supposition that words can 'fix' or stabilize in closure" (NI 63).

"One more day gone, / done, found in / the form of days": there's a sentence you are sure never to hear on *Donahue*, a sentence whose "content" is not extractable from its form. The "One," to begin with, is embedded in both "gone" and "done" on either side of the first line break so that we can virtually *see* the "day" erode before our eyes. But what is "done" is also "found"—the *o* and *n* reappear together with the *d* of *day* to call up the "form of days" once more; indeed, the paragram of "*form—of*" enacts the cycle of the title "Again." Line 4, "It began, it," is another version of this circular process, but the reassurance of cyclicity finds itself challenged by the equally prominent dialectic of "forward, backward, / slow, fast . . . high . . . down." In this context, "No moon. A room in" is almost a palindrome, a "room" being what one has when there is "No moon." Yet the "room in / a hotel" is a transit station, a preparation (note the rhyme of "ground" in line 12 with "found" in line 2 above) "to begin again." Indeed, the line endings in the final tercet make up a three-step unit—"in," "begin," "again"—*in* being the quality that stubbornly inheres in Creeley's "beginning again and again."

"The paragram," writes Steve McCaffery, is "that aspect of language which *escapes* all discourse" (NI 64). Discourse of the sort we meet in lines like "And Ferrente, the dapper Sicilian / coatmaker, laughed. What could / a pants presser know of dignity?" Given the overproduction of such instrumental discourses in late-twentieth-century America, with its glut of junk mail, advertising brochures, beepers, bumper stickers, answering-machine messages, and especially its increasing video coercion (on cross-country flights, it is now customary to show the preview of the film-to-be-shown with the sound on in the entire cabin, and this is only the beginning!), poetry (at least in the industrially advanced countries, the situation in, say, Eastern Europe or Latin America being very different) is coming to see its role as the production of what we might call an alternate language system. Hence the name, pretentious but essentially accurate, Language poetry—a label that, like all group labels, names of *-isms*, and so on, will probably have a limited life span as the designation of a specific poetic school, even as it will, paradoxically, become more significant as we begin to see "Language poetry" as part of a larger movement that began in the sixties. Let me conclude with two examples:

Consider certain emotions such as falling asleep,   I said,

(especially when one is standing on one's feet), as being similar
to fear, or anger, or fainting.   *I* do.   I feel sleep
in me is induced by blood forced into veins
of my brain.   I can't focus.   My tongue is numb
and so large it is like the long tongue of a calf or
the tongue of a goat or of a sheep.   What's more, I bleat.

Yes. In private, in bed, at night, with my head
turned sideways on the pillow. No wonder I say that I *love* to sleep.
(Leslie Scalapino, from *Considering how exaggerated the music is*) [52]

Posit gaze level diminish lamp and asleep(selv)cannot see

MoheganToForceImmanenceShotStepSeeShowerFiftyTree

UpConcatenationLessonLittleAKantianEmpiricalMaoris

HumTemporal-spatioLostAreLifeAbstractSoRemotePossess

ReddenBorderViewHaloPastApparitionOpenMostNotion *is*

blue glare(essence)cow bed leg extinct draw scribe   sideup
even blue(A)ash-tree fleece comfort(B)draw scribe   upside
(Susan Howe, from *Articulation of Sound Forms in Time*) [53]

Both these extracts come from long poetic sequences of the 1980s; both were written by women loosely associated with the Language movement. Their concerns are otherwise quite different. Leslie Scalapino's *hmmmm*, whose opening poem is the eight-line lyric above, is framed as a series of anecdotes of the "So I said and then he said and she said . . ." variety, alternating with short explanatory poems like "I know I am sick . . . when all I can eat is something sweet" (LS 5). In many of the twenty-eight poems in the sequence, the title doubles as the first line, as it does in "Consider certain emotions," so as to initiate a discourse that seems to simulate ordinary speech, with its short phrases, irregular rhythms, and gratuitous repetitions. "I can't focus. My tongue is numb"—these are the sort of locutions a guest on the *Donahue* show might easily use in explaining a particular disorder or state of mind.

But Scalapino uses this confessional model only to turn it inside out. "Satisfied this morning because I saw myself / (for the first time) in the mirror," the narrator tells us in "Seeing the Scenery" (LS 16), but then adds, with a deflationary twist, that she sees herself "in the mirror as a mountain." In "Consider certain emotions," "falling asleep" is compared to "emotions" like "fear, or anger, or fainting." The third noun is at least plausible: fainting is a physical event like sleeping. But how can sleeping be an emotion like fear or anger? The poem presents itself as a logical argument, but the "reasonable" explanation proffered turns out

to be absurd, and besides reason quickly gives way to the simple asser-
tion, "I do." As the anatomy of "sleep" continues, the explanations be-
come more and more farfetched, culminating in "What's more, I bleat.
/ Yes. In private, in bed, at night, with my head turned sideways on the
pillow." In this context, the "No wonder" conclusion is no conclusion
at all; the reader has been given no explanation why the poet says, "I
love to sleep."

Scalapino's choppy, ungainly antilyric thus plays parodically both on
the conventions of the traditional "longing for sleep" poem (e.g., Syd-
ney's sonnet "To Sleep"), as well as on the conventions of modern ex-
pository discourse with its drive to provide rational explanations. The
refusal to name the personae of *hmmmm* (they appear as "I" or "one" or
"you"; as "the man," "the young man," "he," and "she") or to specify
the poems' referents, together with the extensive use of white space and
oddly placed punctuation (sometimes three or four spaces intervene be-
tween the last letter of a word and the comma or period that follows it)
produces a bleak atmosphere of noncognition. Who are these people
and what is happening to them? Edith Jarolim has pointed out that Sca-
lapino's poetry is "cinematic or 'videomatic' in its extensive use of the
quick pan and cut techniques of the nonnarrative, avant garde film or
the rock video: a poem or sequence will scan an event or image and
then move quickly to 'shoot' it from another linguistic angle."[54] Thus
the opening shot of "falling asleep" quickly pans to "standing on one's
feet," at the same time as the tense shifts from past to present and "I"
gives way to "one." Such decentering of the subject foregrounds the ar-
tifice of the verbal process: this is patently not "natural speech" as we
might hear it on *Donahue*.

Susan Howe's *Articulation of Sound Forms in Time*, from which the
second passage above is taken, draws its materials, not, as in Scalapino's
case, from everyday life and observation, but from historical and liter-
ary documents, from archives and letters. The story of the Reverend
Hope Atherton, who, having been separated from the Hatfield militia
he was accompanying on an Indian raid in 1676, surrendered himself to
the Indians only to have them reject him in fear, thinking him "the En-
glishman's God" (see frontispiece and Howe's manuscript note), be-
comes the subject of the poet's meditation on power and marginality
and, by implication, on the marginality of the woman poet (Howe
plays variations on the name *Hope*, which is, of course, usually a wom-
an's name) in America.

In one sense, then, Howe's is a more "referential" text than Scala-
pino's but its actual "articulation of sound forms" is, if anything, even
more fragmented. The poem welds together a series of harsh-sounding

nouns and verbs, all filler (function words, conjunctions, prepositions) being cast out, so as to produce the chantlike rhythm of

ReddenBorderViewHaloPastApparitionOpenMostNotion *is*

where the italicized copula is startling in its disruption of the line's curious drumbeat. First-person reference is conspicuously deleted, the narrative voice being that of the chronicle, but a chronicle in shards or fragments, as if retrieved from a fire or flood and collaged together with other particles. In this context, words often point in two directions: in line 1, for example, it is not clear whether the "gaze" or the "lamp" is said to diminish; again, the person "asleep" may be Atherton or the Mohegans or we as readers whose "selv" is also a reduced particle. In line 2, the coalescence of words referring to the Mohegan raid startlingly culminates in the words "FiftyTree," where we expect to hear "Fifty-three," the "tree" pointing ahead to the "ash-tree" in the final line, even as the "shower" oddly turns into a "fleece."

The next four lines seem to describe Atherton's experience with the Mohegans but each of the words annexed in the linear chain without a space between them (e.g., "ToForceImmanence") is charged with a variety of meanings. We can only say that the stanza refers to the terrible conflict brought on by the "SoRemotePossess" of the colonialist settlers and their priest. Indeed, "SoRemotePossess" works to "ReddenBorder-View"—greed, we might say, leads to bloodshed. The final couplet conveys a catalog of jumbled impressions, most probably the impressions of Atherton on his journey back to "civilization," whose "sideup" finally reveals itself to be "upside" as "(A)" yields to "(B)." But then again, these two isolated words—*sideup* and *upside*—also refer to the "scribe" who "draws" the picture for us—a scribe whose "articulation" of "sound forms" changes in the time-course of the poem.

"Posit gaze level diminish lamp and asleep(selv)cannot see": Howe's intricate network of *p*'s, *l*'s, and *s*'s, of near-rhymes ("level"/"(selv)," "sleep"/"see") and consonantal echoes ("lamp"/"asleep"), binding together words whose grammatical position is generally ambiguous (e.g., "gaze" "level"), produces a dense "writerly" texture ("draw scribe sideup . . . upside") that makes no attempt to simulate speech patterns, whether the Reverend Atherton's or the poet's own. Consciously or unconsciously, the poem's artifice may be a reaction to the media-speak that forms its environment. For imagine a segment of *Donahue* in which the Reverend Atherton is trying to explain his motivations at the time of the skirmish with the Mohegans. "If you ask me, Reverend," says the man in the double-knit suit, "you had no business joining an

army in the first place. You're supposed to be a man of God." "I dis-
agree," says the lady in red across the way, "I think it was a very caring
and compassionate thing to do."

Both parties, no doubt are right. Just as both of them are wrong. Po-
etry, in any case, has moved elsewhere.

3   *Against Transparency: From the Radiant Cluster to the Word as Such*

Replace the image with the word-image.
—Claude Royet-Journoud[1]

The transformation of the speech model which was my subject in chapter 2 goes hand in hand with the changing status of the Image in poetic discourse. Let me begin with a representative passage from Ezra Pound's early *Cantos*:

> Great bulk, huge mass, thesaurus;
> Ecbatan, the clock ticks and fades out
> The bride awaiting the god's touch; Ecbatan,
> City of patterned streets; again the vision:
> Down in the viae stradae, toga'd the crowd, and arm'd,
> Rushing on populous business,
> and from parapet looked down
> and North was Egypt,
>   the celestial Nile, blue deep,
>   cutting low barren land,
> Old men and camels
>   working the water-wheels. . . .[2]

Compare this to the opening of Clark Coolidge's poem *At Egypt* (1988):

> I came here. I don't know you here.
> I say this. I have lost such.
> Plant at the gate. Slant on missing heights.
> Where if I see you you glow. Where no one.
> Here a sun. That the moon.
> Black black, and be sure of it. There is little sure.
> It was a coming which was done.[3]

In Pound's canto, the role of syntax is characteristically subordinated to that of Image, the Image which is famously defined as "that which presents an intellectual and emotional complex in an instant of time," a "radiant node or cluster . . . from which, and through which, and into which, Ideas are constantly rushing."[4] "Great bulk, huge mass, thesaurus; / Ecbatan"—Pound juxtaposes "charged"[5] nouns and noun phrases so as to define his desired "instant of time," the instant when the ancient citadel Ecbatan, Pound's ideal "city of patterned streets," becomes, in the poet's imagination, the place where Danaë receives Zeus in a shower of gold: "The bride awaiting the god's touch."[6] The paratactic mode of the canto locates us in a continuous present: "the clock ticks and fades out," the bride awaits, the crowd, "toga'd" and "arm'd," is seen "Rushing on populous business," and so on. As in the case of film montage, the canto's technique is to produce, as line 4 puts it, "again the vision"; elsewhere, Pound calls it "the method of Luminous Detail" and explains that it is such "'luminous details' which govern knowledge as the switchboard the electric circuit. . . . they gather the latent energy of Nature and focus it on a certain resistance. The latent energy is made dynamic or 'revealed' to the engineer in control, and placed at his disposal."[7]

Luminous detail is regularly associated with two other words: *precision* and *accuracy*. "By good art," writes Pound, "I mean art that bears true witness. I mean the art that is most precise." Whereas, "Bad art is inaccurate art. It is art that makes false reports."[8] But in Pound's practice, the two don't necessarily go together. "And north was Egypt / the celestial Nile, blue-deep, / Cutting low, barren land"—the images are precise but hardly accurate: on the map Egypt is southwest rather than north of Ecbatan (Hamadan). In the context of the canto, however, it hardly matters. Egypt and Ecbatan, the "celestial Nile and the celestial citadel": the juxtaposition is entirely apt, the Image functioning, in W. J. T. Mitchell's words, as "a sort of crystalline structure, a dynamic pattern of the intellectual and emotional energy bodied forth by a poem."[9] In the textual field of the canto, such precise "data" (Pound's term)[10] as the images of the "blue deep" Nile, "cutting low barren land," and the "Old men and camels / working the water-wheels," have the authority of presence. "Your Cantos," Marshall McLuhan told Pound in 1948, when he was writing *The Mechanical Bride*, "I now judge, to be the first and only serious use of the great technical possibilities of the cinematograph. Am I right in thinking of them as a montage of *personae* and sculptured images? Flash-backs providing perceptions of simultaneities?"[11]

Such "perceptions of simultaneities"—Pound's famous ideogrammic method—are notably missing in Clark Coolidge's *At Egypt*. The cited stanza has neither celestial Nile nor old men and camels, neither a "city of patterned streets" nor Zeus coming to Danaë in a shower of gold. Such Egypt-traces as appear—the gate, the "missing heights," the sun and moon—are little more than ciphers, the Image now being neither "accurate" nor "precise," and, in any case, subordinated to what the Russian Futurists called "the word as such." The very title defies our expectations: not "in" or "to" or "from" Egypt, all of which would make good sense, but "at Egypt," a construction that would be marked incorrect on an elementary-school grammar test, unless of course "Egypt" were the prepositional object of an active verb, as in "I am shooting at Egypt."

The opening lines carry on this odd syntactic and verbal momentum. "I came here. I don't know you here. / I say this. I have lost such." We cannot specify "you," "this," and "such," perhaps not even "here," but the abrupt disjunctive declarative sentences convey a sense of disorientation, anxiety, and hyperactivity. In line 3, each of the two short phrases is syntactically and semantically indeterminate: "Plant at the gate" might mean "I saw you planted at the gate," "I planted myself at the gate," "There was a large plant at the gate," and so on; "Slant on missing heights" might refer to the sunlight slanting on the distant "heights," "What I saw gave me a new slant on the missing (because dark?) heights," and so on. The one thing of which we can be sure is that "Plant" rhymes with "slant," a rhyme further heightened by the consonance of *t*'s ("at," "gate," "heights"), the incantatory rhythm here enacting the "otherness" of Egypt even as the words themselves refuse to constitute its image. In any case, "Where" now picks up from "here" without specifying that "here" any further. Does the line mean that I'm in a place where, if I see you, I can observe your glow? In this case "you" might be a mountain. Or again, the line may mean "where you (a lover?) glow (light up) if I see you." Even a "simple" set of phrases like "Here a sun. That the moon" is made strange by the faulty parallelism. Not "Here a sun. There a moon," but "That the moon," which like the title *At Egypt*, allows for a number of constructions, e.g., "Here's the sun. That light must be from the moon"; or again, "That the moon" may be the opening of a sentence like "That the moon will shine tonight is not sure." Indeed, the next line confirms the possibility of such a reading, "Black black, and be sure of it," followed by the qualification, "There is little sure." The stanza concludes "It was a coming which was done." The poet's coming to Egypt, now "done" (completed?). A Second Coming of some sort, perhaps referring to Yeats's poem with its Egyptian setting? A "cold coming," as in Eliot's "Journey of the Magi"? A sexual coming?

Coolidge's lines, I want to suggest, are neither more nor less "difficult" than Pound's but their momentum is certainly different. In the *Cantos*, the images do the work; jostled side by side, juxtaposed, cut, fragmented, especially in the later cantos, the images, precise, allusive, often recondite, create a tightly woven collage surface. In *At Egypt*, such montage of "data"—of luminous details—is replaced by a kind of Wittgensteinian language game. Ordinary words in ordinary constructions—I came here, I don't know you, I say this, if I see you, be sure of it—are denaturalized, decontextualized, so that we must puzzle out their relationships within the given language field. In the case of Pound, we read image against image—in what way is the "great bulk" of the citadel like a "thesaurus"?—whereas in the Coolidge poem, the focus is on the "redundancy" introduced into the information channel itself. For although what Pound calls an "emotional complex" is certainly conveyed, what, if anything, does this stanza "tell" us?

Toward the end of *At Egypt* we read "Egyptian though, Egyptian thought / Egyptians thought when they died / Egyptians thought they died then went / into sky to the east" (AE 73). "Though" (adverb) plus *t* produces an entirely unrelated abstract noun ("Egyptian thought") and then two verbs, the first intransitive ("thought when they died"), the second transitive ("thought they died"). No radiant node or cluster, no directness of presentation, no precision or lucidity. Yet the movement from "though" to "thought," the latter repeatedly bearing a new meaning, displays a concentration, a discrimination among words, that fits Pound's own definition of poetry as language charged with meaning to the utmost possible degree. It is the nature of the *charge* that has so radically changed.

Why, to begin with, no recourse to the *"clear visual images,"* Eliot, writing of Dante, found so central to poetry?[12] Why is the natural (or even the unnatural) object no longer the adequate symbol? Or to come closer to the present, what has happened to the advocacy, on the part of the "Deep Image" poets of the late fifties and early sixties, of a lyric in which, to cite Robert Bly, "everything is said by image, and nothing by direct statement at all. The poem *is* the images, images touching all the senses, uniting the world beneath and the world above."[13]

Reductive as this late version of the romantic image may be (Bly has actively denounced Imagism, restricting the meaning of "image" to the "deep image" that wells up intuitively from the recesses of the poet's subconscious),[14] the assumption that an image-free lyric would necessarily be the lyric of "direct statement" has haunted our poetry from the late eighteenth century to the present. From Blake and Hölderlin to the Surrealists and beyond, the image, in its various incarnations as pictorial representation, metaphor, symbol, or Poundian ideogram, has been understood as the very essence of the poetic. It is by no means my object here to trace the history of the concept of the poetic image, a whole library having grown up around the subject,[15] but to suggest that the current suspicion of "imagefull" language, on the part of the more radical poetries, has a good deal to do with the actual production and dissemination of images in our culture.

   The paradigm shift I wish to describe occurs, so far as American po-
etry is concerned, sometime in the early sixties, and can be measured
by reading George Oppen's *The Materials* (1962), his first book of poems
in twenty-eight years, against another book published in the same year,
William Carlos Williams's *Pictures from Brueghel.* The poems in this
collection, covering the decade of lyric produced after Williams suf-
fered two debilitating strokes, are among his most famous—the title
poem, "The Desert Music," "Asphodel, That Greeny Flower." But what
is often glossed over by Williams's critics is that these poems turn their
back on the very principles that made Williams a central figure in twen-
tieth-century poetics. Take a poem of the thirties like "Nantucket":

> Flowers through the window
> lavender and yellow
>
> changed by white curtains—
> Smell of cleanliness—
>
> Sunshine of late afternoon—
> On the glass tray
>
> a glass pitcher, the tumbler
> turned down, by which
>
> a key is lying—And the
> immaculate white bed [16]

As in the case of Canto V (although its images are not drawn, as are
Pound's, from disparate realms), "Nantucket" foregrounds images ar-
ranged in simple syntactic units: noun phrase (sometimes followed by
short adjectival and participial modifiers) plus noun phrase in paratac-
tic sequence, the poem's camera eye moving with fine precision from
the flowers seen "through the window"—a distance shot—to the white
curtains that link inside to outside, to the items inside the room—glass
tray and glass pitcher, tumbler turned down, the key tantalizingly de-
scribed as "lying down"—and finally zooming in to the "immaculate
white bed," on which no one is lying. There is neither direct commen-
tary on the part of the subject nor discursive elaboration, the implica-
tion being that the images of sight and smell, taste and touch can *reveal*
their own being. But—and here Williams is perhaps closer to Clark
Coolidge than to Vorticist poetics—in the course of the poem, the
image-bearing noun phrases—"Flowers through the window," "Smell of
cleanliness," "Sunshine of late afternoon"—are increasingly absorbed
into the ordinariness of the little connecting words, as in line 8 ("turned
down, by which") and line 9 ("a key is lying—And the"). As Williams
put it in an essay on Gertrude Stein, written the same year as "Nan-

tucket," "everything we know and do is tied up with words, with the phrases words make, with the grammar which stultifies. . . . it's the words we need to get back to, words washed clean." [17]

Williams might well have followed this Steinian precept but the fact is that, increasingly, he didn't. As early as 1936, in a poem like "Perpetuum Mobile: The City," we get passages like the following, from the opening:

> —a dream
> we dreamed
>   each
> separately
>   we two
> of love
>   and of
> desire—
>
> that fused
> in the night (WCWCP 1:430)

Despite their elegant visual layout, these lines display a distrust of the image as bearer of revelatory power, of presence. "A dream we dreamed, each separately, we two, of love and of desire that fused in the night"— here the words, far from being "washed clean" or "Unlinked . . . from their former relationships in the sentence" (SE 116) seem to function as mere counters, as part of the conventional vocabulary of love song and romance. Increasingly, Williams was to become a poet of direct statement so that, in the lyric of his last decade, we read:

> Of asphodel, that greeny flower,
>   like a buttercup
>   upon its branching stem—
> save that it's green and wooden—
>   I come, my sweet,
>   to sing to you.
> We lived long together
>   a life filled,
>   if you will,
> with flowers. So that
>   I was cheered
>   when I came first to know
> that there were flowers also
>   in hell.
>   Today
> I'm filled with the fading memory of those flowers
>   that we both loved. . . . (WCWCP 2:310–11)

"There is no need to explain or compare," Williams had insisted in a diary of 1927 in which he typically attacked "the bastardy of the simile," "Make it and it *is* a poem" (SE 68). Yet in "Asphodel," the proper name is immediately followed by a characterization ("that greeny flower") and then by a simile ("like a buttercup / upon its branching stem") and a qualification ("save that it's green and wooden").

Whether or not we admire this late style, we cannot help but recognize it as a marked departure from *Spring and All* or *The Descent of Winter*, from the Objectivist lyrics of the thirties and early forties, or even from the prose-verse splicings of *Paterson*.[18] Many explanations for the change have been offered, the most obvious one being the biographical. The Williams who wrote the three-step poems of the fifties was a terribly sick man, having suffered two paralyzing strokes followed by months in a mental hospital for treatment of extreme depression. He now wanted, not to experiment but to explain himself as clearly as possible, to set the record straight, as it were. Or again—and this is the account given by Williams's biographer Paul Mariani—"Asphodel" represents a movement *beyond* Imagism, *beyond* Objectivism to a new depth, the depth of rumination in which the flower "without odor" leads the poet through his own hell of memory, a hell in which he must come to terms with his past, especially his frequent adulteries for which he now apologizes to his wife. Robert Lowell, who was in the audience at Wellesley College when Williams, "one side partly paralyzed, his voice just audible, and here and there a word misread," read "Asphodel" to a rapt audience of female students, called the poem "a triumph of simple confession."[19]

But a "triumph of simple confession" can also, of course, be interpreted as a retreat from complexity, from poetic challenge. And what I want to suggest here is that this retreat, psychologically motivated as it no doubt was, given the facts of Williams's situation, was also culturally motivated. Indeed, from our vantage point three decades later, we can perhaps see that the poems in the *Journey to Love* sequence, of which "Asphodel, That Greeny Flower" is the most famous, represent a moment in our history when the Image as "intellectual and emotional complex in an instant of time" had become discredited, even as the poetic modes that "the age demanded" had not yet gathered force.

II

A "triumph of simple confession" (or what Hillis Miller calls "the quiet mastery of supreme attainment") is, in any case, a problematic response to the "pressure of reality" (Wallace Stevens's phrase) associated with the verbal/visual world of the late fifties and early sixties. By 1962, the year *Pictures from Brueghel* was published, there were fifty million television sets in the United States (more TVs than bathtubs) and 500-odd stations on the air twelve to eighteen hours a day.[20] It was the era of slapstick comedy (Sid Caesar, Jackie Gleason, Lucille Ball), of the celebrity host-show (Andy Williams, Johnny Carson, Jack Parr), and of war drama like *The Gallant Men* (the Fifth Army slugging its way to Rome), *Combat* (an infantry platoon on D-Day and after), and *McHale's Navy* (with Ernest Borgnine as the sloppy, if happy, commander of PT-73, anchored off an idyllic South Sea island named Taratupa). TV advertisements, not yet eclipsed by the VCR technology of the eighties, received enormous attention; indeed, advertising in general spawned a world of riveting images made for and by the affluent society in the heyday of its love affair with, as one New York discount house was called, Buy-Wise.

Compare, for example, two Listerine ads (figs. 3.1 and 3.2), the first from 1931 and typical of the predominance of text over image in the magazine ads of the prewar period when radio, and hence the spoken word, still dominated the media. Here the visual image—a drawing rather than a photograph—of an attractive woman fondling her Pekinese dogs takes second place to the "story," a kind of true romance cum cautionary tale about the "minor fault" that can "alter a person's life" as it did in the case of "Miss Nickerson." We learn that "After her debut in June 1904, it seemed almost certain that she would marry a titled young English army officer whom she had met on the Riviera, when the Nickerson yacht had been in foreign waters." But "Nothing came of it," or of any of the other young men who "paid court" to Miss Nickerson. Now past forty with a streak of gray in her lovely black hair, Miss Nickerson lavishes on her little dogs the love that should have been bestowed on her children, had she married! And why didn't she marry? Because— dirty little secret—she has the "unforgivable social fault": halitosis. If only she had used Listerine, all would have been well. And now there's a little still-life of the Listerine bottle, etched against those "bad breath" items—an onion and a fish.

By the early sixties, such moral tales had given way to the second sort of image, a blow-up in triplicate of an attractive woman, glass of Listerine in hand. It is a contrast that appears again and again: consider two ads for washing machines (figs. 3.3 and 3.4), the first, a 1916 ad for the Gainaday Washer-Wringer, advises the middle-class housewife to stop waiting for the proverbial Mary, Ann, or Maggie to "show up" (the racist drawing in the upper left shows the frustrated white housewife waiting for the black laundress, who is only now, presumably behind

What she *really* wanted was Children

Before any social engagement

Many women, otherwise fastidious, neglect to rinse the mouth with Listerine before social engagements. Apparently the matter of halitosis (unpleasant breath) never occurs to them.

Frankly, it should be one's first concern. Because, due to natural processes in even normal mouths, anyone is likely to have halitosis. The insidious thing about this unforgivable social fault is that the victim rarely realizes her affliction. And even a best friend won't tell.

The ideal deodorant

Noted medical authorities, observing Listerine in hospital and private practice, pronounce it ideal as a deodorant.

There is no scientific evidence that other antiseptic mouth washes exceed or even equal Listerine in deodorant power. Indeed recent experiences show that ordinary antiseptics fail to mask in 4 days odors that promptly yield to Listerine.

Does not injure teeth

Too harsh a mouth wash may actually attack tooth structure. Listerine cleanses and protects it.

Harsh mouth washes are also likely to inflame tender tissues of the mouth, physicians say. Listerine's action is healing and stimulating, yet it kills germs in the fastest time science has been able to measure accurately.

Always keep Listerine on your dressing table. It is a pleasant guarantee against offending others. Lambert Pharmacal Company, St. Louis, Mo., U. S. A.

the safe, pleasant deodorant

LISTERINE
ENDS
HALITOSIS

3.1 Listerine ad, 1931, in Robert Atwan, Donald McQuade, and John W. Wright, *Edsels, Luckies, & Frigidaires: Advertising the American Way* (New York: Delta, 1979), p. 28. Subsequently cited as Atwan.

Don't guess about your breath...

gargle LISTERINE and be sure

Anytime, anywhere, anybody can have bad breath, because most bad breath is caused by germs in mouth and throat. Listerine is antiseptic—to kill germs in mouth and throat on contact, by millions. It combines more active ingredients for killing mouth germs and stopping bad breath than any other leading oral antiseptic or mouthwash. Listerine stops bad breath instantly and for hours on end. *You actually feel it working.* **LISTERINE ANTISEPTIC**

3.2 Listerine ad, *Look*, 1962.

Stop Waiting for the Wash-Woman

"Late again. Half the morning gone and the wash isn't even started!"

How many times it happens, doesn't it? How many times the hours grow into days while you wait for Mary, Ann or Maggie to "show up!"

How many times you have to hunt around, through your friends or through the employment agency at the eleventh hour for a substitute!

It is easy to stop this wash-day uncertainty.

Put a Gainaday in your basement and you won't even have to wait for Monday. Any day, any hour, this efficient electric washer and wringer is ready to take care of your heaviest wash or your daintiest laces.

It gives you better than hand-

method results with none of the wear and tear. Its revolving cylinder handles all the clothes as carefully as you handle laces in a wash-pan. It thoroughly cleanses everything from rugs and overalls to the daintiest of fabrics.

You'll like the sturdy, swinging wringer because you can wring the clothes from washer to rinse water, from rinse water to blue water and from blue water to basket without moving the machine. During the last two operations another wash can be going through the machine.

The Gainaday is safe—every working part is entirely covered up, all electric connections are heavily insulated and even the wringer has a safety catch. The Gainaday slides around on the floor as easily as a baby tender.

It's guaranteed for five years.

Write today for a copy of our Picture Story Circular; then we'll tell you how easily you can obtain one of these efficient machines.

Pittsburgh Gage & Supply Co.
3019 Liberty Ave.   Pittsburgh, Pa.

Washer · Gainaday · Wringer

3.3 Gainaday Washer-Wringer ad, 1916, in Atwan, p. 14.

...and it pays off every washday

This 1963 Heavy Duty Laundromat is rigged—you simply can't lose. The Westinghouse Laundromat® Automatic Washer pays back part of its purchase price with every wash because it uses only *half* the bleach and detergent that agitator washers do. (Take a look; every detergent manufacturer says it right on the box!) The Laundromat not only uses less water and detergent but it uses them *more efficiently*—by putting gravity to work. Its revolving tub lifts clothes up through the wash water, then gravity plunges them down for another dousing . . . up and around *fifty-seven* times a minute. The Heavy Duty Laundromat cleans clothes—never customers. It's available only at your Westinghouse dealers. *You can be sure . . . if it's* **Westinghouse**

3.4 Westinghouse Laundromat Automatic Washer, *Look*, 1962.

The Hurry-Up
Breakfast

How much of a man's fortune depends on his breakfast?
A good Breakfast, not too big, goes a long way toward making a man feel good.
When a man feels good he can do his best work.
Now it sometimes (not always) takes time to prepare a good breakfast.
The exception is the breakfast with

Post Toasties

Here's a breakfast that's ever ready to serve instantly—that's delicious—that makes a man (or woman or child) feel good—for it *is* good.
The thin crispy wafers of toasted corn with some milk or cream and sugar (if you like it) should be responsible for a whole lot of success.
Post Toasties start off a good many thousands right each morning.

"The Memory Lingers"

Postum Cereal Company, Limited,   Canadian Postum Cereal Co., Ltd
Battle Creek, Mich., U.S.A.   Windsor, Ontario, Canada

3.5 Post Toasties ad, 1912; in Atwan, p. 198.

schedule, coming up the walk!), and buy her own washer-wringer, de-
picted here in a small image at the center. In the 1962 Westinghouse ad,
text is minimal, the ejaculatory image of coins flying out of the washer
(using a Westinghouse "pays back") into its owner's waiting lap—is
supposed to say it all. Or, to take a third example, compare an early
Post Toasties ad (fig. 3.5), with its conventional drawing, again subordi-
nated to moral tale ("How much of a man's fortune depends on his
breakfast?") to the sixties version (fig. 3.6), which has almost no text at
all (23 words plus the title Post Toasties Cornflakes) but a striking im-
age of two hands shucking a beautiful fresh ear of corn from which,
miraculously, Post Toasties emerge and dribble down the page. The
same transformation is found in soap ads: a 1940 ad for Lifebuoy Soap,
complete with "scientific" chart and little human interest stories (fig.
3.7), would take about five minutes to read in full, whereas the 1962
Lux Beauty Soap ad (fig. 3.8) subordinates a fairly bland text "Lux—
You're Wonderful. . . !" to a ten-inch square color image of a "beau-
tiful" young woman, provocatively gazing at the viewer through the
soap suds. The pink flower in her wet hair, which matches her pink
lipstick, is cropped at the top as if to say that the girl who uses Lux soap
is ready for the taking.

There is another aspect of early sixties imaging that is relevant. In
the typical magazines of the period like *Look*, it is almost impossible
to tell advertising layout from the rest of the magazine. An image of
a palm tree, for example (fig. 3.9), bears the caption "California: a
promised land for millions of migrating Americans." It looks for all the
world like an ad from the California State Tourist Association or per-
haps for Sunkist Orange Juice but it's the lead page of the feature of the
month which is called "California." Further along in this feature-spread,
we come to a page (fig. 3.10) captioned "Design Talent Blooms in the
Wasteland," which spotlights a lady in a beautiful long gown, silhouet-
ted against a dune, on top of which (or behind which) stands her male
companion in evening clothes. The copy below tells us in boldface that
her dress is a James Galanos design. Is it an ad for Galanos? No, just part
of a spread on California fashion. Is there a difference? Not really, as an
ad for a gold brocade Dynasty dress in a 1962 *New Yorker* testifies (fig.
3.11). The subtext, it appears, is that the supposedly informative docu-
mentary article about "the California dream" and the ad for a specific
dress designer are simply two sides of the same coin—the word *coin*
being used here advisedly. Indeed, it is amusing to note that whereas
the man in the Dynasty ad is a tailor, the *Look* photograph man an ele-
gant gentleman-escort, in both cases, the men are subordinated to that
which really counts: not the man, not the woman, but the dress!

3.6 Post Toasties ad, *Look*, 1962.

3.7 Lifebuoy health soap ad, 1940, in Atwan, p. 274.

LUX-YOU'RE WONDERFUL!

Your moisturizing creamy lather lets me
wash without dry skin worries!

cious Lux! Your Moisturizing Creamy Lather is so rich. It moisturizes my skin in a
no cream ever has. Freshens in a way no cream ever does. I can wash without
d of dryness, your creamy lather is so gentle. You soothe. You leave my skin soft,
mooth. Lux—I love you. To me, you're the most wonderful soap in the world!

In five cosmetic
colors
Beauty care of
9 out of 10
Hollywood stars

3.8 Lux beauty soap ad, *Look*, 1962.

CALIFORNIA: a promised land for millions of migrating Americans

This floodlighted palm tree represents one aspect of California. On all the other pages of this issue, LOOK presents—in pictures and words—our soon-to-be largest state in all its important aspects, with an eye to the significance it has for all Americans.

3.9 "California: a promised land," *Look*, 1962.

CALIFORNIA FASHION:

DESIGN TALENT BLOOMS
IN THE WASTELAND

GREAT DESIGNERS usually need the culture and sophistication of Paris, New York or Rome for fashion stimulus. But California's big three of fashion—Galanos, Tassell and Gernreich—flourish in an area some people consider a wasteland, both physically (some 22 million acres of the state are desert and barren) and culturally. They are shown here and on the following page in the desert near Palm Springs with their favorite models wearing their designs. JAMES GALANOS (above) is famous for elegant clothes at sky-high prices. This satin-striped gauze, in stained-glass colors, is splashed with sequins.

continued

3.10 "Design Talent Blooms in the Wasteland," *Look*, 1962.

one man made this dress

He takes a stitch in time, his own time. And there's no sense hurrying him. Chan is a craftsman of the old school. Old? Ancient! He feels you can't be too painstaking with a rich Oriental fabric. And Dynasty uses the richest Oriental fabrics. Cuts them by hand. Finishes them by hand. Gives you clothes from the Orient fine enough for an Eastern princess, smart enough for the ten best dressed women in America. Shown here, pure silk damask sheath with a mere suggestion of sleeve, a pleated obi and its own free-moving jacket. Amber (shown), almond green, Oriental sapphire. Sizes from 8 to 16. About $90.00. Lord & Taylor, New York; I. Magnin, West Coast; Marshall Field & Company, Chicago; Neiman-Marcus, Dallas. At other leading stores throughout the country or write Dynasty, 210 Madison Avenue, New York 16, New York. **DYNASTY**

3.11 Dynasty ad, *The New Yorker*, 1962.

Inevitably, such exchange between image as subject matter and image as sales material has played a major part, not only in the visual arts, where its role has been a commonplace since the advent of Pop art, but in literature as well. I am not talking here about subject matter—the novel or poem "about" consumer culture and commodification—but about the way poetry, for one (and a similar study could be made of fiction or drama), has responded to what we might call the *videation* of our culture. It is by no means, we should note, just a case of the "sensitive" poet reacting against the "vulgarities" of the media: indeed, this "sensitivity" scenario is itself, in large part, a media creation. What really happens, however, is more indirectly channelled.

Consider, for a moment, Williams's references, in "Asphodel, That Greeny Flower," to what we might call current events, references that are quite untypical of Williams's earlier poetry. In book 2 we read:

> The poem
> if it reflects the sea
> reflects only
> its dance
> upon that profound depth
> where
> it seems to triumph.
> The bomb puts an end
> to all that.
> I am reminded
> that the bomb
> also
> is a flower
> dedicated
> howbeit
> to our destruction.
> The mere picture
> of the exploding bomb
> fascinates us. . . . (WCWCP 2:321–22)

It is as if Williams, having seen, as who at the time could not, countless photographs of the famous atomic mushroom cloud (fig. 3.12), feels that he should assimilate this image into his discourse about love ("There is no power / so great as love / which is a sea / which is a garden") and thus tries to make the connection between forms: "the bomb / also / is a flower (WCWCP 2:322). Or again, he brings in the image of the "death / incommunicado / in the electric chair / of the Rosenbergs," observing that "It is the mark of the times / that though we condemn / what they stood for / we admire their fortitude" (WCWCP 2:323).

3.12 Photograph of atomic bomb dropped on Nagasaki, 9 August 1945. The Bettmann
Archive.

3.13 Julius and Ethel Rosenberg, 1953.

Such disjunction between image (the now iconic series of photographs taken of Julius and Ethel Rosenberg before their execution in 1953; see fig. 3.13) and moral commentary exhibits a certain malaise, as if to say that the poet's lifelong image repertoire, with its goldenrod and dahlias, its "black wind" and "mottled" blue sky, its cars and tenement balconies, its old men and young girls caught in memorable postures, or again its collagiste reproductions of love letters and historical documents in *Paterson*, must now include such generic public images as those of "*the* Rosenbergs" or "*the* Bomb." But of course—and this is the crucial point—such images are not drawn from natural observation as in the case of the red wheelbarrow or "young sycamore" or Queen Anne's Lace or from prior literary or artistic sources, as in the case of Pound's Ecbatana or "the bride awaiting the god's touch"; rather, they are images of already manipulated images, in this case newspaper or television images of the atomic blast or of the sentenced Rosenbergs, awaiting their death at Sing Sing. And since the latter are already heavily mediated as part of the political and social process in which they participate, their relationship to the consciousness of the poetic observer becomes problematic.

"Luminous detail," "clear, visual image," "primary pigment," "single jet"—the epiphanic moment when "some form grows radiant"—by the early sixties, when "radiance" had itself become a product sold by most cosmetic firms and soap manufacturers, the image had become a problematic poetic property. The most common reaction, not surprisingly, was what Robert Pinsky has wittily called "a kind of more-imagistic-than-thou attitude," as in the short bardic lyric of Robert Bly:

> I am driving; it is dusk; Minnesota.
> The stubble field catches the last growth of sun.
> The soybeans are breathing on all sides.
> Old men are sitting before their houses on carseats
> In the small towns. I am happy,
> The moon rising above the turkey sheds.[21]

The tone of such poems is self-consciously, indeed aggressively naive, as if to say that if the poet can only verbalize his or her actual sensations, authenticity (the antithesis of the media image) is guaranteed. Hence the present tense, the simple declarative sentences, the reductive "childish" vocabulary. Nature—"the stubble field [catching] the last growth of sun," "the soybeans . . . breathing on all sides," "the moon rising above the turkey sheds"—would seem to exist in its pristine state, at least in the more rural parts of Minnesota. Yet—and this is one of the ironies of the present situation—the context of such poems is not the "real" wilderness of pastoral America but such reading venues as *Bill Moyers' Journal*, which featured Robert Bly on 19 February 1979, the program later published in a 1985 collection called *Transmission: Theory and Practice for a New Television Aesthetics*.

The TV format makes it possible for Bly to be photographed on what Moyers calls "his home ground," namely, "on the shore of Kabekona Lake in Minnesota, and at a farm four hours further south."[22] As Moyers explains: "There's a rhythm to [Bly's] life now. Two weeks a month he spends with his four children near the family farm in southern Minnesota. Four or five days a month he supports himself, barely, by giving poetry readings at colleges and in community forums like Cooper Union in New York. The rest of his time is spent here among the lakes and pines of the north country, where he translates poets from abroad and writes most of his poetry. Robert Bly thinks the best poets finally come home" (CRB 236).

Notice what we might call the *telenostalgia* of this account, the videated nod toward a simpler, pastoral age when, presumably, poets were bards wandering among the lakes and pines and composing their epiphanic lyrics. Indeed, Moyers's little tele-bio-sketch is hardly more "authentic" than the Listerine story about poor Miss Nickerson, the deb who didn't marry because she had halitosis. Who, one wonders, takes care of those four children (and is there a wife?) the other two weeks of the month? And what does it mean to write nature poems that are remunerative only when one descends into the city to read them at colleges and community forums? How does one reconcile these two modes of living?

Moyers, speaking from the TV studio, is especially keen on talking about "the parts of us which grow when we're far from the centers of ambition" (CRB 237). He likes phrases—and Bly helps him along—like "journey into the interior," "peak experiences," and "discovering that third part" "in order to become human" (CRB 239, 240, 245). Along the way, Bly comments on the "grief" caused by the Vietnam War, the horrors of industrialization, and even the "passivity" induced by TV. The program ends with Bly reading a translation of Rilke ("It's a joy to walk in the bare woods. / The moonlight is not broken by the heavy leaves") and the Moyers sign-off: "From Kabekona Lake in Minnesota and Cooper Union in New York, we've been listening to Robert Bly. I'm Bill Moyers" (CRB 259). Time, evidently, for the home audience to go to bed.

Much of what goes by the name of poetry today is processed and packaged in this form. Distinguished from other forms of writing by the sheer weight of their images as well as by the series of breath pauses that signal lineation, "poems" are embedded in what are alternately weighty and witty anecdotes that serve to keep the audience more or less awake and geared up for their next poetic shot. At the same time, the more radical poetries have turned to the deconstruction of image. There are three main ways in which this has occurred: (1) the image, in all its concretion and specificity, continues to be foregrounded, but it is now presented as inherently deceptive, as that which must be bracketed, parodied, and submitted to scrutiny—this is the mode of Frank O'Hara and John Ashbery, more recently of Michael Palmer and Leslie Scalapino and Ron Silliman; (2) the Image as referring to something in external reality is replaced by the word as Image, but concern with morphology and the visualization of the word's constituent parts: this is the mode of Concrete Poetry extending from such pioneers as Eugen Gomringer and Augusto de Campos to John Cage's mesostic works, to the visual texts of Steve McCaffery, Susan Howe, and Johanna Drucker; and (3) Image as the dominant gives way to syntax: in Poundian terms, the turn is from *phanopoeia* to *logopoeia*. "Making strange" now occurs at the level of phrasal and sentence structure rather than at the level of the image cluster so that poetic language cannot be absorbed into the discourse of the media: this is the mode of Clark Coolidge with which I began and of Lyn Hejinian, Charles Bernstein, Rae Armantrout, and Bruce Andrews among others; it comes to us from Gertrude Stein, from whom image was never the central concern, via Louis Zukofsky and George Oppen.[23] And this brings me back, finally, to *The Materials* of 1962.

III

Oppen's famous twenty-five-year silence (he published no book between *Discrete Series* [1934] and *The Materials* [1962]) has often confounded readers: what can it mean, it is asked, to abandon one's chosen art for a quarter of a century? And did the poet's political activism (he worked for Communist party causes on and off for some twenty years) and his years of exile in Mexico reinforce or interfere with his poetics?[24] For my purposes here, the psychology of Oppen's silence is less important than what I take to be its paradoxically positive effect on the poetry. When Oppen resurfaced, Rip Van Winkle–like, in 1958, first in New York and later in San Francisco, he had missed the protracted controversy about the awarding of the Bollingen Prize to Pound for the *Pisan Cantos* in 1948—a controversy that triggered the larger debate about the relationship of poetry to knowledge, of the raw versus the cooked, of Olson's projective verse versus the "closed verse" of the "genteel" tradition. Largely detached from the various schools and having, in the intervening years, read more philosophy (especially Heidegger)[25] than the poetry of his contemporaries, Oppen may well have had less difficulty than, say, Williams, in coming to terms with a world increasingly characterized by what Charles Bernstein has called "imagabsorption"—the "*im-position* of the image on the mind" from without.[26] And indeed, judging from the various essay collections devoted to his work, Oppen's later books—*The Materials*, *This in Which* (1965), *Of Being Numerous* (1968)—have tended to speak to poets who were at least two, sometimes four, decades younger: Bruce Andrews, Donald Davie, Louise Gluck, Robert Hass, Michael Heller, Sharon Olds, Michael Palmer, John Peck, Rachel Blau duPlessis, Robert Pinsky, Ron Silliman, Gilbert Sorrentino, John Taggart, Eliot Weinberger.[27]

But then Oppen, even in his early poetry, displayed little predilection for "direct treatment of the thing," for the image as "radiant node or cluster."[28] Consider the third poem in *Discrete Series*:[29]

> Thus
> Hides the
>
> Parts—the prudery
> Of Frigidaire, of
> Soda-jerking——

> Thus
>
> Above the
>
> Plane of lunch, of wives
> Removes itself
> (As soda-jerking from
> the private act
>
> Of
> Cracking eggs);
>
> big-Business

The early 1930s, when Oppen wrote this little poem, were the years in which the Frigidaire or General Electric refrigerator became a secular icon. "As a protector of health through the prevention of spoilage," writes Roland Marchand, "it served as a benevolent guardian of the family's safety. As the immediate source of a great variety of life-sustaining foods, it acquired the image of a modern cornucopia. No open refrigerator door in an advertising tableau ever disclosed a sparse supply of food. The gleaming white of the refrigerator's exterior suggested cleanliness and purity." Indeed, "the visual cliché of the entrancing refrigerator," wife and husband (the husband was never seen in the vicinity of a refrigerator without his wife), or wife and guests, rapturously contemplating its well-stocked shelves (fig. 3.14), became, says Marchand, a "moment of secular epiphany." [30]

Oppen's little Frigidaire poem deconstructs such moments, not by writing a critique of the consumer culture that produces Frigidaires—that would be much too easy and uninteresting—but by rupturing the very sentence and phrasal units in which the image appears. Indeed, we never "see" the Frigidaire or the soda-jerk or the wives having lunch at the ground-floor soda fountain while big business is presumably conducted in the offices upstairs. "Thus / Hides the / Parts," the poem begins oddly. "Thus," as Harold Schimmel points out in his excellent essay on *Discrete Series*, surprises the reader by its formality, its "uncolloquial nature"; reappearing in line 6, again in isolated position, "Thus" functions, Schimmel notes, as an arrow, road sign, or mathematical symbol, that points us in a particular direction. [31] It is not a signifier pointing toward a particular signified but a relational term.

But what is it that "Thus / Hides the / Parts"? Oppen characteristically omits the subject noun or pronoun. Is it the Frigidaire itself, whose exterior "prudery" (its white walls and door) hides its motor (cf. "All the mechanism is in here" in the GE ad)? Or are the hidden parts the delectable food items placed in the refrigerator? Or do the lines refer to the soda-jerk who prudently cracks the eggs ahead of time and be-

3.14 General Electric refrigerator ad, *Saturday Evening Post*, 24 September 1927, p. 117; from Roland Marchand, p. 270.

hind the scene (a "private act") so that his performance will appear more streamlined? Or to the "big-Business" of the last line, that hides by removing itself (line 9) from its own production as from the "Plane of lunch, of wives" below? The poem invites all these readings, but not to make a didactic point. For the poem itself "Hides / the parts," aligning words so as to create paragrams. "Parts—the prudery" suggests, by its alliteration and word placement that prudery has something to do with hiding one's parts. "Of Frigidaire, of" provides the brand name with a frame that seems to limit its power. The line "Above the" sits above "Plane of lunch, of wives" as if the poet himself were stationed some-where on the balcony, and "lunch" and "wives" are not properly nouns in apposition. The capitalization of "Plane" points back to the capital-ized "Parts" (notice that Oppen doesn't automatically begin a line with a capital letter), and the lower-case "big" in "big-Business" forces us to look hard at that particularly hackneyed phrase.

However one interprets the poem, it is, finally, the "Thus" of lines 1 and 6 that remains most enigmatic. For Oppen never does explain *how* the "parts," whether of Frigidaires or of soda-jerking or of manufactur-ing, are "hidden." His interest is not to produce a clear visual image of a particular scene, a description of lunch at the office building soda foun-tain, but, on the contrary, to see how *words*, taken out of their normal syntactic contexts, can assume new meanings. "Thus / Hides the" in that "thus" contains and obscures the meaning of "the." "Thus / Above the" points to the hierarchy of words within the poem. The apposition of "Cracking eggs" and "big-Business" suggests that the "act / Of / Crack-ing eggs" *is* a big business. And so on.

Syntax, writes Oppen in his "Daybook" (the entries are undated): "a careful packing of a poem to avoid mere shuffling, a deadening, to avoid destroying a word by its relationships."[32] Which is to say by the wrong relationships. "Those who are not very concerned with art," writes Op-pen, "want poems or pictures to record for them something they already know—as one might want a picture of a place he loves" (DBK 29). But, as he puts it, again in his "Daybook" (DBK 25), preparatory to its incor-poration in the poem "Route": "Words cannot be wholly transparent. And this is the 'heartlessness' of words" (GOCP 186). "Heartless" in the sense of being uncompromising, unwilling to engage in rituals of tran-scendence, of otherness. It is interesting to compare Oppen's refusal of transparency, his repeated insistence that "the word is a solid" (DBK 25), to Pound's 1915 definition of Image:

> The Image can be of two sorts. It can arise within the mind. It is then 'subjective'. External causes play upon the mind, perhaps; if so, they are drawn into the mind, fused, transmitted, and emerge in an Image unlike

themselves. Secondly, the Image can be objective. Emotion seizing upon some external scene or action carries it intact to the mind; and that vortex purges it of all save the essential or dominant or dramatic qualities, and it emerges like the external original.[33]

"Purged" by the vortex, the Image, as Pound said elsewhere (LE 33), "stands clean," a substitute, as it were, for the "external original," which it resembles. It is this still-Modernist faith in the image as analogy that Oppen calls into question in the poems of the sixties that begin with *The Materials*. "Image of the Engine," one poem is called, but its descriptive Whitmanian opening soon dissolves into phrases like "What ends / Is that" (GOCP 20). In another poem (no. 21 of "Of Being Numerous," GOCP 162) that starts out as a quintessentially Objectivist lyric with its emphasis on thingness, on "the brick / In a brick wall / The eye picks / So quiet of a Sunday,"[34] Oppen abruptly "drops" the brick and, pointedly avoiding the pictorial or tactile, skips a line and places, all by itself, a proper name that may or may not be the "you" of lines 5–6:

> Here is the brick, it was waiting
> Here when you were born
>
> Mary-Anne.

The ordinary name Mary-Anne, three syllables bearing two short *a*'s surrounded by white space, has an odd opacity. For we don't know any more about Mary-Anne than we do about the brick: the name evokes no image, tells no story; indeed the address to Mary-Anne seems to interrupt the poet's rumination about the past and leave its meaning suspended.[35] What relatedness there is exists on the level of sound rather than meaning: *Mar*-y picks up the sound of "There" in line 1 so that anaphora brings us full circle: "There"—"Here"—"Here"—"Mar-y."

From Image to the "'heartlessness' of words": consider now what happens in a short poem from *The Materials* deceptively called "The Hills":

> That this is I,
> Not mine, which wakes
> To where the present
> Sun pours in the present, to the air perhaps
> Of love and of
> Conviction.
>
>   As to know
> Who we shall be. I knew it then.
> You getting in
> The old car sat down close
> So close I turned and saw your eyes a woman's
> Eyes. The patent

> Latches on the windows
> And the long hills whoever else's
> Also ours. (GOCP, 54)

The title "The Hills" leads us to expect some sort of description—an image, perhaps, of how "the hills" of childhood have changed ("Tintern Abbey") or of where the poet is stationed ("I stood tiptoe / Upon a little hill"), or of the relationship of the hilly landscape to the speaking subject, as in H.D.'s "The Helmsman":

> We wandered from pine-hills
> through oak and scrub-oak tangles
> we broke hyssop and bramble,
> we caught flower and new bramble-fruit
> in our hair: we laughed
> as each branch whipped back,
> we tore our feet in half buried rocks
> and knotted roots and acorn-cups.[36]

In Oppen's poem, such concretion is notably absent: the only adjective used to describe the "hills" is found in the penultimate line and it is hardly very descriptive: "the long hills." But then the whole poem has only four adjectives—"long," "present," "old," and "patent"—and no more than twelve nouns; it is composed primarily of deictics, the "little words I like so much" as Oppen called them,[37] as in that first unsparing and flatly monosyllabic line, "That this is I," followed enigmatically by the disclaimer "Not mine."

"That this is I, / Not mine, which wakes"—here the possibilities of syntax rather than of image or metaphor are put into play. In line 1, the dependent (dependent on what?) clause challenges the reader to fill in the gaps. For instance:

I know that this is I.
I can't believe that this is I.
How strange that this is I.
How ironic that this is I.
I must face the truth that this is I.

And the next line can be read as follows:

It can't be mine, this body which is now waking up to the morning sunshine.

It is not mine, this household now coming to life in the morning sunshine.

It is not mine, the "I" which the sun awakes; I have no control over my self.

And so on. This is not to suggest, however, that Oppen's lines don't "say" anything. For however one chooses to read these opening words, they convey a tone of extreme disorientation, as if their speaker were cut off, not only from others but from his own inner being. "That this is I"—four syllables with four stresses, like a monotonous drumbeat that demands to be heard, and which, for that matter, the poet instantly seems to retract with the words "Not mine." The abruptness of the opening suggests that the speaker is waking up in a strange place and that he has momentarily lost all sense of self and of bodily weight. The "present / Sun pours in the present": the repetition is not gratuitous, stressing as it does the recognition that this is indeed the light of common day, the harsh and full daylight. Nor is what awaits at all certain: the "air" is only "perhaps" (the word coming at the end of the long fourth line is emphatic) the air "Of love and of / Conviction." And anyway, love does not necessarily insure conviction or vice versa.

The opening of the second visual unit ("stanza" seems too strong for this irregular block of type) is almost as enigmatic. "As to know / Who we shall be" can mean "I am not so presumptuous as to know / Who we shall be." Or again it may be a question: "Who is so wise as to know / Who we shall be?" These deictics, in any case, now give way to a more traditional image: a memory, evidently, of the poet's beloved (or, more specifically, as we know from the other poems, his wife Mary) in the early days of their courtship, getting into his "old car" and sitting "close / So close I turned and saw your eyes a woman's / Eyes." The scene is hardly remarkable: one thinks of a dozen old films in which a lovely young woman gets into a man's car and looks into his eyes: Claudette Colbert, for example, flagging a ride with Clark Gable. Or the standard sixties ad (fig. 3.15), in which the beautiful couple (the man of course at the wheel) is seen, driving their new Thunderbird through the green and verdant hills of a luscious America.

But just when the reader settles into the romance plot, something jars. The "woman's / Eyes" (the line break oddly separating the eyes from the rest of her person) are now placed in apposition to "The patent / Latches on the windows." What sort of collocation can this be? Latches are what lock the windows; patent latches are inscribed with their brand name; "patent" also connotes patent leather which is black and shiny. Thus the line "Eye. The patent" oddly relates Mary's eyes to black and shiny little machine parts with a brand name, parts that shut the speaking subject *inside* the machine itself. Somehow, although we don't know how, the memory has a painful edge; when the poem concludes, "And the long hills whoever else's / Also ours," the pleasure of return (here are the familiar hills!) remains muted.

Thunderbird Turnpike The deep velvet feel of a Thunderbird's springs, the balanced poise of its weight, open new roads to adventure. Find a hidden, rutted byway where ordinary cars would hesitate . . . a Thunderbird's supple tread smooths it into a tawny ribbon. The miles have a new meaning in a four-passenger car with this solid heft, these contoured foam rubber seats, this silent evidence of utter quality. Every road beckons when you move with such cradled ease, behind the absolute authority of Thunderbird power. Can you imagine what it is to feel every lane transformed into a secret turnpike? It only happens in Thunderbird Country. Your Ford dealer will show you the way. *unique in all the world*

3.15 Ford Thunderbird ad, *Look*, 1962.

If one knows Oppen's biography, "The Hills" can be read as an elegiac poem recounting the poet and his wife's return, after many years, to the hills of San Francisco where they had been young, a return that is bittersweet and fraught with memories of early love but also of constriction. But "The Hills" is not so much "about" this return as it is about the despair of not knowing what one once thought one knew. Just when "the little words" seem to be pointing toward *things*—"You getting in / The old car sat down close"—the syntax undermines their momentum. "The patent / Latches on the windows": suppose "patent" is read as a noun, "latches" as a verb. How, then, do we characterize the remembered car ride?

"The question 'What is a word really?'" says Wittgenstein in *Philosophical Investigations*, "is analogous to 'What is a piece in chess?'"[38] In following the Wittgensteinian precept that "the meaning of a word is its use in the language" (PI 43), that "naming" is at best "a *queer* connexion of a word with an object" (38), Oppen's work suggests that perhaps we have had, at least for the moment, a surfeit of luminous detail. Consider, for example, the transformation of a topos like the cat poem from Christopher Smart's *Jubilate Agno* ("For I will consider my Cat Jeoffry") to Baudelaire's mysteriously erotic *Les Chats* to Williams's brilliant tracking (1930) of the cat's movement as it climbs over "the top of / the jamcloset / first the right / forefoot / carefully / then the hind" and "step[s] down / into the pit of / the empty / flowerpot." By the sixties, the image of the cat had become a popular logo. Take the widely disseminated image used to advertise Lanvin's My Sin (fig. 3.16). This ad juxtaposes the image of a black furry cat, shaped like a large black ball (no paws visible), staring with "mysterious" green eyes into the middle distance. Silhouetted against the big cat-ball, whose shape it replicates, is the circular concave Lanvin perfume flask on whose surface is the silhouette, Greek-vase style, of a giant robed person (perhaps a goddess?) putting hands on a much smaller androgynous figure who is evidently the sinner. "My Sin," reads the caption, "a most provocative perfume." What dark secret love, one wonders, lies behind this pseudo-stroy?

Increasingly, so far as the media are concerned, the image is supposed to say it all. Here (fig. 3.17) is a two-page spread from a 1989 *New York Times Magazine*, nostalgically depicting the adult's idealization of what young boys should be like—two lads in tweeds and caps, at home, or at least visiting, at a beautiful farm. The whole ad has only five words, "Polo / Ralph Lauren / for Boys." But the reduction of verbal text goes hand in hand with the increasing complexity of image-making. The Ralph Lauren "picture" immediately connotes New England and hence elegant East Coast country living, the Ivy League, and so on. But

3.16 Lanvin My Sin ad, *Look*, 1962.

3.17 Polo ad, *New York Times Magazine*, September 1989.

look again. The trees behind the barn look like California cypresses, with eucalyptus to their right: the photograph was probably shot in Northern California. But then again the landscape is so generalized it could be any part of the country. New England, that is to say, can belong to all of us. Then, too, the Polo boys, far from riding horses around the corral or picnicking next to a gorgeous waterfall as in this 1962 Salem cigarette ad (fig. 3.18), simply sit on what seems to be a front or back stoop of an ordinary clapboard house. The storm door behind them seems to have a little hole in it—as storm doors of ordinary houses often do. Ralph Lauren clothes, the image tells us, are within anyone's reach.

From here it is just a step to the ingenious Nissan ad for the new Infiniti luxury car (fig. 3.19), an ad often spread across two or even three pages. Here there is only one word—the name "Infiniti" (*i* not *y* in that this is a special version of the larger thing)—and no car at all, only boundless fields and fences, with the open forest behind them. The text, "scientific" and informative, comes on a separate page and is meant to be read only *after* one is hooked on the image. But the image of what? What does the absent signifier, the Infiniti car, have to do with these miles of fenced pastures? Evidently the automobile, once a large noisy machine that spluttered and roared, took up space and polluted the environment, is now an invisible magic carpet, by means of which we fly across those fields, jumping whatever fences get in our way. Driving the

3.18 Salem cigarette ad, *Look*, 1962.

3.19 Nissan Infiniti ad, *New York Times Magazine*, October 1989.

Infiniti, says the ad, will make you feel a part of Nature, pure and simple. No crowds, no traffic, no roadblocks, no mean streets to negotiate—only an empty paradise.

Such powerful images challenge poetic discourse to deconstruct rather than to duplicate them. They prompt what has become an ongoing, indeed a necessary dialectic between the simulacrum and its other, a dialectic no longer between the image and the real, as early Modernists construed it, but between the word and the image. Here, for example, is the first poem in Rae Armantrout's *Precedence* (1985). Its title is "Double," and its "hills of home" are not even, like Oppen's "long hills," "Also ours":

> So these are the hills of home. Hazy tiers
> nearly subliminal. To see them is to see
> double, hear bad puns delivered with a wink.
> An untoward familiarity.
>
> Rising from my sleep, the road is more
> and less the road. Around that bend are pale
> houses, pairs of junipers. Then to *look*
> reveals no more.[39]

"To *look* / reveals no more." In that case, it is time, as Armantrout suggests, to let the words themselves "see double."

4   *Signs Are Taken for Wonders:*
The Billboard Field as Poetic Space

Now the letter and the word which have rested for centuries in the flat bed of
the book's horizontal pages have been wrenched from their position and have
been erected on vertical scaffolds in the streets as advertisement.
—Walter Benjamin, "Zentralpark"[1]

It is the highway signs, through their sculptural forms or pictorial sil-
houettes, their particular positions in space, their inflected shapes, and their
graphic meanings that identify and unify the megatexture. They make verbal
and symbolic connections through space, communicating a complexity of
meanings through hundreds of associations in a few seconds from far away.
Symbol dominates space. . . . Architecture defines very little: The big sign
and the little building is the rule of Route 66.
—Robert Venturi, Denise Scott-Brown, and Steven Izenour, *Learning from Las Vegas*[2]

4.1 From *Learning from Las Vegas*, p. 5

In the billboard culture of the late twentieth century, the "successful"
text is one that combines high-speed communication with maximum
information. Here, for example, is what the Venturis call the "heraldry"
of the Las Vegas Strip (fig. 4.1), with its promise of food, shelter, gaso-
line, and even, in the spirit of Brecht Mahagonny, "free aspirin" to com-
plete the nocturnal cycle. "Free aspirin" is followed by the words "Ask
us anything," and, in much smaller letters, the signature of "Jay G.
Manning, Union Oil Dealer." Ask an oil dealer "anything": it is a pros-
pect that, to say the least, gives one pause.

    Learning from Las Vegas appeared in 1972; since then, the more bill-
boards, highway signs, advertising posters, and media spreads that have
come to compete for our attention, the more "subtle" these minitexts
have become. Here is a recent Parliament cigarette ad from the *New
York Times Magazine* (fig. 4.2), which depicts an attractive young
couple, silhouetted against an Ionic column on a breathtakingly gor-

93

geous terrace cum ocean view, the painter's easel (tactfully, it is not clear whether his or hers) to one side. The caption reads:

THE
PERFECT RECESS

Re·cess (Webster) : A break from activity for rest or relaxation.
Re·cess (Parliament) : A unique filter for extra smooth taste and low tar enjoyment.

To read these words in their context is to have some sense of what has happened to Imagist doctrine in the course of the eight decades since its inception. Exact treatment of the thing, accuracy of presentation, precise definition—these Poundian principles have now been transferred to the realm of copywriting. But advertising being what it is, the "exact" definition of the word "RECESS" (further complicated by the pun on "Parliament") and the matching of word to image finds itself on the same page as the inscription, placed on top of the second Ionic column in a white coffin-shaped box framed in black like an obituary card:

> SURGEON GENERAL'S WARNING: Cigarette
> Smoke Contains Carbon Monoxide

What kind of "PERFECT RECESS" can it be that includes this ominous warning? Is the topos here "Carpe diem"? A last puff on that enticing Parliament before being overcome by its lethal fumes? Or perhaps *Liebestod*? The artist-lovers doomed to succumb to the final solution of carbon monoxide? Of such absurdities is the postmodern world of advertising heraldry made: in this particular case, the legal injunction to provide the warning runs headlong into Philip Morris's zeal to disseminate one of its products: hopefully, so the copywriters may have reasoned, the "big picture" will draw attention away from the nagging, legally imposed moral message.

Or take another billboard text (fig. 4.3), this time for a more neutral product: Gap sportswear. On a black background, in widely spaced white letters we read:

CURRENT

IT'S WHEN THE CIRCUITS HUM,

OR BLOW, AT YOUR COMMAND.

GAP CLASSICS, POWER TOOLS

FOR INDIVIDUALS OF STYLE.

And centered beneath this, in three-inch widely spaced white letters, the isolated word **G A P.**

Current, circuits humming, power tools, black and white—what sort of electronic network is referred to here? Turn to the facing page and the expectation is wholly dispelled: the big picture is of the celebrated postmodern artist Robert Longo, and the current always switching is no more than a vibration from the "Gap mock turtleneck," that Longo is wearing. The sophistication of the two-page spread and the

4.2 Parliament ad, *New York Times Magazine*, 4 February 1990, p. 69.

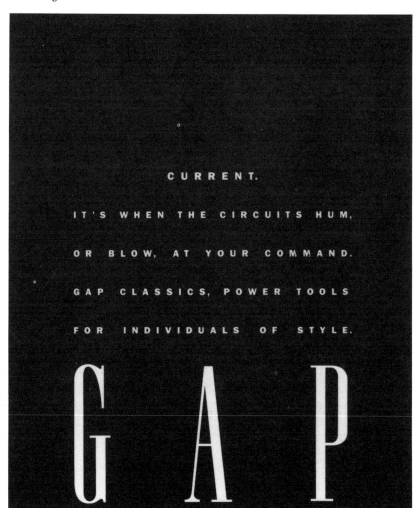

4.3 Double-page ad for GAP, *New York Times Magazine*, 4 February 1990, pp. 16–17.

services of the "star" artist as well as of the photographer Matthew Rolston—these are enlisted in the cause of selling a mass product, a turtleneck shirt priced at $18.

What role has such sign inflection played in the shaping of recent art discourse? According to *Learning from Las Vegas*—and the Venturis' argument is a powerful one—no artist (in their case, architect) can

Gap mock turtleneck 516, as worn by
ROBERT LONGO, artist.
Photographed by Matthew Rolston.

afford not to learn from the "existing landscape," not to study its semiotic. In the case of architecture, this means, of course, understanding how a given building complex relates to its location vis-à-vis the moving automobile, rather than the individual pedestrian, from whose vantage point it is seen. Here is their description of a typical A&P supermarket:

On the commercial strip the supermarket windows contain no merchandise. There may be signs announcing the day's bargains, but they are to be read by pedestrians approaching from the parking lot. The building itself is set back from the highway and half hidden, as is most of the urban environment, by parked cars. The vast parking lot is in front, not at the rear, since it is a symbol as well as a convenience. The building is low because air conditioning demands low spaces, and merchandising techniques discourage second floors; its architecture is neutral because it can hardly be seen from the road. Both merchandise and architecture are disconnected from the road. The big sign leaps to connect the driver to the store, and down the road the cake mixes and detergents are advertised by their national manufacturers on enormous billboards inflected toward the highway. The graphic sign in space has become the architecture of this landscape. Inside, the A&P has reverted to the bazaar except that graphic packaging has replaced the oral persuasion of the merchant. (LL 9)

As an analysis of the semiotic of contemporary supermarket structures, the Venturis' discussion is extremely persuasive. But from their perspective, such architecture, like the giant revolving neon signs on the Las Vegas strip, is not only meaningful but normative. Thus the second part of *Learning from Las Vegas*, "Ugly and Ordinary Architecture, or the Decorated Shed," tries to make a case for a custom-designed architecture that will erect structures that look like what they are, that make, in other words, no pretense to "transcend" the ugly and ordinary facts of daily life. The Venturi Guild House, for example, an apartment house for the elderly in downtown Philadelphia (fig. 4.4), is built of "technologically unadvanced brick, the old-fashioned, double-hung windows, the pretty materials around the entrance, and the ugly antenna not hidden behind the parapet in the accepted fashion, all are distinctly conventional in image as well as substance, or, rather, ugly and ordinary." (LL 70). But the architects have added pop detail that ironizes this situation. Over the front entrance, a huge sign bears the building's name. According to the authors, this Guild House sign "*denotes* meaning through its words; as such it is the heraldic element *par excellence*. The character of the graphics, however, *connotes* institutional dignity, while contradictorily, the size of the graphics *connotes* commercialism" (LL 71). Guild House is at once of its time and place (ugly and ordinary) and yet, so the architects claim, the symbolism of its exterior decoration makes it something more as well.

The case for rapprochement with "popular culture" made here is seductive: no longer, the Venturis suggest, can architecture retreat into some idyllic pastoral world, removed from the urban and commercial megastructure of late twentieth-century communication and transpor-

4.4 Guild House, Friends' housing for the elderly, Philadelphia, 1960–63; Venturi and Rauch, Cope and Lippincott Associates. From *Learning from Las Vegas*, p. 66.

tation systems. But there are also difficulties with this position. What the Venturis take to be the witty irony of the "commercial" lettering and spacing of the Guild House sign, for example, is surely lost on the apartment house's elderly inhabitants: for them the facade merely reinforces the ugly and ordinary of the building's interior. More important: if pop culture is to provide the artist's norms, why pay an expensive architect to design a building that will be largely indistinguishable from tract housing? Indeed, the Venturis' notion that plastic flowers might as well be placed at the front entrance because that is, so to speak, what "they" want, is at least as elitist a concept as the high art/mass art distinction that postmodern critics are calling into question. Which is to say that the artwork, however implicated it is in its actual cultural moment, is never just another neon sign used to point us to the entrance of the Stardust Motel or the Texaco station. Not surprisingly, the commissions the Venturis have received in recent years have been primarily to build public structures (wings to existing museums, e.g., the National Gallery in London, the Oberlin Art Museum in Ohio, the Princeton Museum, and university lecture halls), rather than mass housing and office or storefront space, let alone custom-built homes. The "decorated shed," it seems, is hardly designed for those who actually own one.

If the populist claim for "learning from Las Vegas" is thus dubious,[3] the Venturis' analytic framework does provide some fascinating clues to the "look" poetic texts are assuming in the late twentieth century. For by analogy, the lesson for poetry would be that the standard print format associated with the word "poem" (justified left margin, ragged right margin, a block of type to be read from left to right and top to bottom and surrounded by white space, a format still ubiquitous in the "poems" printed in *The New Yorker* or *Poetry* magazine or *American Poetry Review*) is by no means the inevitable or the only one. Indeed, as the "look" of the standard poem begins to be replicated on the billboard or the greeting card, an interesting exchange begins to occur.

Consider, for example, the following billboard sign spotted by the Venturis in Philadelphia (LL 52):

O. R. LUMPKIN. BODY-

BUILDERS. FENDERS

STRAIGHTENED.

WRECKS OUR SPECIAL-

TY. WE TAKE THE DENT

OUT OF ACCIDENT.

If lineation is, as is generally assumed, the minimum requisite for poetry, however "free" its verse form, then this is certainly a poem and not the worst one at that. Lineation, after all, forces the reader to relate "lumpkin" to "body" and "builders" to "fenders," while "straightened" appropriately gets a line all to itself. Line 4 contains an inadvertent double entendre: "wrecks," not followed by the auxiliary verb (are) is likely to be taken as a verb. What is it at Lumpkin's Body Shop that wrecks our "special- / ty" (or special "T")? And now comes the piece de resistance: the morphological word play, "We take the dent / out of accident." Surely, the next time we have an accident, this memorable punning will stick in our minds and draw us to O. R. Lumpkin rather than some other body shop.

How does the artist react to such displays of verbal skill? Perhaps, as the Belgian artist Marcel Broodthaers posited, by making signs that cannot be "read," at least not in the usual sense. Between 1968 and 1970, Broodthaers made a series of 30-odd vacuum-formed plastic reliefs, in appearance like oversize license plates (see figs. 4.5 and 4.6) called *In-*

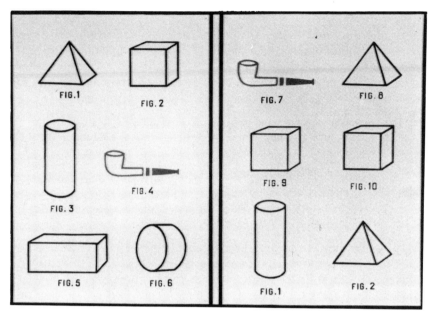

4.5 Marcel Broodthaers, *Livre tableau*, 1969–70. Paint on vacuum-formed plastic; 85 × 120 cm. Courtesy Galerie Michael Werner, Cologne. (See *Marcel Broodthaers*, p. 136)

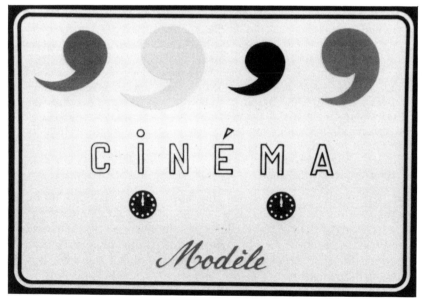

4.6 Marcel Broodthaers, *Cinéma modèle*, 1970. Paint on vacuum-formed plastic; 85 × 120 cm. Courtesy Galerie Michael Werner, Cologne. (See *Marcel Broodthaers*, p. 136).

dustrial Poems. The "subject" of these curious *plaques en plastique* or rebuses, as Broodthaers called them, is "a speculation about a difficulty of reading that results when you see this substance. . . . Reading is impeded by the imagelike quality of the text and vice versa." And he explains:

> The stereotypical character of both text and image is defined by the technique of plastic. They are intended to be read on a double level—each one involved in a negative attitude which seems to me specific to the stance of the artist: not to place the message completely on one side alone, neither image nor text. That is, the *refusal to deliver a clear message*. . . . The way I see it, there can be no direct connection between art and message, especially if the message is political, without running the risk of being burned by the artifice.[4] (My italics)

The "double level" of which Broodthaers speaks refers literally to the fact that, whereas vaccuum-forming is usually used specifically to make signs that must be easily read,[5] in the *Industrial Poems*, the surfaces of the raised forms (letters, printers' signs, formal images) are painted, each one in two combinations of colors, one the reverse of the other (e.g., if one side of the plaque is red on white, the other will be white on red). Accordingly, the "message" cannot be separated from the medium. As Benjamin H. D. Buchloch explains:

> The casting process not only allowed for a complete integration of typographic and formal elements in one continuous surface, but also destroyed the redeeming features of that negative white space that the traditional page format and the ground of the collage or montage still had to offer. Thus, erasure of language in these panels results as a "natural" consequence of their fabrication in a casting process where language appears literally blinded (blind-stamped), and where it acquires the status of the relief at the cost of readability. Poetic text, artistic object, discursive classification, and institutional demarcation are all literally made "of a piece," and of one material; in their final format they are framed as mere advertisement and, in their final form, they are contained as mere object (another art commodity). (BHDB 88)

Thus a plaque like *Livre-tableau* (fig. 4.5) can be seen as a kind of reductio ad absurdum of what is surely its parent text, Magritte's *Ceci n'est pas une pipe* (fig. 4.7). If the latter asks epistemological questions about ways we relate the visual signifier (the painted pipe) to the verbal signifier (the word *pipe*) and, in turn, to the object signified, Broodthaers' red-outlined pipe (on the "negative" it is white on red) is labelled "FIG. 4" in the left-hand panel but "FIG. 7" in the right and it has also changed position, as have the other geometrical figures. Since the plaque therefore supplies no useful information, it cannot function as a

4.7 René Magritte, *La Trahison des images* (*Ceci n'est pas une pipe*), 1928–29. Oil on canvas; 25 3/8 × 37 inches (64.5 × 94 cm). Los Angeles County Museum of Art; purchased with funds provided by the Mr. and Mrs. William Preston Harrison Collection.

signboard, but neither does it make the slightest concession to aesthetic value, as had been the case in Futurist or Dada typography. The aim, on the contrary, seems to be to force the viewer/reader to "see" what he or she in fact always does see (a page of figures in a geometry textbook; a classroom poster) as if for the first time.

The point may be clearer if we consider a comment Broodthaers made about his *moule* (mussel) "sculptures" (see fig. 4.8, *Moules sauce blanche*). Asked by an interviewer whether his mussels were perhaps symbolic, "a dream of the North Sea?" Broodthaers replied, "A mussel conceals a volume. When the mussels overflow the pot, they are not boiling over in accord with a physical law, but follow the rules of artifice whose purpose is the construction of an abstract shape" (TTF 41). "Rules of artifice" is the key phrase here: only by observing such rules, the artist implies, can the "refusal to deliver a clear message" be fully realized.

But the "construction of an abstract shape" can take many forms. "I thought," we read on the opening page of John Ashbery's *Three Poems*, "that if I could put it all down, that would be one way. And next the thought came to me that to leave all out would be another, and truer, way."[6] If Broodthaers's strategy is, so to speak, to "leave all out," its complementary mode is that of putting it all down. One of the most interesting examples of such "information overload" is Steve McCaf-

4.8 Marcel Broodthaers, *Moules sauce blanche*, 1967. Casserole, mussel shells, paint. 50 × 36 × 36 cm. Collection Mr. and Mrs. Isy Brachot. (See *Marcel Broodthaers*, p. 130.)

fery's 1989 text *The Black Debt*.[7] Open this book (the title is Hegel's
term for writing), and you will find a continuous block of large bold-
face type that covers 119 pages (no paragraphs, no breaks, but justified
left and right margins created by adjusting the spacing of the letters) and
is called "Lag," followed by a second such block of 80 pages called "An
Effect of Cellophane." "While the large type," says McCaffery on the
dustjacket, "may be an aid to the visually impaired, it will hopefully
bring into play the materiality of reading as a first order physical encoun-
ter rendering the negotiation of the lines a highly visceral experience."

Certainly *The Black Debt* cannot be read "normally." The typeface
and continuous print call to mind signboards, tickertape, and elec-
tronic mail: one all but expects the text to go off screen even as one is
looking at it. Again, this is a text that is neither, strictly speaking,
"prose" nor "verse," the "measure" being the absolute equality of line
lengths in the block. And within that block, individual phrases and sen-
tences are usually quite grammatical even though there is usually no
logical connection between them.

"In vain," says Samuel Johnson in the epigraph from Boswell's *Life*,
"shall we look for the *lucidus ordo*, where there is neither end or object,
design or moral, *nec certa recurrit imago*."[8] For Johnson, such absence
of the Horatian *lucidus ordo* (he is talking to Boswell about the "tire-
some repetition of the same images" in Macpherson's pseudo-epic *Fin-
gal*) is of course a fault; a poem without design or moral, where no
definite image recurs, cannot be good. But for a poet like Steve McCaf-
fery, living in the late twentieth century, *lucidus ordo* and *certa imago*
belong to the world of FREE ASPIRIN and THE PERFECT RECESS, poetry
now being that discourse that defers reading. Thus McCaffery's first text,
appropriately called "Lag," consistently resists the reader's attempts to
overcome its partition and segmentation and to make the individual
phrases cohere into some sort of "meaningful" narrative (fig. 4.9).

The only punctuation mark used in "Lag" is the comma, that politest
and weakest of breaks in continuity, whose traditional function, the
OED tells us, is to "separate the smallest members of a sentence," so as
to "make clear the grammatical structure, and hence the sense of the
passage." Ironically, the phrasal syntax of "Lag" is indeed quite clear—
"a red envelope" is a noun modified by an indefinite article and an
adjective; "the rain stood up" has a subject noun modified by definite
article followed by an intransitive verb, and so on—but semantically,
the segments often make no sense individually and even less, when they
are related to one another. Indeed, each phrase acts to restrain the
larger flow of which it is a part, only to call attention to itself as a co-
nundrum to be solved.

SENTENCE NOT SENTENCE, A
RED envelope, the rain stood up, the
prolonged cosseting or a silhouette
the customer knows, dead drunks
arriving at a gate, these enormous
movements of soap intact and called
a breakdown on the road, winter-
thorn but a floating crow in flight, as
secondary systems round the kitchen,
a list of old socks, independent with
dessert then pushing a chair to the
left, setting this down well in advance
of the middle limp before the brat,
dawning night waned, a way of doing
coke, binoculous interior on inspected
coffee, when an ashtray's cracked, an
evanescent need to fill and putty tra-
vails on a tray, waking at eight to an
echo, three means a half inch width,
nine seven four two five, the cracking
of spokes codes this distance, whis-
pered vowels due to laxity, whole
lengths of paragraphs in prose, pas-
sions building sounds, them and the
name of Howson on a truck, all the

11

4.9 Steve McCaffery, *The Black Debt*, page 11.

On the opening page (and this pattern will remain consistent throughout), the poet's phrasing ranges from a simple statement of negation, *a* ≠ *a* ("SENTENCE NOT SENTENCE" or, in its more complex punning variant on subsequent pages, "absinthe not absence," "miasma not my asthma," and so on); definition ("three means a half-inch width"); and the listing of numbers (nine seven four two five, evidently the digits of a zip code, phone number, bar code, etc.) to simple declarative sentences with past-tense verbs ("the rain stood up"; "dawning night waned"); noun phrases ("a red envelope," "a list of old socks," "a way of doing coke," "the lengths of paragraphs in prose") and gerunds ("waking at eight to an echo"); "when" clauses ("when an ashtray's cracked") and "as" clauses ("as secondary systems round the kitchen"); and statements of discrimination ("the prolonged cosseting or a silhouette the customer knows"; "winterthorn but a floating crow in flight"), in which the second term is regularly missing.

On first inspection, the reader is likely to take this page as a kind of Chomskyan exercise in nonsensicality, a phrase like "waking at eight to an echo" violating, as I said a moment ago, not grammatical but semantic convention. One wakes at eight to an alarm or a phone call or a pat on the head or a kiss, but not to an echo. Or would it after all be possible? Certainly, if one were asleep in, say, a ravine. Or if *echo* were a brand name, on the order of Walkman or Sprite or Tide—those natural referents that advertising culture has increasingly made its own. What makes the phrasing of "Lag" so strange is that the more these "meaningless" phrases are probed, the less nonsensical they turn out to be.

Consider the five opening phrases of "Lag." (1) "SENTENCE NOT SENTENCE": the text begins with a statement of aesthetic: what you read, McCaffery suggests, will be written in sentences but they will not be the sentences you are used to reading even though you are now sentenced to do so. (2) Red envelopes are not common (except for valentines, Christmas cards, and so on), but every envelope we send or receive in the mail is "read." (3) Rain doesn't "stand up"; it falls; then again, when it rains very heavily, it looks as if the drops are standing up on the windshield or the windowpane. In the next phrasal unit, (4) the word "cosseting" stands out, a literary word common enough in the Victorian novel, but now nearly obsolete, especially in American English. Like Beckett, McCaffery is fond of interjecting the odd archaism or obscure learned word into what is otherwise highly contemporary idiom. "Prolonged cosseting" (being petted, indulged, caressed) is just what takes place in elegant clothing boutiques, when the seasoned "customer" hits upon a "silhouette" (perhaps her own?) she "knows" and likes. Is the customer envious of someone else's silhouette? Or does the dress, cosseting the customer's own body, produce the desired "silhouette"? (5) "Dead drunks arriving at a gate" initially sounds like a contradiction in terms: to be "dead drunk" means to be out cold and hence not "arriving" anywhere—at least not on one's own steam. Perhaps the dead drunks are in the paddy wagon, arriving at the police station or jail gate. On the other hand, if we take the phrase literally, the reference may be to drunks who are dead, corpses being carted to a hospital emergency room. And finally, if we take a matter-of-fact view of the situation, it is not at all impossible for even those who are "dead drunk" to stumble somehow to the gate, say, of a shelter.

Such "language games" bring to mind the Wittgenstein of *Philosophical Investigations*, for example, "When we say: 'Every word in language signifies something' we have so far said *nothing whatever*; unless we have explained exactly *what* distinction we wish to make."[9] McCaffery, one of whose previous books of poetry is called *Evoba*,[10] takes the Wittgenstein theorem that "the meaning of a word is its use in the language" (no. 43) to its absurdist extreme. For what does "use" mean in the public space of billboards and TV discourse? To whom, for example, does the sign "O. R. Lumpkin, body builders . . . wrecks our specialty" speak? Hardly to those who have just been involved in a wreck (and hence are not exactly in a billboard-reading frame of mind) but rather to those who are experiencing normal driving conditions. "Wrecks" are thus not really O. R. Lumpkin's "specialty." Rather, the body shop's aim is literally to "take the dent out of accident" and put it in the driver's subconscious so that, if a wreck occurs, O. R. Lumpkin will come to mind.

It is such sleight-of-hand (or should I say sleight-of-sign) that McCaffery is parodying in "Lag." Watch out, the text seems to be saying, when you read those headlines, those cigarette ads, or road signs: the "message" may not be what you think it is. Or, conversely, a seemingly obscure statement may be the bearer of a perfectly ordinary message. In reading the sixth phrase on page 1, for example, one's first reaction is likely to be that there is no reason why "these enormous movements of soap intact" should be "called a breakdown on the road," or why these two phrases are connected by "and." But the "breakdown" makes perfect sense if we think of the "movements of soap" as a van shipment, the cartons of soap evidently remaining intact despite the breakdown. The use of "but" in the next phrase is similar: we need only supply a phrase like "[I thought it was] winter-thorn but [what I saw was] a floating crow in flight." And that would make good sense except for the fact that "winter-thorn" is not in the *OED* (does it refer to a dark thorn, seen against a wintry sky or perhaps against white snow?) and that it has, at the literary level, the inescapable connotation of "Winterbourne" (the hero of Henry James's *Daisy Miller*). And further: look at the sound structure of this phrase—

w*í*nter- / th*ó*rn but a fl*ó*ating cr*ó*w *in* fl*í*ght—

with its formal iambic pentameter, its elaborate alliteration and assonance.

But, the skeptical reader may say at this point, even if what you say is true: so what? Why should McCaffery expect us to play along while he spins out his little riddles and word games? And even when his seemingly arbitrary and disconnected phrases reveal narrative patterns (e.g., in line 11 "dessert," and "pushing a chair to the left," may be said to prepare the scene for "a way of doing coke," "inspected coffee," and an "ashtray" that's "cracked" in lines 14–16),[11] it may still be objected that such puzzle-making is hardly the stuff of real poetry. Where, after all, is the imaginative transformation of the material? And where is the response of the lyric self?

Here again I turn to Wittgenstein. "The aspects of things that are most important for us are hidden because of their simplicity and familiarity. (One is unable to notice something because it is always before one's eyes)" (no. 129, p. 50e). Perhaps the best way to read "Lag" is as one poet's lyric road map whereby the all-too-familiar is made strange. Its strategy is to place the reader, along with the author, in the position that we are now actually in as we drive the freeways, shop on the mall, push our carts through the supermarket, or watch the evening news. To give just one example: shortly after I had read "Lag," I was listening, on the car radio, to a call-in political program on KPFK (Pacifica). An irritated caller was complaining that whites don't give credit to the achievements of black people. "For instance," he said, "Richard Stokes invented the stop watch." "Yes," said the host. The caller corrected himself: "I mean the stop light." The host said "yes" again as if it made no difference, the issue being, of course, not the fact of the particular invention but the question of white racism. Stop light, stop watch—they're all "inventions," aren't they? Or, in McCaffery's parodic version: "absinthe not absence" (12), "Hanoi not annoy" (24), "commerce not commas" (35), "theodicy not the Odyssey" (50), "letters spray not let us pray" (81).

In "Lag," puns, palindromes, anagrams, and number series, placed at set mathematical junctures (e.g., one per so-and-so many lines of text), alternate with stock phrases to present a world whose seeming "normalcy" regularly gives way to short-circuit. What could be simpler, for example, than "a list of old socks" (11)? Any child can understand what the words mean. But—and here is the "lag"—what *is* a list of old socks? Even if anyone wanted to make one, how would one do it, socks being so limited in color and material. We might say "three pairs of navy blue ski socks," but then how would we further specify the items in this category? By referring to the pair of navy blue ski socks that has a hole in the heel? Or again, a phrase like "continuing to have a nice day" sounds almost like the injunction we hear at every supermarket checkout counter or bank teller's window, except that no one ever raises the issue of "continuing" to "have a nice day," since *having* a nice day means you're going to *have* one—or does it? One thing is sure: the person who tells you to "Have a nice day" won't be around to find out whether indeed you are having it. And this is why the locution "continuing to have a nice day" sounds so absurd.

"In vain," the Johnson epigraph tells us, "shall we look for the *lucidus ordo*, where there is neither end or object, design or moral, *nec certa recurrit imago*." In "Lag," each phrase is no sooner articulated than it gives way to the next, usually quite unrelated phrase. There is no "clear image," no master narrative, no expository pattern, not even an autobiographical thread to provide a constant. Yet once we get the hang of McCaffery's "prose," its *ordonnance* is seen to be quite reasonable. "Impersonal" as this text is, it is by no means unemotional or uninvolved. We learn nothing—at least nothing direct—about McCaffery's (or his narrator's) personal life, his opinions or ruminations. Nonetheless I would posit that "Lag" projects a highly particularized way of looking at things, of processing the most diversified information fields—geology and genetics, archeology and advertising, classics and commercials—that is finally as recognizable in its particular ways of negotiating with knowledge as is the more personal lyric consciousness we expect to find in poetry. Indeed, the poem gives the lie to the *nec certa recurrit imago*, for items do have a way of reappearing: the "red envelope" of page 11 turn up on page 16 in the "letter falling from its reader's hands," the "list of old socks" (11) in the recognition that "this foot is a sock," and so on. On the last page of "Lag" we read, "how does one reach the end of language," and the answer, of course, is that one doesn't, since "being is the word that writing shatters" (119). Thus the poem can end only with negation—"Nature not Nietzsche"—followed by a final comma, which is followed by white space. The comma suggests continuity: the "black debt" continues to be paid.

The mode of "Lag," and of its companion piece "An Effect of Cellophane," owes more, I think, to eighteenth-century satire, especially to Swift, than to the Romantic poetry we still take as normative. The poet appears here as cultural critic, but a critic who must fictionalize his materials so that they will appear in their true horror and absurdity.

The visual dimension plays a key role: as we open *The Black Debt*, perhaps at random, we are confronted by the seemingly endless print block of contemporary writing and try to make out the words and phrases. On page 35, for example, I caught the words "come back for martinis." Then my eye moved up a line and I realized that it's "a come back for martinis"—a total shift in meaning. Read the print block up or down, forwards or backwards, McCaffery suggests, and you will come to see how vulnerable we are to prefabricated messages, bogus claims to authority, and endless dubious prescriptions like "going up in a plane and not coming down until wet." The hermeneutic "lag" is thus the forced delay that makes us see what is really happening, that, for example, "not coming down until wet" implies that the plane is coming down into a rainstorm or crash landing, say, into the Long Island Sound.

About a third of the way through "Lag" (p. 37), we read:

> by the letters big we announce a giant, the cite of myopia snapping
> this thread, grammatical, grief, ground, guessing

The "letters big" of billboard land are always announcing giants, whether the Giant Foods Supermarket or Big Mac or the Pep Boys: such signs are the site as well as the "cite" of "myopia snapping this thread." But the alliterative sequence "grammatical, grief, ground, guessing" suggests that finally we can undo such "grammatical, grief," that it can prepare the "ground" for our "guessing." What McCaffery calls his "rhizomatic writing" works to enact this process.

II

McCaffery's earliest work comes out of the Concrete movement, which he encountered during his undergraduate years in England in the late sixties.[12] *Carnival* (1967–70), for example, has been described by its author as "essentially a cartographic project; a repudiation of linearity in writing and the search for an alternative syntax in 'mapping'."[13] A mask is placed on a piece of paper; "the writing commences on the mask, moves over onto the undersheet, then back onto the mask. The mask is then removed and thrown away. This leaves a broken, fragmented text." Further, since the mask induces the text to bleed off the edge of the page, the text links up with the other treated undersheets to create, when the perforated pages are detached, an interlocking flat surface (a square of four) to be "read" spatially rather than temporally. Thus *Carnival* challenges the sequentiality of the normal book; indeed, the irony is that one has to destroy the book in order to read it.

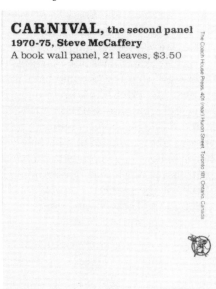

CARNIVAL, the second panel
1970-75, Steve McCaffery
A book wall panel, 21 leaves, $3.50

The Coach House Press, 401 (rear) Huron Street, Toronto 181, Ontario, Canada

Instructions
Buy two copies. Keep one on your bookshelf.
Take the other & tear each of the 16 text pages
carefully along the perforation. The panel is
assembled by laying out the pages in a square
of four.

4.10 Steve McCaffery, *Carnival, The Second Panel*

The panels themselves explore language at its most basic physical level: script and grapheme. Panel Two (fig. 4.10), for example, places typewritten text in what McCaffery calls "agonistic relation with other forms of scription: xerography, xerography within xerography . . . electrostasis, rubber-stamp, tissue texts, hand-lettering and stencil." "The

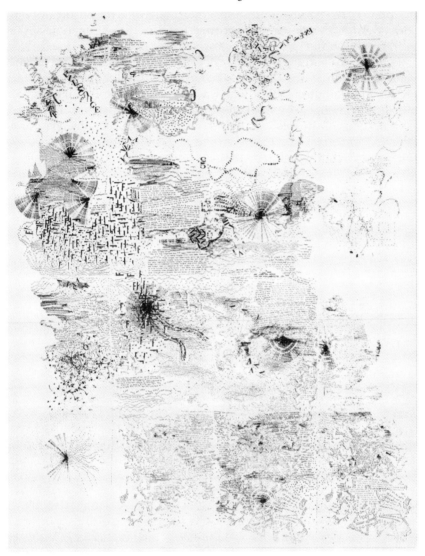

thrust," he explains, "is geomantic—realignment of speech, like earth, for purposes of intelligible access to its neglected qualities of immanence and non-reference."[14] And even though, as McCaffery came to see later, the "actual content of the writing [was] incredibly naive," the project, he feels, was a useful experiment both in "spontaneous composition" ("The nature of the format didn't allow me the opportunity to correct errors, or to revise the writing") and in the elimination of the unitary subject in favor of "polyglossia" (BPN 72–73).

Even at this early stage, then, McCaffery's visual poetics was motivated by linguistic and theoretical concerns rather different from those of, say, Ian Hamilton Finlay, who was one of his mentors. Take, for example, the famous *Wave-rock* (1966), whose text, made up entirely of permutations of the two title words, is sandblasted into blue glass and designed to be placed where the light can shine through it as it does when a wave hits a rock (fig. 4.11). As a site-specific sculpture, Finlay's "large glass" is extremely attractive, but what about the text? Mary Ellen Solt comments:

> the letters of the words "wave" and "rock" are topographically related to the form of wave and rock and . . . the word "wave" moves toward the word "rock." This is accomplished by appeal to our normal impulse to read from left to right. There is no dislocation in the placement of the letters: all of the "w's," "a's," "v's" and "e's" are placed directly on top of each other. Space created by left-out letters is used to convey the textural quality of the wave. But the poem actually happens in the crashing of the two words together. . . . the letters are thrown out of line without destroying their rock-like solidity. . . . The crash is caused by the conflict between the normal movement of the reading eye and the stronger abnormal impulse to read in the opposite direction. . . . after we notice the crashing together of the words, we notice instability of "o" in rock" which seems to float between the two directional reading impulses.[15]

Finlay himself has further noted that in the clash of the two words *wave* and *rock*, a third, *wrack* is born, and that "the thickened stems of the letters suggest, visually, seaweedy rocks." Thus the two "opposing forces" presented in "equipoise" are "resolved" in the context of the poem (see MES 296).

Such talk of "equipoise" and "resolution" points to the difference between the earlier utopian phase of Concrete poetry and its later more iconoclastic version, between what is sometimes called "clean" and "dirty" Concrete.[16] In its first or formative phase, as Rosmarie Waldrop notes in her short, brilliant essay, Concrete poetry presented itself as "first of all a revolt against [the] transparency of the word," a demand that we must *see* words rather than merely *read* (see through) them. Concrete poetry "makes the sound and shape of words its explicit field of investigation"; it is "*about* words."[17] Further, in its concentration on the physical material of which the poem or text is made, its use of "graphic space as a structural agent" (MES 7), the "verbivocovisual" poem, as the Noigandres group of Brazil referred to the Concrete poem,

is able to eliminate subjectivity—what we now call the author func-
tion—in favor of material construction.[18]

But—and this can be seen in the case of one of Eugen Gomringer's
modest "constellations" like *silencio* (fig. 4.12) as easily as in an elabo-
rate art construct like Finlay's *Wave-Rock*—despite its elimination of
"transparency" so important to later poets and visual artists, and
despite its alleged "isomorphism" (content = form),[19] such "clean" Con-
crete poetry has always been open to the charges of a certain reduc-
tionism. In the case of *silencio*, for example, much has been made of
the blank space at the center of the configuration, a space supposedly
equivalent to the "silence" conveyed by the verbal sign.[20] But quite
aside from what semioticians have criticized as the "iconic fallacy" of
Concrete poetry,[21] it is a question whether such Gomringer "constella-

4.11 Ian Hamilton Finlay, *Wave-rock*, 1966. University of California, San Diego, La Jolla.
(Reproduced from Mary Ellen Solt, *Concrete Poetry*, p. 207.)

tions" as *silencio* or *wind* (fig. 4.13), charming and witty as they are, especially the first time we read/see them, can continue to hold our attention. Finlay's *Wave-rock* is more elaborate and more visually impressive but even here, the minimalist gesture can be read as perhaps too comfortable a retreat from what Stevens called the "pressure of reality." What *about* wave and rock (or even wrack)? one wants to ask; what about the clash of opposing forces?

```
silencio silencio silencio
silencio silencio silencio
silencio          silencio
silencio silencio silencio
silencio silencio silencio
```

4.12 Eugen Gomringer, *silencio*, 1953. (From Solt, *Concrete Poetry*, p. 91.)

4.13 Eugen Gomringer, *wind*, 1953. (From Solt, *Concrete Poetry*, p. 93.)

The denial, so to speak, of the connotative properties of language goes hand in hand with another difficulty, namely, the ambivalence this Concrete poetics displayed toward the related visual poetics of advertising and the media. For Gomringer, whose poetics grew out of an early concern with painting, graphics, and industrial design (see MES 8), a rapprochement between visual poetry and commercial art seemed not only possible but desirable. As he put it in his 1954 manifesto "From Line to Constellation," "the language of today must have certain things in common with poetry, and . . . they should sustain each other both in form and substance. In the course of daily life, this relationship often passes unnoticed. Headlines, slogans, groups of sounds and letters give rise to forms which could be models for a new poetry" (MES 67). And two years later, "Concrete poetry is founded upon the contemporary scientific-technical view of the world and will come into its own in the synthetic-rationalistic world of tomorrow" ("Concrete Poetry," MES 68).

The Brazilian Noigandres group, on the other hand, allied itself more closely with radical politics: in particular, Decio Pignatari wrote Concrete poems that could be regarded as constituting a critique of

4.14 Decio Pignatari, "beba coca cola." (From Solt, *Concrete Poetry*, p. 108.)

advertising. In the well-known *beba coca cola* ("drink coca cola"; fig. 4.14; MES 108), for example, Pignatari permutates the phonemes and morphemes of the ubiquitous slogan—"beba" (drink) becomes "babe" (drool); "coca" becomes "caco" (shard) and then "cloaca" (the common passage for fecal, urinary, and reproductive discharge)—the columnar arrangement emphasizing the disjunction between the advertiser's (and by extension, the imperialist U.S.'s) imperative ("beba") to the potential consumer and the product Coca-Cola itself. In placing "babe" directly below "beba," Pignatari suggests that "drinking" has become mere "drooling"; the same strategy turns "cola" into "caco," the broken coke bottles seen as the shards of a doomed civilization, and finally into "cloaca," with the suggestion that drinking Coca-Cola is at best a form of infantile regression and at worst the consumption of ex-

4.15 Augusto de Campos, *Codigo* logo, 1973.

crement. Further, as Rosmarie Waldrop notes, right before the "cloaca" line, "caco" and "cola" are transferred to the "beba" column, "negating the spatial separation that seemed to separate the product from the consumer. The sides are interchangeable; those who drink are no better than those who manipulate them into drinking" (RW 146).

One may conclude that the thirteen little words (each has only four letters except for "cloaca" which has five) that make up Pignatari's poem are arranged in much more complex and ingenious ways than one would suppose, and that here, at least, is a meaningful critique of imperialist politics. But even Waldrop, who reads *beba coca cola* with such care, remarks that "there is no mistaking the message of this anti-advertisement" (RW 146). The Concrete poem as antiadvertisement, in other words, is perhaps not all that different from the Concrete poem as proto-advertising logo—in both cases, the reader, ostensibly free to construe the poem in a variety of ways, is actually constrained by the author's guidelines.

Not surprisingly, then, Concrete poetry of this type has, in recent years, been moving in the direction of industrial design and the making of lovely objects (greeting cards, posters, signs) for personal and social use. "It has been argued," writes Claus Clüver, "and not necessarily with tongue in cheek, that the most representative (and perhaps even the most exciting) art form of our age is the advertising logo. Why not create a logo advertising modern poetry, modern art, and the modern view of man as 'homo semioticus'?" (CCL 39). And he gives as an example Augusto de Campos's logo in the form of a labyrinth, designed in 1973 for the literary magazine *Codigo* (fig. 4.15),[22] explaining that "as a visual sign, it can be read as a representation of a globe, which is a representation of the world: 'All the world's a code,' to paraphrase Shakespeare. But this text does not only draw on the verbal and visual sign systems, it also employs two verbal languages, for in the center of the code/globe/world we read GOD, unless you want to have it backwards, which would make you into a cynic, for Greek 'kynos' means 'DOG'" (CCL 39).

I have no quarrel with this interpretation of what is, as Clüver himself points out, an especially pleasing and ingenious advertising logo. The question remains, however, whether the conflation of Concrete poetry and advertising isn't a kind of dead end for the former; such texts as "CODIGO," after all, function primarily as recognition symbols: as soon as we see them, we know a particular object (in this case a literary magazine) is in question because only that particular object has just this (and no other) emblem. But is "CODIGO" all that different from such witty California license plates as the following (figs. 4.16 and 4.17)?[23]

4.16 License plate, *Los Angeles*, p. 128.

4.17 License plate, *Los Angeles*, p. 129.

Indeed, it seems that the call for what Eugen Gomringer has characterized as "reduced language," for "poems . . . as easily understood as signs in airports and traffic signs," [24] runs the risk of producing "poems" that *are* airport and traffic signs. But if this is the downside of Concretism, we must remember that the Noigandres poets and related European and American groups were the first to recognize fully that, given the sophisticated print media, computer graphics, signposts, and advertising formats of our culture, all writing—and certainly all poetic writing—is inevitably "seen" as well as "seen through" or heard. Indeed, by the eighties, when home laser printing, with its availability of letter sizes, appearances, and fonts, had become a reality, visual poetics could turn its attention to ways of foregrounding the materiality of the text without sacrificing semantic complexity or cultural critique. McCaffery's *The Black Debt* is a case in point. [25] I now want to look at a very different way of visualizing text: Johanna Drucker's *The Word Made Flesh*, written, or more accurately produced, in the winter of 1988/89.

III

In the special issue on "Close Reading" for *Poetics Journal* (1982), Johanna Drucker chose as her text a billboard advertising the latest Toyota Celica, as seen from a moving car at four different locations: Oakland, Alcatraz, San Francisco, and New York, respectively. The essay intentionally contains no reproduction of the billboards so that the reader can only go by the author's ecphrasis. A first "reading" produces the text "Performing Art" and a long swash behind the vehicle which reads as motion, swiftness, speed. [26] The words are initially tantalizing: "Performing art. The gerund in what sense: insistent? suggestive? descriptive. . . . an oblique comment on performance art. Using the association with the notion of the avant-garde to increase its commercial potential. The supposed disdain for marketing, familiar inversion, guarantee of value" (82).

The billboard depicts an object as if in motion and "a statement with a hook and the associations thus provoked." Each time Drucker's gaze now meets this familiar sign, she notices a little more: the "background clear but so neutral it doesn't qualify," but that, on closer inspection, has "bands of different intensity running through it," the "taillights and parking lights, as sources of luminosity," and finally, the man sitting at the steering wheel, "head a ghost presence, hands stiffly extended to grasp the wheel . . . the individual in relation to the machine, unrelated to the street/highway" (84). But—and this is, I think, the point of Drucker's "close reading" of the Toyota sign—once one has accounted for all its elements, "the image is uninteresting, uncomplex," "total surface"—indeed a mere mirror for the product itself, "so that the final reading, as the first, is of a surface with a highly reflective finish" (84).

Such "surface images," images "to be read quickly," provide the impetus for what Drucker does in her own artist's books, especially in her recent *The Word Made Flesh.*[27] As in *The Black Debt*, the aim is to produce a text that cannot be "looked through," but in Drucker's case, visual (as opposed to verbal) syntax becomes a central device. "An argument could be made," she writes in an essay called "Hypergraphy," "that the semantic value of language is much less unique to it than the syntactic conventions, and that the available means for communicating word values such as morning, sadness, or exit are considerable, whereas the means for constructing a prepositional relation 'of' or 'to' of a sequence of tenses or a conditional are essentially impossible within the visual realm."[28]

The frontispiece of *The Word Made Flesh* bears the title, in big block letters:

A L 'I N T E R I E U R D ᴱᵁ ᴸᴬ L A N G U ᴱᴬᵍᴱ

and Drucker's poem physically enacts that journey. To begin with, the mode of production is itself part of the work's meaning. *The Word Made Flesh* is printed in a very limited edition (55 copies) on Mohawk Superfine paper, the big block letters having a thick, almost furry surface as if they were living animals. But unlike the avant-garde artist's book of the early century, Drucker's doesn't boast a single illustration, a single pictorial equivalent to the text. Rather, it is the alphabet itself that is made flesh, the letter being seen in all its visual potential, as if to say that, desensitized as we are by the endless billboard discourse around us, we have almost forgotten the astonishing power of the alphabet to create human meanings.

The first (unnumbered) page bears the single letter "I," in normal print-size, at the center of the page. It could be a Roman numeral one or the first-person pronoun. In any case, on page 2 (fig. 4.18), this "I" is placed next to a giant black "T" (the first letter of "The Word Made Flesh"), which will appear four more times and then be followed by the remaining letters of the title. The letters spell "it," but visually the very small "I" seems all but lost in white space next to the oppressive presence of the heavy black "T," a stolid figure, a treelike form, its "limbs"

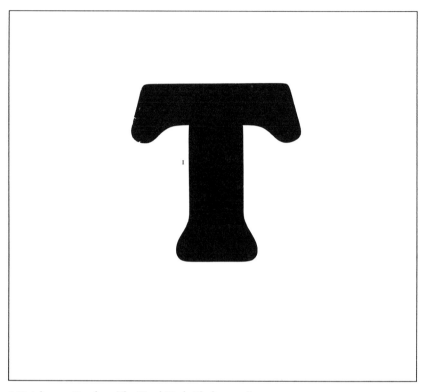

4.18 Johanna Drucker, *The Word Made Flesh*, page 2.

outspread, or perhaps a giant black gate. On page 3 (fig. 4.19), the construction of "it" is impeded by the introduction of two new units: "the tongue" (small typeface) and "lay" (the size of "I"). We can read this in a variety of ways: "I lay" (underneath the "**T**" or impeded by its heavy weight), "I lay the tongue," "the tongue lay." Next (fig. 4.20) still surrounded by white space, the giant "**T**" swallows up the little "t" of "the" to produce "[T]he tongue / LIES / on the [T]ABLE." What is curious here is that the "**T**" is part of "the" and "table" (it looks like a table too) but cannot be joined to "lies," "tlies" not being a word in English. Perhaps "lies" has to remain separate, this being a text that will soon have to do with truth/falsehood and with the sex act. On the fifth page (fig. 4.21), in any case, the big "**T**" is again shared by "the" ("the tongue") and "table," but the "THE" of "ON THE TABLE," now printed in a different type face, tall and elegant, modifies five different nouns, as follows:

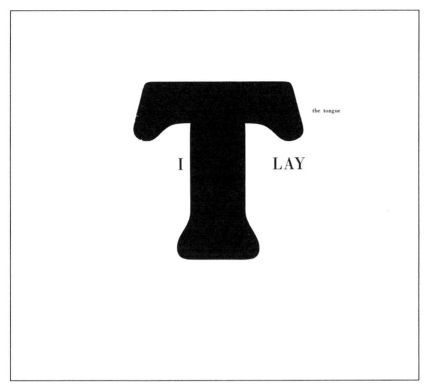

4.19 Drucker, page 3.

> The tongue [lies] on *the* table writing, writhing, spelling out *the* breath
> of its efforts in an unseemly desire to be seen. A stick taken up in defense
> of *the* world marks *the* struggling back of *the* folds of skin

Note that I put "lies" in brackets because it may not be part of this syntactic unit at all: its position suggests that the description of the erotic writing process, "a stick taken up in defense of the world" with the ensuing "struggling back of the folds of skin" may be regarded by the author as no more than *lies*. In any case, here are the beginnings of a cryptic narrative that questions the relation of writing to sexuality.

It is on the next page, the final one bearing the "**T**" of *The Word Made Flesh* (fig. 4.22) that what we might call the subtext enters: the black-letter text (exactly like the one above) is now etched against a background of red letters, spaced so that word boundaries tend to disappear. This "red text," anticipated by the red rice paper page inside the

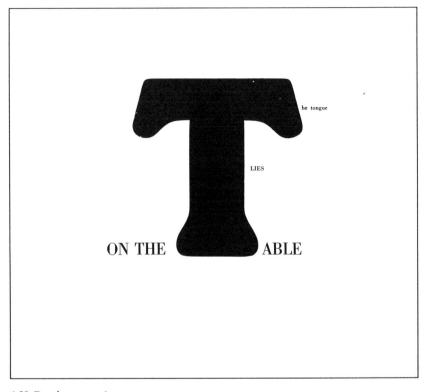

4.20 Drucker, page 4.

cover, may be said to represent *l'intérieur de/du la langue/language* of the frontispiece; it is, so to speak, the "Flesh Made Word" that compliments the "Word Made Flesh."[29] If the reader "corrects" the spacing, the red text reads as follows:

> All the waters, elements and primal fishes broke through air around us into tongues. How was the trace of displacement into pale air made into speech by a breaking wave of chance? All th[e] nights, broken glas

and the text continues onto the next page, beginning with the final "s" of "glass": "s and starstruck children woke to find themselves enslaved by authoritarian structures."

At the same time, however, the red writing is always interrupting (or being interrupted by) the black text: "broke through air around us into tongues," for example, can also be read as "broke through at the

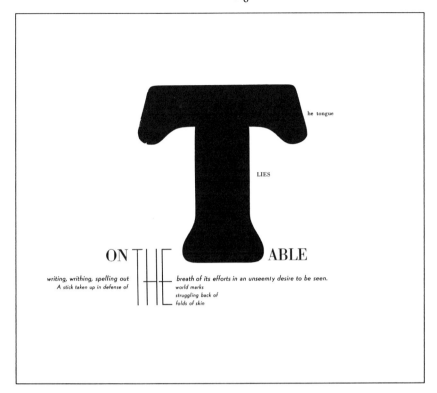

4.21 Drucker, page 5.

tongue," and the "breaking wave of chance" collides with "the folds of skin." It is thus difficult to talk of text and context; rather, there are a number of things going on at the same time: (1) a textbook on evolution, describing the transformation of fish into air-breathing mammals with tongues, their "membrance tautened to transparence"; (2) a stilted quasi-Victorian tale, perhaps a children's book, that has to do with "primal fishes," "pale air," the "breaking wave of chance," nights of "broken glass," and, on later pages, the "liquid pulse of laughter struggling in the small veins," and so on; (3) an economic discourse with reference to "authoritarian structures," "shelves of supermarkets," "tales of trading," "a primitive economy"; and (4) weaving in and out, a series of elusive sexual references, from "ripeness was a matter of appetite" to the "sticky fingers of engagement" and the "attendant fantasies that flushed our wistful flesh."

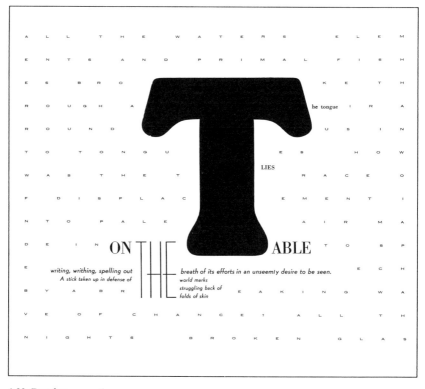

4.22 Drucker, page 6.

As the text evolves, the black foreground lettering becomes more and more elaborate, the word literally being made "flesh," as the huge replicas of **T, H, E, W, O, R, D, M, A, D, E, F, L, E, S, H** are described as "naked," "wheezing," "lie[ing] back," "feeling," "glowing," "speaking," "throbbing," and soon. Yet, even as the giant letters act as magnets, subordinating everything in their path to their powerful pull, the letters and words themselves break down paragrammatically, morphemes within words being foregrounded so as to call attention to themselves. On the "**E**" page (fig. 4.23), for example, the word "assets" is printed so that it also contains "ass" and "as"; on the same page, the passage beginning "which rise up rigid" culminates in the reference to a "tautened transparency which separates memory from fact"—or is it "from act"? Thus, although the "narratives" contained in the **A** (black) and **B** (red) texts continue from page to page, they cannot be "read" in a linear way. Moreover, the overdetermination of the black letters and word

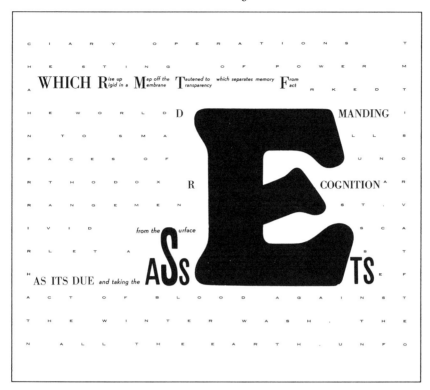

4.23 Drucker, page 8.

groups is regularly countered by the underdetermined "words" in the red texts.

On the second line of the "**E**" page (see fig. 4.23) and continuing on to the next, "**W**" page, for example, we read:

> The sting of power marked the world into small spaces of unorthodox arrangements, vivid scarlet as the fact of blood against the winter wash, then all the earth unfocused energy and wandering eyes made their way into the pulse of a primitive economy and waited there for the ice to crack on our surface of time.

After the initial *m* of "marked," continuity is broken by the superimposition of the black text, "Which rise up rigid in a map off the membrane." But even without the black text, the prose cited above has something of the oddity of Steve McCaffery's "Lag." Its syntax is perfectly straightforward, but the commas connect phrases that seem to

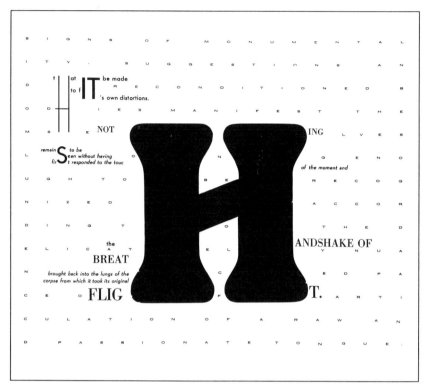

4.24 Drucker, page 21.

belong elsewhere. Why, for example, are the "small spaces of unorthodox arrangements" "vivid scarlet as the fact of blood against the winter wash"? Whose "wandering eyes" make their way "into the pulse of a primitive economy" and where is it that the ice is about to "crack on our surface of time"? "Poetic" as such phrases are, their noncoordination produces a situation in which the conventionally *poetic* appears as an odd memory, a standard obscured by the spacing of the letters which makes the very act of reading extremely difficult.

As we proceed through Drucker's book, we thus experience the word made flesh right before our eyes, as the big black block letters participate in elaborate skin games. At the same time, the word's flesh is unmade as other letters sink back into the larger gene pool of the alphabet. On the final page (fig. 4.24) the giant "**H**" is part of "notHing," "toucH," "Handshake," "breatH," and "fligHt," its incarnation measured against the textuality of the words:

signs of monumentality. Suggestions and reconditioned bodies manifest themselves long enough to be recognized according to the delicately nuanced pace of articulation of a raw and passionate tongue.

Here the "articulation" of the "raw and passionate tongue" is finally given *breath* and *touch*. Foreground and background, text and context change places as the word, indeed the letter, assumes life and takes *fligHt*, a "reconditioned" body, made new, so the black letters tell us, by the "handshake of breath."

IV

"The materiality of language," writes McCaffery in an essay on bill bissett's "writing outside writing," "is that aspect which remains resistant to an absolute subsumption into the ideality of meaning. . . . To see the letter not as phoneme but as ink, and to further insist on that materiality, inevitably contests the status of language as a bearer of uncontaminated meaning." [30] From John Cage's *Lecture on Nothing* and Jackson Mac Low's *The Pronouns* to Susan Howe's *Articulation of Sound Forms in Time* and Madeleine Gagnon's *Poélitique*, experiments with the visualization of poetic text—with calligramme, anagram, paragram, collage, overprint, erasure, found text, mesostic text—have proliferated. "Even writers who had never or seldom experimented with concrete techniques," observes Caroline Bayard, have "abandoned regular margins and straight-lined verse" (CB 163). More accurately, since the question of margins, regular or irregular, is of secondary importance, what Bayard means is that even more traditional poets now display an "awareness of space as a graphic and signifying agent."

But—and I shall conclude with a caveat—just as Concrete poetry all too easily turned into the "pretty" layout of posters and greeting cards, so the deconstruction of billboard discourse is subject to its own simplifications. This is the case, to my mind, with the now highly fashionable artworks of Barbara Kruger, whose huge billboard photographs have been extravagantly praised as using, in the words of Frederick Garber, "advertising's classic synecdoche to subvert the social constructions that advertising builds." [31] In works like the famous *We Won't Play Nature to Your Culture* or *I am your almost nothing*, Kruger juxtaposes photographic image to signpost slogan so as to create, according to her admirers, subtle and ironic feminist critiques of the dominant patriarchal culture. In *Your life is a perpetual insomnia* (fig. 4.25), for example, the "you" is the image of a man, his head cropped below the hairline, his eyes covered by the left hand, and his attire the "correct" business regalia—expensive pin-striped shirt and tie, multiple rings, hints of gray hair in the eyebrows—a power status that evidently goes hand in hand with a life that is "perpetual insomnia." Indeed, such little details as the unbuttoning of a single wrist button and the wearing of what looks like a wedding ring on the third, not ring, finger suggest the disorder lurking behind the order.

Garber argues, with great ingenuity, that Kruger's is by no means the easy target corporate man, that, on the contrary, she is satirizing "our public visual discourse that urges us to identify people who look like this with wealth, class and power. . . . the action turns sourly self-reflexive because the figures who create such clichés, whether of men or women, are precisely those power figures whom this stereotype recalls. 'You' has made the original image and Kruger turns it into his sardonic autobiography, revising it into a mirror in which he sees both himself and his stereotype at once."

My difficulty with this and related readings is that the alleged deconstruction of the stereotype often seems just as stereotypical as its object. "Public visual discourse" does not necessarily urge us to identify men in pinstripe shirts and paisley ties, men whose hair is graying and brow knitted, with wealth and power; on the contrary, as we see in the GAP ad (fig. 4.36), public visual discourse is much more sophisticated than that. Thus it is a good question whether *Your life is a perpetual insomnia* subverts gestures of mastery, as the artist and many of her admirers would have us think, or whether Kruger's text doesn't inadvertently reinforce a cliché of her own—the cliché that men of the power elite inevitably live a meaningless nightmare existence. What is even more problematic: it is not clear how or why the artist who makes these observations is not herself tainted by the reification endemic to the discourse of patriarchy. From what position of authority, in other words, does Kruger operate so as to maintain her bemused distance from the horrors and inequities her work invokes?

As I was mulling over these questions, I received in the mail a postcard (fig. 4.26 recto and verso) offering a Kruger silk screen called *Business as usual*, with its indictment of ladies' fur-coat culture, mounted on an otherwise ordinary canvas tote bag so as to make it a desirable commodity worth $50.00, the proceeds going to the Printed Matter bookstore on SoHo's Wooster Street. However worthy the cause (Printed Matter is a fine small-press publisher of verbal/visual books), this particular appropriation of the Kruger collage makes *Business as usual* a doubly ironic slogan.

It is frequently argued that commodification of this sort is so endemic to our culture that the artist is inevitably absorbed into its process. But if this is the case, the kind of head-on "oppositionality" we

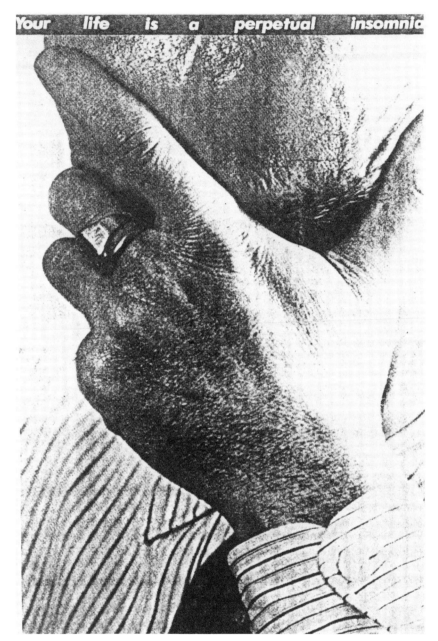

Your life is a perpetual insomnia

4.25 Barbara Kruger, *Your life is a perpetual insomnia*. Courtesy of Mary Boone Gallery, New York.

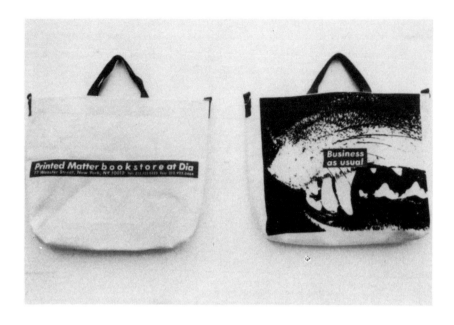

Printed Matter b o o k s t o r e at Dia

Bulk Rate
U.S. Postage
Paid
Ann Arbor Mich
Permit No. 87

NOW AVAILABLE
FROM PRINTED MATTER!
A Book-Bag by BARBARA KRUGER

- two color silk-screen
- heavy natural canvas
- small inside pocket with velcro flap
- detachable nylon shoulder strap
- big! 15 × 18" with 3" gusset

Each $50.00

trade discounts available

Marjorie Perloff
1467 Amalfi Drive
Pacific Palicades, CA 90272

Order by phone or mail using your
Visa or Mastercard.

tel. 212.925.0325
fax. 212.925.0464

photo: Nancy Linn

Printed Matter bookstore at Dia
77 Wooster Street   New York NY 10012

4.26 Nancy Linn, photograph of front and back of a canvas book bag with Barbara Kruger silk-screen on postcard from Printed Matter bookstore at Dia, 77 Wooster Street, New York, N.Y. 10012.

find in Kruger's work becomes a questionable possibility. Indeed, what the more stringent aesthetic of the 1990s has come to recognize is that, given the advertising industry's own self-consciousness, its ability to undo its own existing clichés—the "successful man," say, now being depicted as wearing a T-shirt rather than a coat and tie—art discourse must work, not just to reverse the "commercial" stereotype, but to undo its own presuppositions about the stereotype in question. Not all successful businessmen, after all, are alike.

To put it another way: are we sure that, as Broodthaers noted when he declared that "Art is commercial. My aim is equally commercial" (MB 49), we don't ourselves participate in *Business as usual?* In McCaffery's "Lag" we read the sentence "You check the map I must have bought"—a marvelous synecdoche of the narrator's capacity or for that matter, anyone's capacity—to deny complicity. After all, I must have bought a map! But what if I didn't? Then "you" will have to check it anyway. And it will be up to "you" to see that the car gets where it's going.

"The *preconceived idea* of crystalline purity," said Wittgenstein, "can only be removed by turning our whole examination round" (PI no. 107, p. 46e). It is that "turning round" that transforms "examination" (as in *Learning from Las Vegas*) into artistic performance. As Johanna Drucker puts it on the opening page of *Through Light and the Alphabet:*

> All our conversations were in language and according to conventions the others could be party to, but this one took off on its own trajectory to mind the business being left out of the accounts. The world was too amorphous for repose inside of sweet articulation.

5   *The Return of the (Numerical) Repressed:*
From Free Verse to Procedural Play

In organic poetry the metric movement, the measure is the direct expression of the movement of perception. And the sounds, acting together with the measure, are a kind of extended onomatopoeia—i.e., they imitate, not the sounds of an experience . . . but the feeling of an experience, its emotional tone, its texture.
—Denise Levertov, "Some Notes on Organic Form"[1]

The exhaustion of tradition, represented by rules, is the starting point in the search for a *second foundation*, that of mathematics.
—Jacques Roubaud, "Mathematics in the Method of Raymond Queneau"[2]

Constraint is . . a commodious way of passing from language to writing.
—Marcel Bénabou, "Rule and Constraint"[3]

Free verse = freedom; open form = open mind, open heart: for almost half a century, these equations have been accepted as axiomatic, the corollary of what has come to be called, with respect to poetic language, the "natural look." "The line comes (I swear it)," announced Charles Olson in "Projective Verse" (1950), "from the breath, from the breathing of the man who writes at the moment that he writes."[4] "Trouble with conventional form (fixed line count & stanza form)," said Allen Ginsberg in 1961, "is, it's too symmetrical, geometrical, numbered and pre-fixed—unlike to my own mind which has no beginning and end, nor fixed measure of thought . . . other than its own cornerless mystery—to transcribe the latter in a form most nearly representing its actual occurrence."[5] And lest we conclude that Olson and Ginsberg represent a particular Projectivist or Beat sensibility rather than the dominant poetic discourse of the period, consider Robert Lowell's explanation, in his *Paris Review* interview of 1961, of the turn toward free verse that characterized the *Life Studies* poems of 1959: "I couldn't," says Lowell, sounding not unlike Ginsberg, "get my experience into tight metrical forms. . . . I felt that the meter plastered difficulties and mannerisms on what I was trying to say to such an extent that it terribly hampered me."[6] Even as sophisticated an analyst of poetic form as Anthony Easthope suggests that a "necessary condition" for the postmodern overthrow of the bourgeois subject, of the Cartesian ego, is "the use, as in Pound's *Cantos*, of 'free verse,'" where the rhythm can, as

134

Pound puts it, "correspond exactly to the emotion or shade of emotion to be expressed." "This exact correspondence," remarks Easthope, "cannot take place when the abstract pattern of pentameter is imposed throughout and when closure of the syntagmatic chain tries to run everything together."[7]

The fidelity of verse form to the actual arc of feeling, the notion that rhythm, sound repetition, and lineation can enact the process of discovery, that they can mime what Robert Duncan called, in the title of his 1960 collection, "the opening of the field," can be traced back, of course, to Whitman and, more immediately, to D. H. Lawrence, whose Preface to the American Edition of *New Poems* (1918) is a remarkable manifesto calling for "free verse" as the "direct utterance from the instant, whole man," as the "soul and the mind and body surging at once, nothing left out." As Lawrence expressively put it:

> Free verse toes no melodic line, no matter what drill-sergeant. . . . We can get rid of the stereotyped movements and the old hackneyed associations of sound and sense. We can break the stiff neck of habit. . . . free verse has its own *nature*, that . . . is neither star nor pearl, but instantaneous like plasm. . . . It has no finish. It has no satisfying stability, satisfying to those who like the immutable. None of this. It is the instant; the quick. . . . For such utterance any externally applied law would be mere shackles and death. The law must come new each time from within.[8]

In his own best poems, as I have argued elsewhere,[9] verse form is, as Lawrence described it, determined by the simulation of a particular utterance, the voice of an "I" that alternately cajoles, teases, and hectors his nameless interlocutor, using linear patterns that loop back and forth to enact the "gradual pulsing to and fro" of consciousness coming to awareness.

But in the last decade or so, the "freedom" of free verse has come in for some serious questioning. Robert Hass, for example, has remarked somewhat sadly (even as he has continued to write predominantly in free verse) that whereas "free verse" once "had something to do with [the] revolt against some alternative formal principle that feels fictitious," "Now, I think, free verse has lost its edge, become neutral, the given instrument."[10] Which is to say that free verse has become quite simply the lyric norm. In a recent *American Poetry Review* (March–April 1990), for example, every one of the sixteen poets represented (and this includes the Czech poet Miroslav Holub, the Brazilian Adélia Prado, and the Irish Eavan Boland, as well as such U.S. poets as Marvin Bell, John Koethe, Debra Gregerman, Diane Swan, and Lucien Stryk) writes free verse.[11] Indeed, students coming to poetry today are increas-

ingly taught that if a given text is lineated, then it's a "poem," no mat-
ter how the lines are constituted.[12] The question of meter, of syllable
and stress count, of quantity is thus thrust into the background.

Given this situation, it is not surprising that a group of younger poets
who call themselves "New Formalists" have launched a campaign to
revive "meter," by which they mean almost exclusively iambic pen-
tameter. Brad Leithauser, for example, dismisses free verse as showing
"signs of fatigue" and declares that "Anyone who loves poetic form, and
has worked hard within it, knows that the iambic line is still a loded-
gold mine." Indeed, the iamb is the unit that "feels right."[13] A similar
case is made by David Dooley in an essay called "Iambic in the 80s,"
which discusses the use, by contemporary poets of three metrical forms:
blank verse, rhymed satiric quatrains, and the sonnet (CC 116–28). And
Timothy Steele insists that "Fine metrical composition makes a sen-
suous appeal to the ear and mind that no other kind of composition
makes."[14]

But such formulations—and there are many in the various New For-
malist manifestos—are based on a premise that will not stand up to
scrutiny, namely, that there are no cultural, ideological, or social con-
straints placed upon metrical choice, that, on the contrary, metrical
choice is wholly "free" and that hence traditional forms are there for
the using. If, by this reasoning, I feel like writing heroic couplets on
Monday, Spenserian stanzas on Tuesday, and free verse on Wednesday,
depending on my mood, my subject matter, and so on, I can do so
at will. "Even in an age remarkable for its science," writes Timothy
Steele," our individual and collective well-being and happiness depend
on how thoughtfully and sensitively we respond to qualitative issues in
human experience. . . . Poetry preeminently supplies this guidance"
(MM 293), the implication being that "science" and "poetry" are some-
how on different planes and that the latter "answers" to the former
without being implicated in its assumptions or hypotheses.

The notion that we can somehow revive and reproduce the exact
metrical forms of earlier centuries flies in the face of common sense.
Even Timothy Steele, after all, would probably be reluctant to suggest
that the Augustan heroic couplet bears no relationship to other phe-
nomena in early eighteenth-century English culture, that the couplet
might just as easily have been used by, say, the *Beowulf* poet. But the
implications are much broader: indeed, as Henri Meschonnic has shown
so forcefully in his *Critique du rythme*,[15] there is no prosodic form that
isn't, at least to some degree, historically bound and culture-specific.
The dominance of the alexandrine in French poetry from the seven-
teenth to the late nineteenth century, for example, has to do, not with

the intrinsic value of a twelve-syllable line, governed by specific rules as to caesurae and stress, but with specific relationships between poetry and discourse.[16] Similarly, as Anthony Easthope has argued, a seemingly neutral and omnipresent form like iambic pentameter in English is not without ideological base. First used by Chaucer in the fourteenth century, the pentameter then went underground, reemerging in Wyatt and Surrey's adaptations of the Italian sonnet in *Tottel's Miscellany* (1557), and quickly becoming *the* verse form, replacing earlier accentual verse, where stress-count was not necessarily matched by the proportional number of syllables per line. And Easthope observes:

> On the one side, as the name proclaims, iambic pentameter reaches back to the quantitative metre of Greek and Latin and the model of binarily contrasted syllables arranged in "feet"; on the other, the non-metric intonation approximates to the abstract pattern and thus the native language is brought into relation with the classical model. . . . The ascendancy of pentameter relegates the older accentual metre to a subordinate or oppositional position in which it has remained ever since: the appropriate metre for nursery rhymes, the lore of schoolchildren, ballad, industrial folk song and even, more recently, the football chant. (AE 65)

How the Renaissance model, say, the iambic pentameter sonnet, gradually gives way to the rhetorical model of the heroic couplet, the "transparency" model of Romantic blank verse with its identification of the reader with the speaker so that "enunciation" itself is "semanticized" and made "iconic" (AE 9), and finally the modernist collage of Pound's *Cantos*, where the pentameter and linearity itself break down into a fragmented surface that "foregrounds and insists upon the materiality of the signifier" (AE 140), is convincingly, if somewhat schematically, demonstrated by Easthope.

But what happens after modernism? Easthope suggests that we have now moved from the "free verse" of Eliot (actually not at all free but a series of deviations from established norms)[17] and the fragmented collage surface of the *Cantos* to what he calls *intonational metre*, which is to say the mimesis of actual speech, whose intonation "is determined phonetically, syntactically, and semantically" (AE 153). Easthope talks of the "tone-units" of contemporary poetry, these units being more or less the "breath-groups" (Olson) or "utterances" (Lawrence) of earlier proponents of free verse. But, as Easthope himself notes, "Intonation can only be defined for speech, not writing, since writing can always be spoken aloud in different ways" (AE 153).

And therein lies the rub: as the speech-based poetics of midcentury has given way, more and more, to the foregrounding of the materiality of the written sign itself,[18] a prosody based on intonational contours has become increasingly problematic. The emphasis on the moment of enunciation (at best variable and transitory) now seems a questionable procedure, whether for the poet or the reader. For such "momentary" or "instantaneous" rhythm suggests that there is first an experience, something lived and felt *out there*, and only then and secondarily its verbal rendering.[19] But this doctrine goes counter to everything poststructuralist theory has taught us: if writing is regarded, not as the linear representation of a prior "full" or "originary" speech, but as what Derrida calls a "sequence of differences," a sequence in which the phonemic, graphemic, and ideographic elements of language are brought into play,[20] then we may expect to find a poetic composition that is neither conventionally metrical on the one hand, nor breath-determined or "intonational" on the other.

What does such "writerly" prosodic form look like? One possibility—and this is probably the most common postmodern practice—is to take the existing meters and stanza forms and to treat them parodically. A witty poem by John Ashbery called "The Songs We Know Best," for example, begins as follows:

> Just like a shadow in an empty room
> Like a breeze that's pointed from beyond the tomb
> Just like a project of which no one tells—
> Or didja really think that I was somebody else?
>
> Your clothes and pantlegs lookin' out of shape
> Shape of the body over which they drape
> Body which has acted in so many scenes
> But didja ever think of what that body means?[21]

The thrust of such parody is strongly intertextual: we read Ashbery's rhyming tetrameter quatrains, not only againt pre-Raphaelite and nineties love poems with their ballad stanzas and their predictable rhyming of "breeze" and "trees," "room" and "tomb," "shape" and "drape," but also against those familiar popular songs that refer to shadows "in an empty room," to breezes blowing "from beyond the tomb," to mysterious body shapes and mistaken identities. All such allusions are gently mocked in Ashbery's "song we know best" even as they are recalled with great fondness. Ashbery uses sonnet and sestina, haiku and pantoum in similar ways, but what is not always understood is that his free verse and prose poems, which make up the bulk of his work, are also send-ups of various sorts. "Business Personals," for example, which I discuss in detail in the next chapter, is a kind of mock-Whitmanian ode, its long and loose (6- and 7-stress) free-verse lines positing the Sublime only to deflate and burlesque it in intricate ways.

A second way of approaching the question of metrics—and this will be my subject here—is to maintain the counting principle inherent in meter but to count, not feet or stresses or vowel lengths or even syllables, but some other more elusive quantity. What has been called *constraint* or *procedurality* is not equivalent to the concept of *rule* in traditional metrics, where the choice of, say, *ottava rima* sends a definite signal to the audience that every stanza will have eight lines of iambic pentameter, rhyming *abababcc*. Rather, a procedural poetics, which can, incidentally, apply equally well to "prose" and "verse" (the distinction between them being much less important than the concern for language as a site of paragrammatic play, of the sedimentation of verbal, phonemic, and graphemic traces in interaction), is primarily *generative*, the constraint determining, not what is already fixed as a property of the text, but *how* the writer will proceed with his composition. Since the notion of *procedurality* has been developed most fully by the French literary group called Oulipo, the acronym for the Ouvroir de littérature potentielle founded at Cerisy-la-Salle in 1960 by Raymond Queneau and François Le Lionnais, I shall begin with this important alternative poetics.

II

Oulipo, as its name indicates, was designed not as a movement but primarily as a workshop, whose members—poets, novelists, scientists, mathematicians, philosophers—could come together to discover new ways of creating literature. Its early membership included such important writers as Italo Calvino, Jacques Roubaud, Georges Perec, and the American Harry Matthews, and while there may be no direct relationship or exchange between Oulipo on the one hand and American "procedural" texts like Zukofsky's *80 Flowers* or Cage's *Roaratorio* on the other, the links between these poetics are worth examining.

Consider, for example, Georges Perec's reinvention of the *lipogram*, which may be defined, according to *Larousse* (see OU 98), as "a literary work in which one compels oneself strictly to exclude one or several letters of the alphabet" (*lipo* comes from *leipo*, 'I leave'). Although the lipogram was an important form in antiquity,[22] it evidently went into eclipse in the nineteenth century: the *Robert*, for example, ignores the word, an omission which prompts the following commentary from Perec:

This lexicographical ignorance is accompanied by a critical misappreciation as tenacious as it is contemptuous. Exclusively preoccupied with its great capitals (Work, Style, Inspiration, World-Vision, Fundamental Options, Genius, Creation, etc.), literary history seems deliberately to ignore writing as practice, as work, as play. Systematic artifices, formal mannerisms (that which, in the final analysis, constitutes Rabelais, Sterne, Roussel . . .) are relegated to the registers of asylums for literary madmen. (OU 98)

What Perec calls "systematic artifice" is not just game playing. For one thing, as Jacques Roubaud has posited, "a text written according to a constraint must speak of this constraint"; indeed, "a text written according to a mathematizable constraint must contain the consequences of the mathematical theory it illustrates" (OU 12). In the case of Perec's novel *La Disparition*, for example, the lipogram used (the exclusion of the letter *E* throughout) functions at the thematic as well as the "lettrist" level since this is a novel about disappearance: thus, says Roubaud, the novel is "both the story of what it recounts and the story of the constraint that creates that which is recounted" (OU 12).

But even if the constraint thus serves a double function, what is its advantage over more "normal" methods of constructing a literary text? And isn't the Oulipo device—whether lipogram, palindrome, algorithm, or the "S + 7" method[23]—a form of fancy rather than imagination, of game-playing rather than art? Perhaps the best way to understand the Oulipian emphasis on procedurality is that, as Marcel Bénabou puts it, constraint "forces the system out of its routine functioning, thereby compelling it to reveal its hidden resources" (OU 41). And again, "Linguistic constraints . . . directly create a sort of 'great vacuum' into which are sucked and retained whole quantities of elements which, without this violent aspiration, would otherwise remain concealed. . . . the paradox of writing under constraint [is] that it possesses a double virtue of liberation, which may one day permit us to supplant the very notion of inspiration" (OU 43).

What Bénabou means, I think—and other Oulipians like Jacques Roubaud bear this out—is that whereas a rule (e.g., "a Petrarchan sonnet has fourteen lines made up of an octave [rhyming *abba abba*] and a variable sestet [e.g., *cdecde*]") creates a certain stasis, in that the projected poem must fit into a particular preexistent mold, a constraint, which ideally gives rise to a single text only, can, as Roubaud says, "tend toward multiplicity."[24] It prompts the author to let the concealed phonemes and morphemes of a given text come to the surface and create their own configurations, thus allowing for what Warren Motte calls "the maximal motivation of the literary sign" (OU 17).

Saturation, by this account, is a matter, not of "authentic" emotion or "important" subject matter, but of verbal resonance.

"Never," cautions Georges Perec in *Espèces d'espaces* (1974), "use the word 'etcetera'," [25] an injunction that might be the epigraph for a manual on the poetics of constraint. In *La Vie mode d'emploi* (*Life: A User's Manual*), it would seem at first that Perec, refusing the "etcetera," describes each individual atom, that he subordinates nothing. The scene is a single apartment house at 11 rue Simon-Crubellier in Paris; each of the novel's ninety-nine chapters describes in the most minute detail the furnishings and activities in a given room of the apartment block (see fig. 5.1). [26] The individual stories (*La Vie mode d'emploi* is subtitled *Romans* not *Roman*) sometimes intersect, sometimes give way to narratives of former inhabitants, sometimes remain isolated; all the characters, as well as the real people referred to, are listed in the Appendix, which also contains a chronology of those lives touched on in one way or another by their residence at 11 rue Simon-Crubellier or their relationships to those who have lived there. And further, as the Postscript tells us, the book contains dozens of found texts (not identified as such in the novel), ranging from extracts from Sterne and Stendhal to Mann and Proust, to Borges and Butor, to fellow Oulipians like Calvino, Queneau, and Roubaud.

At one level, then, we can read *La Vie mode d'emploi* as a kind of *Arabian Nights*, a storehouse of exciting narratives dealing with love, revenge, murder, mistaken identity, fraud, and family hatreds, interwoven with the contemporary plot in which the eccentric English millionaire Bartlebooth invents for himself an entirely useless lifetime project designed to leave no traces (it involves a 50-year regimen for painting watercolors in specific sites around the world, watercolors that can then be transformed into jigsaw puzzles which Bartlebooth must solve, whereupon their backing will be removed and they will be returned to the place of origin where they will be erased so that the process comes full circle), a project that involves the inhabitants Valène, Winckler (minor artists), Morellet (an ex-laboratory assistant), Mme Hourcade (an ex-factory worker), and the servant Smautf. But what makes *La Vie mode d'emploi* such a startling work is that we never come to know these characters and that their lives, far from making "sense" or cohering in any normal way, simply take on certain shapes. Indeed, the elaborately minute descriptions of items in a given room (say, the picture postcards in X's collection or the engravings in Y's) do not characterize their owners, as would such items in, say, a Balzac novel; on the contrary, the more we are made to see, the less we know. "Perec's method," says Josipovici, "actually destroys the delicate bal-

						Morellet	*Simpson Troyan Troquet*
Honoré	SMAUTF	SUT-TON	ORL-OWSKA	ALBIN			PLASSAERT
HUTTING	GRATIOLET		CRESPI	NIETO & ROGERS	*Jérôme*	*Fres-nel*	BREI-DEL · VAL-ÈNE
Brodin – Gratiolet							*Jérôme*
CINOC	DOCTOR DINTEVILLE						WINCKLER
Hourcade	*Gratiolet*						*Hérbert*
RÉOL	RORSCHACH				STAIRS		FOULEROT
Speiss							*Echard*
BERGER	*Grifalconi*						MARQUISEAUX
	Danglars						*Colomb*
BARTLEBOOTH							FOUREAU
	Appenzzel						DE BEAUMONT
ALTAMONT							
MOREAU							LOUVET
SERVICE ENTRANCE	MARCIA, ANTIQUES		*Claveau* OFFICE NOCHÈRE	ENTRANCE HALL			*Massy* MARCIA
CELLARS		BOILER ROOM	CELLARS	LIFT MACHINERY		CELLARS	CELLARS

11 RUE SIMON-CRUBELLIER
Names of previous occupants are given in italics.

5.1 Georges Perec, *11 Rue Simon-Crubellier*, in Perec, *Life: A User's Manual*, page 501.

ance of foreground and background on which novels depend for their effect of reality" (GJ 183).

The key to Perec's hyper-description—his endless cataloguing of detail—is the jigsaw puzzle described in the Preamble:

> the perceived object . . . in the present case, a wooden jigsaw puzzle—is not a sum of elements to be distinguished from each other and analysed discretely, but a pattern, that is to say a form, a structure: the element's existence does not precede the existence of the whole, it comes neither before nor after it, for the parts do not determine the pattern, but the pattern determines the parts: knowledge of the pattern and of its laws, of the set and its structure, could not possibly be derived from discrete knowledge of the elements that compose it. That means that you can look at a piece of a puzzle for three whole days, you can believe that you know all there is to know about its colouring and shape, and be no further on than when you started. The only thing that counts is the ability to link this piece to other pieces. . . . as soon as you have succeeded . . . in fitting [it] into one of its neighbors, the piece disappears, ceases to exist as a piece.[27]

This account of the jigsaw puzzle may strike us as simple common sense: we all know that individual puzzle pieces—the so-called "little chaps," "double crosses," or "crossbars"—have no identity until they are connected. But what we usually don't acknowledge is that even the "realist" novel provides status for the individual "piece" only via the larger pattern and that, moreover, someone is calling the shots:

> every move the puzzler makes, the puzzle-maker has made before; every piece the puzzler picks up, and picks up again, and studies and strokes, every combination he tries, and tries a second time, every blunder and every insight, each hope and each discouragement have all been designed, calculated, and decided by the other. (LUM, unnumbered Preamble, 191).

This argues for an intentionality and artifice quite alien to the notions of organic form, which I cited at the beginning of this chapter—Denise Levertov's sense of "measure," for example, as the "direct expression of the movement of perception." And indeed *Life: A User's Manual* is itself conceived as a puzzle, "designed, calculated, and decided by the other." For the movement from one apartment to another in the novel is based on the knight's tour problem in chess. As Perec's English translator David Bellos explains it, this is the tour the knight, moving one square in one direction and two squares in a direction at right angles to the first, would have to follow so as to travel right around the 8×8 chessboard touching every square once only. Perec extends the board, making it a 10 × 10 grid (see fig. 5.2): the hypothetical knight's tour thus dictates the order of the chapters' unfolding.[28]

But the chess game doesn't quite work. There are 100 squares on a 10 × 10 grid and yet the novel has only 99 chapters. The bottom left-hand square (1,0) remains empty: nothing, presumably, happens here. Chapter 65 occupies square (2,8), chapter 66 square (3,9). But something is missing: to get from (2,8) to (3,9), the knight would have to move through (1,0)—the empty square. Perec, as both Bellos and Josipovici note, has thus introduced a "deliberate imperfection," a Lucretian *clinamen*—an error or bend. For what should be chapter 67 thus becomes 66 and accordingly 100 is never reached, even as Bartle-

	1	2	3	4	5	6	7	8	9	0
1	59	83	15	10	57	48	7	52	45 Plassaert	54
	Hutting									
2	97	11	58	82	16	9	46	55	6	51
3	84	60	96 Dinteville	14	47	56	49	8 Winckler	53	44
4	12 Réol	98	81	86	95	17	28	43 Foulerot	50	5
5	61 Berger	85	13 Rorschach	18	27	79	94	4	41	30
6	99	70	26 Bartelbooth	80	87	1	42	29	93	3
7	25	62 Altamont	88	69	19	36	78	2 Beaumont	31	40
8	71	65 Moreau	20	23	89	68	34	37 Louvet	77	92
9	63	24	66 Marcia	73	35	22	90	75	39	32
0	*	72	64	21	67	74	38	33	91	76

5.2 Georges Perec, *11 Rue Simon-Crubellier*, as refigured by David Bellos, "Georges Perec's Puzzling Style," *Scripsi*.

booth fails to complete the project of reassembling the 500 puzzles (see DB 66–69).

The numerical rule and its deflection thus control the intricate and puzzling structure of Perec's novel. Number games play a major role throughout: for example, each chapter refers, in one way or another, to the grid-square reference numbers of each room: in chapter 61 ("Berger, 1"), for example, which is at grid square (1,5), a "sideboard of indeterminate style" bears "a bottle of Pastis" 51 (LUM 291); again, in chapter 64 ("In the Boiler Room, 2"), whose grid square is (3,0), Olivier hides the wireless set in a chest "whose slightly sloped top was pierced with holes that had originally been numbered −03" (LUM 303). And, perhaps most intriguingly of all, the final chapter (99), which makes clear that Bartlebooth dies without completing 61 of the 500 puzzles, is located at grid square (1,6).

There are many other kinds of number games (and alphabet games, charts, puzzle grids) in this novel, but Perec's purpose is not just to dazzle us with his showmanship, his trickery. For the purpose of all these puzzles is, as Bellos points out, to prevent "even the most careful *natural* reader" from seeing the structure or armature of the whole until after he or she has finished reading the book. Thus Perec's "puzzle hides, as a jigsaw does, what it also reveals very clearly once you have seen it" (DB 76). Indeed, one of the revelations is that the author, supposedly absent from this most impersonal of novels, has been there all along in the person of the painter Valène (one of Perec's first pseudonyms in the 1950s) and that when, in chapter 51, we scan the numbered list of items to be included in Valène's depiction of 13 rue Simon-Crubellier, the word that emerges from what is a giant reverse diagonal acrostic is the word *âme* (âme or 'soul'). Contrived, tricky, Daedalian as is the artifice of *Life: A User's Manual*, perhaps the text's ultimate contrivance is to teach its "users" that the soul cannot be controlled, that the puzzle before us cannot be solved. Indeed, the empty square (1,0) is there to remind us of the indeterminacy of the puzzling process.

III

What do such "empty squares" and numerical schemes have to do with postmodern American poetry? In 1974, as his great long poem *"A"* was nearing completion, Louis Zukofsky drew up an outline for a new project to be called *80 Flowers*:[29]

> *Plan.* Beginning at 70 to finish for my 80th birthday a book of songs called *80 Flowers*.

Substance. Only those flowers I have actually seen and whatever botany I can learn in 10 years. . . .

Form. 8-line songs of 5-word lines : 40 words to each poem growing out of and *condensing* my previous books. . . .

As to "40 words" c.f. Old Testament; *tetraktys.* . . . Also adding integers $4 + 0 = 4$. Eight lines $= 2 \times 4$. . . . Eight 8-line songs per year would $= 8^2 = 64$, and adding integers again $= 10$ (years); 8×10 years $= 80$. . . .

"Number-tumbling," Michele J. Leggott comments on this schema, "is usually near the heart of Zukofsky's poetry. . . . Numbers are something to work against, a form to transform as number-generated writing takes on its own life, spawning more numbers, other ratios" (RZ 14). In the Old Testament, Leggott notes, forty has a special value as the number of years in a generation (Judges 3:30, 5:31), whereas the sacred *tetraktys* (see fig. 5.3), the subject of a long passage in "*A*"–19, is the Pythagorean figure of divinity, the triangle based on the fact that 10 is the sum of the first four integers (1, 2, 3, 4), its three sides enclosing the universal 1 (the "central fire") at the center. *Tetraktys* was Pythagoras's name for deity; it is also, Leggott observes, "the root of tetragrams that contain the god-head's name in four letters," e.g., JHVH, Zeus, Jove, Deus, Gott, Deva, Dios, Odin, and Lord (RZ 15, 383). The tetraktys thus supplied Zukofsky with both 10 and 4; 4×2 or 8 is the Pythagorean number of love, and turned on its side, the infinity symbol (RZ 16). And 10 divided by $2 = 5$ (the sacred pentangle) which gives us the 8×5 of each "Flower."[30]

The result looks like this:

> Starglow
>
> *Starglow* dwarf china rose shrubthorn
> lantern fashion-fare airing car-tire crushed
> young's churching old rambler's flown
> to sky cane cut back
> a crown transplanted patient of
> drought sun's gold firerimmed branched
> greeting thyme's autumn sprig head
> happier winter sculpt white rose   (CSP 325)

"Starglow" (*Starglo*) is a rare cream-colored miniature rose, producing fragrant blooms with pointed petal tips (RZ 93); Zukofsky's rose, Leggott suggests, is a hybrid of *Starglo* and *Rosa chinensis minima*, "the fairy rose (faery rose? fiery rose?)," which is a "dwarf shrub with small, single or double, rose-red flowers," similar to the Baby Rambler (hence the "dwarf china rose shrubthorn"), which, when cut back, renews itself with new canes ("to sky cane cut back"). Zukofky's highly condensed and elliptical poem presents this dual rose or rose-graft (white/

red, cultivated/wild) as lighting up the dark ("lantern fashion-fare air-ing"; "lantern" relates to the various other lights in the poem: sun, fire, star, moon), but also subject to being crushed under a cruel "car-tire." But the "sculpt white rose" of the final line seems to survive such setbacks; "greeting" the sprig of thyme, cut back for winter, it rises ("flown / to sky") in the poet's imagination, etched againt the "sun's gold firerimmed" radiance.

This is at best a cursory reading of "Starglow," [31] but it should be ade-quate for our purposes here, the question being why Zukofsky cast his flower poem in this particular mold, this 8 × 5 (8 lines, 5 words per

5.3 Sacred tetraktys, as sketched by Joseph K. Perloff.

line) grid. We should note, to begin with, that according to conventional scansion, "Starglow" would have to be labelled a "free verse" poem, its stress count ranging from four ("to sky cane cut back") to seven ("lantern fashion-fare airing car-tire crushed"), its syllable count from 5 (line 4) to ten (line 2). Visually, too, for that matter, the line lengths are quite irregular.

Why, then, the Pythagorean scheme? In a very interesting essay called "Approaching *80 Flowers*," David Lévi-Strauss argues that Zukofsky's organization is not of lines or feet or even of rhythmic units or cadences, as is normal in poetry, but of *words:* "In adhering to a 5-word count in the line, words are freed of the usual subservience to demands of syntax. The entire arrangement becomes more spacious, less linear. Words begin to move in several directions at once, in a grid—40 units to each poem, each word a unit." And Lévi-Strauss adds, "Words, unbridled, flex, shift from noun to verb to adjective to sounder, break to form other words, recombine, all still held in the suspension of *words together.* A multiplication of precise relationships between words, this 'flowering.'"[32] If, in other words, we think of each flower poem as a 40-space grid, each space occupied by a single word, we can read the poem, not only from left to right, but from top to bottom and vice versa, creating new relationships between word units. Thus *Starglow* in line 1 goes with "lantern" directly beneath it, the "crown" of line 5 points directly to "sun's gold" in line 6, and so on. Syntactic relations are held to a bare minimum: almost all function words are removed as are active verbs (there is not a single one in "Starglow"). The poem is made up of elaborate noun and adjectival phrases, with heavy compounding as in Hopkins; often it is impossible to tell whether a given word is a noun or an adjective ("churching" in line 3), a gerund or a present participle (e.g., "greeting" in line 7). Indeed, syntax is subordinated to sound, which is the feature foregrounded; consider a line like

lantern fashion-fare airing car-tire crushed

with its alliteration of *f*'s and *c*'s, its elaborate assonance of short *a*'s, its rhyming on "fare," "air," "car," its consonance of "-tern," "car," "tire." So much chiming does this line contain that when the harsh sounding of *crushed* is introduced at its very end, the reader is jolted and propelled forward to the place where "crushed" meets "churning" and then "cut back."

The grid, writes Rosalind Krauss, "is what art looks like when it turns its back on nature. . . . the grid is the means of crowding out the dimensions of the real and replacing them with the lateral spread of a single surface."[33] But what is curious about Zukofsky's grid poems is

that their geometric order is always at war with the "nature" to be re-
jected: as in the case of Perec's 10 × 10 chessboard, the grid becomes the
occasion for a curious jostling, exchange, and disjunction. The past
participle "branched" in line 6, for example, encourages us to read the
"-ead" right beneath it as a matching past participle, even though it is
the kernel of the noun "head." Or again, words that should go together
like "winter" and "white" ("winter white") are separated by a particle
like "sculpt." The words thus act, as Lévi-Strauss suggests, as *chords*—a
new quantitative measure (DLS 88). The 8 × 5 grid, with its allusions
to the tetraktys and other Pythagorean and biblical figures, becomes, as
in the case of *Life: A User's Manual*, an unpredictable system. A poem
about roses: what could be more banal? And yet, in Zukofsky's hands, it
becomes a galaxy of interlocking and magnetic words.

IV

A year after Zukofsky's death in 1978, IRCAM at the Centre Pompidou
in Paris aired the first production of John Cage's *Roaratorio: An Irish
Circus on Finnegans Wake.*[34] Like *80 Flowers* and certain sections of
Zukofsky's *"A," Roaratorio* and Cage's other mesostic texts, of which
the most recent is *I–VI* (the Charles Eliot Norton Lectures given at Har-
vard in 1988–89),[35] present a challenge to the dominant free verse aes-
thetic of the period. But whereas Zukofsky's poetic experiments remain
largely cult works, little known by the public or, for that matter, by the
world of Norton Anthology discourse, Cage's are widely known, pri-
marily because of his fame as a composer, an avant-gardist, a "great
figure" in the art world. At the same time, Cage's poetics remain at least
as misunderstood as Zukofsky's, primarily because we have not yet
formed an adequate conception of what is meant by the term *chance
operations.*

The common wisdom about Cage's texts is that, in the words of
Edward Rothstein, recently reviewing *I–VI* for the *New Republic*, "they
are randomly put together." Cage, as Rothstein typically explains his
technique, "once used the *I Ching* as his instrument of liberation—thus
giving the choices of tones and phrases a semi-mystical aura as he
tossed sticks according to the ancient Chinese oracle. But the aura
evidently became less convenient the more exotic Cage's techniques
became. Now he depends on a computer program for assistance, its spit-
out numbers determining the locations of words and ideas and sounds."
And further, in referring to the *mesostic* rule, which organizes the text
of *I–VI*, Rothstein remarks: "Between any two consecutive capital
letters in the randomly chosen words . . . Cage insists that neither letter

may appear in lower case. *This rule is purely lexicographical: it means nothing,* particularly since the words with the capitalized letters are arbitrarily chosen." [36]

One wonders what Rothstein thinks Cage means when he explains in the Introduction to *I–VI* that, in any given line, he adds "all the wing words from the source text . . . within the limit of forty-five characters to the right and the same to the left," and admits, "Then I take out the words I don't want" (*I–VI* 2). Again, consider the basic rule for the creation of *Roaratorio,* as Cage presents it in the printed text:

> Taking the name of the author and/or the title of the book as their subject (the row), write a series of mesostics beginning on the first page and continuing to the last. Mesostics means a row down the middle. In this circumstance a mesostic is written by finding the first word in the book that contains the first letter of the row that is not followed in the same word by the second letter of the row. The second letter belongs on the second line and is to be found in the next word that contains it that is not followed in the same word by the third letter of the row. Etc. . . . Do not permit for a single appearance of a given letter the repetition of a particular syllable. Distinguish between subsequent appearances of the same letter. Other adjacent words from the original text (before and/or after the middle word, the word including a letter of the row) may be used *according to taste,* limited, say to forty-three characters to the left and forty-three to the right. [37]

Chance operations, even though the phrase is Cage's own, is a highly misleading term for what actually happens in a mesostic text like *Roaratorio.* True, the mesostic words themselves may be generated by an arbitrary counting device (e.g., "find the first *J* not followed by an *A* in *Finnegans Wake*), or as they are in *I–VI,* by elaborate computer operations based on the *I Ching;* but such nonintentionality, as Cage has repeatedly explained, must be understood as a form of *discipline,* forcing the artist to break with ego, with habit, with self-indulgence. [38] A given writing project is said to use chance operations in that, at its outset, Cage has no idea what words the *I Ching* (or its computer version, the Mesolist) will generate, what words, that is to say, he will have to use. Once the chance-generated letters and words are in place, however, their presence provides the poet with rules that cannot be broken. Like Perec's 10 × 10 chessboard square or Zukofsky's 8 × 5 lyric stanza, then, the mesostic text is the very opposite of random; it is, on the contrary, rule-generated, the clinamen, to use the Oulipo phrase, being that the "wing phrases" in each line are written *according to taste,* following Cage's stated purpose of "taking out the words I don't want."

Let us see how this works in practice. *Roaratorio* is a series of mesos-

riverrun, past Eve and Adam's, from swerve of shore to bend of bay, brings us by a commodius vicus of recirculation back to Howth Castle and Environs.

Sir Tristram, violer d'amores, fr'over the short sea, had passencore rearrived from North Armorica on this side the scraggy isthmus of Europe Minor to wielderfight his penisolate war: nor had topsawyer's rocks by the stream Oconee exaggerated themselse to Laurens County's gorgios while they went doublin their mumper all the time: nor avoice from afire bellowsed mishe mishe to tauftauf thuartpeatrick: not yet, though venissoon after, had a kidscad buttended a bland old isaac: not yet, though all's fair in vanessy, were sosie sesthers wroth with twone nathandjoe. Rot a peck of pa's malt had Jhem or Shen brewed by arclight and rory end to the regginbrow was to be seen ringsome on the aquaface.

The fall (bababadalgharaghtakamminarronnkonnbronntonnerronntuonnthunntrovarrhounawnskawntoohoohoordenenthurnuk!) of a once wallstrait oldparr is retaled early in bed and later on life down through all christian minstrelsy. The great fall of the offwall entailed at such short notice the pftjschute of Finnegan, erse solid man, that the humptyhillhead of humself prumptly sends an unquiring one well to the west in quest of his tumptytumtoes: and their upturnpikepointandplace is at the knock out in the park where oranges have been laid to rust upon the green since devlinsfirst loved livvy.

Die erste Seite aus *Finnegans Wake* von James Joyce.
The first page of *Finnegans Wake* by James Joyce.

I

wroth with twone nathandJoe
A
Malt
jhEm
Shen

pftJschute
sOlid man
that the humptYhillhead of humself
is at the knoCk out
in thE park

Jiccup
the fAther
Most
hEaven
Skysign

Judges
Or
deuteronomY
watsCh
futurE

pentschanJeuchy
chAp
Mighty
cEment
and edificeS

the Jebel and the
crOpherb
flYday
and she allCasually
ansars hElpers

3

4

5

Die vertikale Zahlenreihe gibt die Seiten des *Finnegans Wake* von James Joyce an. Die über die Textseiten
verstreuten Interpunktionszeichen wurden aus dem Originaltext herausgelöst.
The margin numbers indicate the pages of *Finnegans Wake* by James Joyce. The scattered punctuation
marks were extracted from the original text.

5.5 John Cage, *Roaratorio*, page 29.

tics on the name JAMES JOYCE, generated by a "writing through" of *Finnegans Wake*—a reduction, Cage tells us, of its 626 pages (in the standard edition) to 41 or, in terms of tape time, to one hour.[39] Here is the opening page of the *Wake*, as reproduced by Cage in the text edition of *Roaratorio* (fig. 5.4), followed by the first page of Cage's own text (fig. 5.5).

Notice here that although the choice, say, of the first word, "nathandjoe" (see fig. 5.4, line 12, for the first *J* in the text) is generated by rule (choose the first word in *Finnegans Wake* containing a *J* not followed by an *A*), the inclusion of "wroth with twoone" as the left-hand wing phrase is purely Cage's decision. Indeed, it is quite possible to follow Cage's mesostic rule qua rule and produce a different version. For example:

> nathandJoe
> rot A peck
> Malt had
> jhEm or
> Shen
>
> the pftJschute
> erse sOlid
> humptYhillhead
> knoCk
> thE park
>
> of false Jiccup
> the fAther of fornicationists
> Most high
> hEaven
> the Skysign
>
> Judges had
> numbersOr
> deuteronomY   (one
> for to watsCh
> futurE

In my version, the variety of pitches and long vowels that constitutes the "signature" of the original disappears as does the rhythmical mock-Irish chant of "wroth with twoone nathandJoe." More important: the duality of Joyce's "twone" (two-in-one), which literally refers to the alternate biblical fathers, Wise Nathan and Chaste Joseph, but here in Cage's stanza also modifies "jhEm / Shen," that is, the twin ("twoone") sons, Shem and Shaun, of the novel's hero, H. C. Earwicker—this duality motif is lost in my version. (Even if my version retained "twone," for that matter, creating, say, the line, "with twone nathandJoe rot," I would lose the ominous opening on the emphatic word "wroth.") Furthermore, Cage's "writing through" also creates its own meanings, as in "Judges / Or / deuteronomY" (Joyce's text reads, "before joshuan judges had given us numbers or Helviticus committed deuteronomy"), meanings that are neither random nor entirely rule-bound but freely constructed.

Klaus Schöning, who produced *Roaratorio* at IRCAM and Cologne and edited the bilingual text edition, makes the following notation about form in his 1981 performance diary:

> "A fugue is a . . . complicated genre; but it can be broken up by a single sound, say from a fire engine" (from *Silence*).
> Paraphrase: *Roaratorio* is a more complicated genre; it cannot be broken up by a single sound, say from a fire engine. (R 19)

This provides a useful point of entry into Cage's complex *Hörspiel:* it is a work that cannot be interrupted. And further: a work designed "to suggest the complexity of *Finnegans Wake*" (R 75). Asked by Schöning if the use of Anthony Burgess's abridged version of the *Wake* would not have made his task easier, Cage responds: "No, no. The short *Finnegans Wake* tries to give you the gist or story of it. But the story of it is exactly what it isn't" (R 75). The aim, in other words, is never to follow "a single line," but to produce simultaneous layers of sound and meaning that correspond to the complexity of the parent text.

How to structure this complexity? Whereas the *Wake* is a cycle, beginning in the middle of one sentence and ending in the middle of another that can be combined with the first, a cycle based on Vico's theory of history and the circle of Indian Karma, the *Roaratorio* is a "circus" ("there is not one center," says Cage, "but a plurality of centers," R 107), in which everyone can participate (*oratorio* thus becoming *roaratorio*). What prevents this "circus" from being a free-for-all, however, is the observance of rule, the 5 × 2 "stanza" pattern created by the vertical mesostic "line" made of the ten letters *J A M E S J O Y C E*. If this letter-string recalls a rhyme scheme (say, *ababb cdcdd*), it is also very different, its *aural* and *visual* elements refusing to cohere. The name JAMES JOYCE, visible as a column on the page, is not heard at all when the poem is read aloud; conversely, the sounded *e* in "jhEm" or "hEaven" transforms the silent *e* of *James*, just as the /z/ phoneme of *James* can become the /s/ of "Skysign" and the diphthong /oy/ of *Joyce* can supply both the open /o/ of "sOlid" and the short /i/ of "humptYhillhead." Indeed, the *sprechstimme*, chanting, singing, and whispering used by Cage in the actual performance of the text are never fully present in the written version. Thus the normal hierarchy of speech and writing collapses. For is Cage's written text to be regarded as the secondary representation of his speaking and chanting? Or is the written text primary and the recital just one possible externalization?

Like Zukofsky's 8 × 5 stanza in *80 Flowers*, Cage's mesostics call into question the possibility of syntacticality. "Thoreau," remarks Cage, "said that when he heard a sentence, he heard feet marching. And I think that sentences still clearly exist in *Finnegans Wake*. Whereas in ancient Chinese language the sentence—as we know it—doesn't to my mind exist, because you're uncertain . . . whether a noun is a noun, or whether it's a verb or . . . an adjective. So that you don't know the relationship of the words. And a single poem can move as a single word in Joyce . . . a single poem can move in many different directions to appeal to the understanding" (R 85).

The poetic, for Cage, is thus a matter of making "it less like sentences" (R 85). Consider the following extracts:

Joyce: The great fall of the offwall entailed at such short notice the
           pftjschute of Finnegan, erse solid man, that the humptyhillhead
           of humself promptly sends an unquiring one well to the west in
           quest of his tumptytumtoes; and their upturnpikepointandplace
           is at the knock out in the park where oranges have been laid to
           rust upon the green since devlinfirst loved livvy.

Cage: pftJschute
                                sOlid man
                    that the humptYhillhead of humself
                          is at the knoCkout
                             in thE park

Despite all its punning, compounding, rhyming, phonemic play, and onomatopoeia, Joyce's sentence relies on grammatical logic: the Humpty-Dumptyan fall off the wall brought about the "pftjschute" of Finnegan, the once-solid man, his head coming to rest at the Hill of Howth, his upturned toes at Castle Knock in Phoenix Park, where the invading Orangemen ("oranges") have been laid to rest ("rust") upon the Green ever since the first Dubliner ("devlinfirst") loved the river (Anna) Liffey. Joyce's text can be "translated" in this way, even if no paraphrase can exhaust its possible meanings.

Cage's stanza rejects even this much logic, transforming the narrative into a word grid, where each unit ("pftJschute," "sOlid man," etc.) calls attention to itself. The "knoCk out / in thE park" becomes, first and foremost, a crash of spirants and stops—/p/, /f/, /t/, /th/, /s/, /sh/, /d/, /k/—so to speak "knocking out" the nasals and liquids and drumming the long and short vocalic /u/ of "PftJschute," "humpt-," and "humself" and the /ah/ of "sOlid" and "knoCk" into the listener's consciousness. At the same time, the elimination of connectives, realigns meanings: "pftJschute" now stands as a kind of appositive to "sOlid man," a "humptYhillhead of humself," whom the very next stanza further identifies as "Jiccup / the fAther." And whereas in Joyce, the subject of "is" (line 4) is the "upturnpikepointandplace," in Cage, the verb refers directly to Finnegan, the "sOlid man," the "humptYhillhead of humself."

The effect of such condensation is to produce a text that defies any sort of linear reading. And further: the individual words and word groups are defamiliarized by the "musical" soundings of the piece, the intricate layering of drumbeat and thunderclap, waterflow and birdsong, Irish dance tune and frog croak, that weaves in and out of the composition even as the voice, first heard as a solo, continues its recitation. In his desire "to make a music that was free of melody and free of harmony and free of counterpoint," Cage has "used [the] text [of *Finnegans Wake*] as a ruler" (R 89), transforming visual location into the temporality of sound. The actual procedure is extremely intricate, but we might review the main steps, as Cage outlines them.

The first step was to make a tape recording of the recital of the text, "using speech, song, chant, or *sprechstimme*, or a mixture or combination of these" (R 173). This provided "a ruler in the form of a typed or printed text and in the form of a recited text, both of them measurable in terms of space (page and line) and time (minute and second), by means of which the proper position . . . of sounds [might] be determined." The word "Jiccup" in the third stanza, for example, is measured spatially at 4:11 (page 4, line 11), and temporally as 14 seconds into the hour.

The next step was to make a list of places mentioned in the *Wake* as those places are identified in Louis Mink's *A Finnegans Wake Gazetteer* and a list of the page and line where the mention of each is made. Since there are so many places cited, Cage decided to limit the total number to 626 (the number of pages in his copy of the *Wake*), and these 626 places were selected by chance operations and tabulated. Next Cage commissioned as many people as necessary to go to the place in question and make a recording of between thirty seconds and five or ten minutes. The recording was to be made simply by "accept[ing] the sounds which are in the place you go to" (R 119); Cage himself traveled around Ireland with friends recording sounds of, say, dogs barking or chickens cackling or the wind blowing as the church bells ring. These sounds are then arranged along a ruler, again made by measuring the page and line where the place name appears in the *Wake* and transferring the ruler from space to time.

The place names thus generate one set of sound tracks. A second one was made by listing all the sound references in the book (fig. 5.6), reducing them by chance operations, and establishing families of sounds (as in fig. 5.7). These sounds are again transferred from their spatial position to a temporal one: for example, the reference to "the song of sparrownotes on his stave of wires" (FW 136, l. 35) means that we hear sparrows singing at the corresponding point in time (c. 13 minutes) on the hour-long tape. But note—and this is very important—that at the point where we hear the sparrow song, the spoken mesostic text, which does not, of course, include all the sounds listed, is by no means referring to it. Cage would find such an obvious correspondence between the sign and its referent much too uninteresting.

Finally, a whole program of "relevant musics" was recorded on yet another multitrack tape. Joe Heaney, "the king of Irish singers," was enlisted to perform and he urged Cage to include four Irish instruments— "the flute, the fiddle, the bodhran, which is a drum, and the Uillean pipes," the latter to be played by the Dublin musician Seamus Ennis (R 92–93). Thus, while Joe Heaney sings such familiar Irish songs as "Dark is the colour of my true love's hair" and "Little Red Fox," Seamus Ennis plays "The Boys of Blue Hill" or the "Derry Hornpipe" on his pipes, even as variations on jigs, reels, and Irish drum songs alternate with mazurkas and polkas.[40]

Place-related sounds, sound-references in the *Wake*, and actual musical sounds—these are finally superimposed on one another by a series of mathematical operations, the collection of sixteen multitrack tapes being reduced to a single one. "The material," says Cage, "is then a plurality of forms"; it has "what Joyce called 'soundsense'" (R 103). But doesn't it matter, Schöning asks Cage, that the sound track often drowns out the reciter's voice so that the words cannot be understood? From Cage's perspective this is no problem, for "this is our experience in life every day. Wherever we are a larger amount of what we have to experience is being destroyed every instant. If for instance . . . you go to a museum where you would think that you have . . . peace and quiet as you are looking at the Mona Lisa someone passes in front of you or bumps into you from behind" (R 101–3). Accordingly, the layering of sounds in *Roaratorio* is meant to resemble, not "white noise," as one of Cage's composer friends suggests, but what Cage calls "black noise," which is to say, "a sphere of sounds coming together." But in keeping with the circus format of the whole, these sounds never coalesce or

132

LISTE MIT GERÄUSCHEN AUS *FINNEGANS WAKE* (KAPITEL I)
Die Zahlen geben Seite und Zeile im Original von James Joyce an.

LISTING THROUGH *FINNEGANS WAKE* (CHAPTER I)
The numbers show the page and line from the original edition by James Joyce.

03.04	*violer d'amores*
.09	*avoice from afire bellowsed mishe mishe*
.15–17	*(bababadalgharaghtakamminarronnkonn-*
	bronntonnerronntuonnthunntrovarrhoun-
	awnskawntoohoohoordenenthurnuk!)
	christian minstrelsy
04.02–03	*Brékkek Kékkek Kékkek Kékkek! Kóax Kóax*
	Kóax! Ualu Ualu Ualu! Quaouauh!
.07	*apeal*
.08	*a toll, a toll*
.10–11	*with what strawng voice of false jiccup!*
05.03	*larrons o'toolers clittering up*
.03–04	*tombles a'buckets clottering down*
.09	*Hohohoho*
.11	*Hahahaha*
.15	*thunder of his arafatas*
.16	*that shebby choruysh of unkalified*
	muzzlenimiissilehims
.31	*fargobawlers*
.32–33	*megaphoggs*
06.06	*all the uproor from all the aufroofs*
.11	*lute*
.16–17	*duodisimally profusive plethora of*
	ululation
.18–19	*And the all gianed in with the shout-*
	most shoviality
.21	*Some in kinkin corass, more, kankan keening*
.22	*Belling him up*
.24–25	*E'erawhere in this whorl would ye hear sich a din again?*
.25–26	*With their deepbrow fundigs and the dusty fidelios*
.28	*Tee the tootal of the fluid hang the twoddle of the*
	fuddled, O!
.29	*Hurrah*
.36	*baywinds' oboboes shall wail him*

5.6 John Cage, "Listing through Finnegans Wake (Chapter 1)," from *Roaratorio*, page 132.

CATEGORIES AND NUMBER OF ALL SOUNDS USED IN *ROA-RATORIO*
(Hand-written facsimile: Poster (9))

A. LISTING THROUGH FINNEGANS WAKE:

	Part I	Part II
Thunderclaps	6	4
Thunder rumbles and earthquake sounds	29	27
Laughing and Crying (Laughtears)	64	100
Loud voice sounds (shouts, etc.)	31	22
Farts	5	5
Musical instruments (short)	66	96
Bells, clocks, chimes	28	42
Guns, explosions	32	36
Wails	7	11
Animals and particular birds	56	113
Music (instrumental and singing)	57	145
Water	34	24
Birds (in general)	16	18
Singing	64	72
	495	715
		495
B. PLACES		1210
		1083
Grand Total		2293

5.7 John Cage, "Categories and Number of All Sounds Used in Roaratorio" from *Roaratorio*, page 147.

merge; they retain their individual identities. Nor do the sounds heard in any sense "accompany" the words or provide a musical setting. On the contrary, word, melody, natural sound, animal cry, waterfall, and thunderclap remain independent of one another even though the sounds chosen by mathematical calculation exist somewhere in Joyce's text. It is accident, that is to say, whether the hoot of an owl happens to coincide with a reference to the "dEprofundity / of multimathematical immaterialitieS" (R 58) or, say, with an account of how "girlsfuss over him pellmale their *Jeune premier* / mussing his frizzy hAir" (R 60).

How, then, does a rule-generated text like *Roaratorio* position itself vis-à-vis the dominant poetries (or, for that matter, the dominant musical compositions) of the period? On the one hand, Cage's procedurality can be characterized as an extreme formalism—the subjection of natural speech, free expression of emotion, the true voice of feeling and so on—to elaborate ordering systems. The superimposition of the sixteen multitrack tapes, the precise arithmetical notions, the exact transfer of a 626-page grid to a 60-minute tape segment, the consistent observation of the mesostic rule, even the transfer of the internal punctuation to the larger field of the page itself[41]—all these operate according to the chosen constraint. On the other hand, and this is perhaps the trickier aspect of Cagean procedurality, the text produced by the constraints in question has little resemblance to one that observes the rules of versification. Take, for example, the third stanza of Yeats's "Stream and Sun at Glendalough":

> What motion of the sun or stream
> Or eyelid shot the gleam
> That pierced my body through?
> What made me live like these that seem
> Self-born, born anew?[42]

Yeats's balladlike stanza has five lines, with the rhyme structure $a_1a_3b_3$ a_1b_3. Despite its subtle rhetorical variations from the iambic tetrameter and trimeter base (e.g., the trochaic reversal and caesura in "Self-born, born anew"), the stanza uses sound repetition (both rhythmic recurrence and rhyme) to enforce meaning, the continuity of the former counterpointing and underscoring the complexities of the latter.

But in a *Roaratorio* stanza, say,

> Jest
> gregArious
> field Marshal
> princE
> myleS the slasher in his person (R 39)

the generating rule creates no perceptible repetitions (although the use of *James Joyce* means that each 5-line unit begins with a line having a *J* in it), no parallel sound tracks, no regular chiming as in "stream" / "gleam" or "through" / "anew." And no doubt this "burying" of the device is intentional, an attack, as it were, on the technological base of the printed book, whose typography has ideally been, in Richard Lanham's words, "as transparent as a crystal goblet," and whose "linear flow was not, except incidentally, interrupted by iconographic information." [43]

The production of a written text on an electronic screen, on the other hand (and that production is complicated, in Cage's case, by the layering of the verbal text with the sound texts produced on the multitrack tapes) creates a very different cultural artifact. "The transparent surface," writes Lanham, "which guarantees the identity and stability of the conceptual life becomes opaque and volatile, dynamic not static"; the electronic word surface is "put into continual play," challenging the reader/listener to interact with it (RLEC 32). In this context, procedurality provides a set of controls for the poet and, by extension, for the reader/listener who may perceive, often quite suddenly, what the "secret" constraint is. The resulting verse form is neither metrical nor free; the linear and syntactic forward drive of a poem like "Stream and Sun at Glendalough," moving as it does to the climactic question about the possibility of rebirth, is replaced by a preselected time frame (in this case, a standard one-hour radio time slot), within which time/space are nowhere symmetrical but everywhere saturated. Like the Koch snowflake or similar figure of fractal geometry, Cage's composition presents "infinite length crowding into finite area." [44]

V

In the past decade, procedurality in the Zukofsky and Cage tradition has become more common as poets have increasingly tried to come to terms with what Ron Silliman has called the "limiting claustrophobia" of the free-verse model (DRS 34). Silliman himself used the Fibonacci number series (1, 1, 2, 3, 5, 8, 13, 21. . .) in composing his long prose poem *Tjanting* (1981); the Fibonacci series, he explains, helped him to create an "oppositional series of paragraphs" (a kind of image of "class struggle"), for the series begins with two ones, which "permitted the parallel articulation of two sequences of paragraphs but also determined that their development would be uneven" (DRS 36). Thus whereas the first #1 generates paragraphs with 1, 2, 5, 13 . . . 4181 sentences each, the second has 1, 3, 8, 21 . . . 2584. Another procedural device used in *Tjanting* is that "each paragraph . . . repeat[s] every sentence of its previous occurrence," the repeats being rewritten "so as to reveal their con-structedness, their artificiality as elements of meaning, their otherness" (DRS 36). When, for example, "Poppies grew out of the pile of old broken-up cement" (paragraph #7) reappears in #9, the construction is inverted: "Out of the rockpile grew poppies." And in #11, we read, "Out of rock piled groupies." [45] The permutations of the text's leitmotifs here and in other Silliman works like *The Chinese Notebook* (which is orga-nized into 223 numbered paragraphs, a format based on Wittgenstein's *Philosophical Investigations*) or *2197* (which has 13 individually titled sections of 13 paragraphs or stanzas, each with 13 sentences, each sen-tence in each section modifying a similar sentence in each of the other 12 sections) [46] create a dense constructivist surface, the "I"'s conscious-ness being, so to speak, "fractalized," so as to heighten the "artifice of absorption."

A related process characterizes Lyn Hejinian's remarkable *My Life*. When this "autobiography" was first written in 1978, it had 37 sections, one for each of Hejinian's then 37 years, and each section had 37 sen-tences. [47] The (unnamed) number assigned to each section governs that section's content: thus 1 has its base in infant sensations, in 9 the refer-ences are to a gawky child, in 18 someone is "hopelessly in love," in 22 there are allusions to college reading, in the form of Nietzsche, Darwin, Freud, and Marx. It is not that these sections are "about" the year in question, for each is a collage made up of numerous interpolations—memories and meditations, axioms and aphorisms. Nevertheless, in the course of the narrative, the references gradually shift from childhood to adolescence to adult thought and behavior.

The writing of a life, Hejinian believes, has no beginning, middle, or end: it goes on as long as the author lives. Accordingly, in 1986 when she turned 45, Hejinian revised *My Life*, adding eight sections to the narra-tive as well as adding eight new sentences to each section, these eight spliced into the text at irregular intervals. [48] Here, for example, is 29, with the eight new sentences distinguished from the rest for convenience:

> *Yet we insist* The windows were open and the morn-
> *that life is full* ing air was, by the smell of lilac and
> *of happy chance* some darker flowering shrub, filled with
> the brown and chirping trills of birds. As
> they are if you could have nothing but
> quiet and shouting. Arts, also, are links.
> I picture an idea at the moment I come
> to it, our collision. Once, for a time, anyone might have been
> luck's child. Even rain didn't spoil the barbecue, in the backyard
> behind a polished traffic, through a landscape, along a shore. Free-

dom then, liberation later. She came to babysit for us in those
troubled years directly from the riots, and she said that she dreamed
of the day when she would gun down everyone in the financial dis-
trict. That single telephone is only one hair on the brontosaurus.
The coffee drinkers answered ecstatically. If your dog stays out of
the room, you get the fleas. In the lull, activity drops. I'm seldom
in my dreams without my children. MY DAUGHTER TOLD ME THAT
AT SOME TIME IN SCHOOL SHE HAD LEARNED TO THINK OF A POET AS A
PERSON SEATED ON AN ICEBERG AND MELTING THROUGH IT. IT IS A
POETRY OF CERTAINTY. In the distance, down the street, the prac-
ticing soprano belts the breeze. As for we who "love to be as-
tonished," money makes money, luck makes luck. Moves forward,
drives on. CLASS BACKGROUND IS NOT LANDSCAPE—STILL HERE AND
THERE IN 1969 I COULD FEEL THE SCOPE OF COLLECTIVITY. It was the
present time for a little while, and not so new as we thought then,
the present always after war. Ever since it has been hard for me to
share my time. The yellow of that sad room was again the yellow
of naps, where she waited, restless, faithless, for more days. THEY
SAY THAT THE ALTERNATIVE FOR THE BOURGEOISIE WAS GULLIBILITY.
CALL IT WATER AND DOGS. Reason looks for two, then arranges it
from there. But can one imagine a madman in love. Goodbye;
enough that was good. There was a pause, a rose, something on
paper. I MAY BALK BUT I WON'T RECEDE. Because desire is always
embarrassing. At the beach, with a fresh flush. The child looks
out. THE BERRIES ARE KEPT IN THE BRAMBLES, ON WIRES ON RESERVE
FOR THE BIRDS. At a distance, the sun *is* small. There was no proper
Christmas after he died. That triumphant blizzard had brought the
city to its knees. I am a stranger to the little girl I was, and more—
more strange. BUT MANY FACTS ABOUT A LIFE SHOULD BE LEFT OUT,
THEY ARE EASILY REPLACED. One sits in a cloven space. Patterns
promote an outward likeness, between little white silences. The
big trees catch all the moisture from what seems like a dry night.
Reflections don't make shade, but shadows are, and do. In order
to understand the nature of the collision, one must know some-
thing of the nature of the motions involved—that is, a history. He
looked at me and smiled and did not look away, and thus a friend-
ship became erotic. Luck was rid of its clover.

This particular section has as its epigraph or leitmotif one of the op-
timistic clichés we associate with Hejinian's mother: "Yet we insist that
life is full of happy chance." It begins, like many of the childhood sec-
tions, with a pleasant nature image: windows open, morning air, smell
of lilac, chirping birds. But the mood is meditative, the time evidently
"those troubled years" when babysitters came "directly from the riots."
Indeed, further down the page we learn that it is 1969, when "I could

feel the scope of collectivity." The text presents us with small children, including a daughter who "had learned to think of a poet as a person seated on an iceberg and melting through it." Yet, from another angle, the narrator thinks of hers as a "poetry of certainty." Being a poet, in any case, takes place against the "yellow of naps," and against what seems to be a new love relationship, a "friendship [that] became erotic."

In this context, the eight new sentences play a curious part. Not only don't they stand out; once inserted into the text, they are wholly absorbed into its momentum so that it is impossible to tell where the seams are. Some of the phrases provide new information (like the date 1969), some carry on the image patterning, like "The berries are kept in the brambles, on wires on reserve for the birds." The point, I think, is that, as Hejinian puts it in the eighth new sentence, "many facts about a life should be left out, they are easily replaced." This is precisely what her own text does: a given "fact of life" will be "replaced" or at least recontextualized so as to take on somewhat different meanings by being inserted between a new X and Y. And yet, as in a jigsaw puzzle or mosaic, the replacement strategies don't alter the fact that the "pieces" are very similar—cut, as it were, from the same cloth.

At one level, then, *My Life* is an elaborate, one might say Oulipean, number game, with its 37 × 37 (or 45 × 45) square, each number having the appropriate tempo and mood assigned to it. And furthermore, the formal patterning is heightened by the repetition of the short italicized phrases placed in the white square that begins each section, phrases that are then permutated throughout the text, appearing and reappearing in different contexts. In 29, for example, we find the leitmotif of 1 ("A pause, a rose, something on paper") and 2 ("As for we who 'love to be astonished'"), embedded in the text, as indeed they are throughout *My Life*.

Why such formal artifice in what is usually taken to be a genre as "natural" as autobiography? I shall come back to this question but first I want to look at the text at the level of microstructure and see how the individual units themselves are structured and how they function in the larger picture.

The images invoked in this passage are largely the sort every little girl would notice and later remember: the wallpaper with its "pattern of small roses," "the white gauze curtains which were never loosened," the ominous "shadow of the redwood trees" outside the window and the sunset reflected in it, the "little puddle" that is sometimes "overcast," indicating cloudy weather, the uncle with the wart on his nose and his "jokes at our expense" and the deaf aunt who is "nodding agreeably." And further: there are the proverbs that adults recount to

A pause, a rose,
something on paper
A moment yellow, just as four years later, when my father returned home from the war, the moment of greeting him, as he stood at the bottom of the stairs, younger, thinner than when he had left, was purple—though moments are no longer so colored. Somewhere, in the background, rooms share a pattern of small roses. Pretty is as pretty does. In certain families, the meaning of necessity is at one with the sentiment of pre-necessity. The better things were gathered in a pen. The windows were narrowed by white gauze curtains which were never loosened. Here I refer to irrelevance, that rigidity which never intrudes. Hence, repetitions, free from all ambition. The shadow of the redwood trees, she said, was oppressive. The plush must be worn away. On her walks she stepped into people's gardens to pinch off cuttings from their geraniums and succulents. An occasional sunset is reflected on the windows. A little puddle is overcast. If only you could touch, or, even, catch those gray great creatures. I was afraid of my uncle with the wart on his nose, or of his jokes at our expense which were beyond me, and I was shy of my aunt's deafness who was his sister-in-law and who had years earlier fallen into the habit of nodding, agreeably. Wool station. See lightning, wait for thunder. Quite mistakenly, as it happened. Long time lines trail behind every idea, object, person, pet, vehicle, and event. The afternoon happens, crowded and therefore endless. Thicker, she agreed. It was a tic, she had the habit, and now she bobbed like my toy plastic bird on the edge of its

7

children: "Pretty is as pretty does," or such lessons in necessity as "See lightning, wait for thunder." Even the "moment yellow," which later turns "purple" is the staple of "girls' books" and *Seventeen* magazine: what could be more banal, more everyday than such references to childhood?

But of course there is something else going on here. As against the conventional autiobiography, Hejinian's everywhere undermines sequence: *b* does not follow *a*, and the connectives are often missing. And further, this is an autobiography that provides almost no direct references to the basic facts—what city the poet lives in, where her father works, where she goes to school, whom she marries, how old her children are, and so on. True, we can surmise that the story opened some time in the early forties, since the narrator's father is returning from the war. Or again, in 29, the assumption is that father has died—"There was no proper Christmas after he died"—especially since 28 contains the sentence "I wanted to carry my father up all those stairs." But even these central "events" remain shadowy, peripheral—events that take place, so to speak, at the outer edges of the screen whose real focus is on something else.

That something else may be defined as the creation of a language field in which "identity" is less a property of a given character than a fluid state that takes on varying shapes and that hence engages the reader to participate in its formation and deformation. The scene is set by the first italicized phrase, *A pause, a rose, something on paper.* Are the "pause" and the "rose" nouns in apposition or do they refer to the same thing? The consonantal endings (z) link the two monosyllabic words, but even then, we can't specify their meaning or relate them with certainty to the "something on paper." When the phrase recurs in the third section, it is embedded in images of plant, animal, and insect life:

> As if sky plus sun *must* make leaves. A snapdragon volunteering in the garden among the cineraria gapes its maw between the fingers, and we pinched the buds of the fuschia to make them pop. Is that willful. Inclines. They have big calves because of those hills. Flip over small stones, dried mud. We thought that the mica might be gold. A pause, a rose, something on paper, in a nature scrapbook. What follows a strict chronology has no memory. (ML 13)

Here the phrase makes sense as referring to something seen on the page of a scrapbook, something one pauses over. But the next appearance of the phrase comes in a comic account of Mother's way of eating pudding, "carving a rim around the circumference of the pudding, working her way inward toward the center, scooping with the spoon, to see how far she could separate the pudding from the edge of the bowl before the center collapsed, spreading the pudding out again, lower, back to the edge of the bowl." "You could tell," adds the narrator, "that it was improvisational because at that point they closed their eyes." That what was improvisational? The pudding-eating ritual just described or something quite different? And why would improvisation make one want to close one's eyes? Because one has seen it all before and it's boring? Because the improvisation is frightening? There is no way to tell and, in any case, the scene now "cuts" to the familiar "*A pause, a rose, something on paper.*"

The recurrence of these leitmotifs (e.g., *What is the meaning hung from that depend? The obvious analogy is with music*, or *Like plump birds along the shore*) has an oddly reassuring effect. It is the poet herself who is pausing to put "something on paper," something that is her written offering, her "rose." In the course of *My Life* these phrases become markers, signposts around which much that is confusing in one's life can coalesce. "What is the meaning hung from that depend?" can be taken as an epigraph for the whole text even as "the obvious analogy is with music" fits any number of "analogies" that come up in the narrative, and there are dozens of bodily forms that emerge "Like plump birds along the shore."

Indeed, throughout *My Life* the italicized *phrase-making* serves to remind us that, as Hejinian put it in the title of an early book of poems, "Writing [is] an aid to memory." It is the act of writing itself that transforms *Everygirl* into the author of the autobiography. Let us go back to the opening page for a moment and see how this process works. *My Life* opens with a classic Hollywood shot: the "purple moment" when the baby girl at the top of the stairs sees the front door open on Father, returning from the war, evidently (for this is what adults tell the child later) "younger, thinner than when he had left"—all this against the background of rose-patterned wallpaper and white gauze curtains. But the Hollywood shot would not include the sentence, "In certain families, the meaning of necessity is at one with the sentiment of pre-necessity." The remark is gently satiric, pointing to the family's need to predict what will happen, to control future events, to plan the transformation of "pre-necessity" into "necessity." And this sentence is, in its turn, followed by the terse, "The better things were gathered in a pen"—a sentence open for a wide range of interpretations, for example:

The better toys were gathered in the playpen.
The better dishes (the good china) were kept in a special closet.
The better *objets d'art* were kept in a cordoned-off area, as untouched as the windows behind the white gauze curtains.

And so on. However we read "better things" and "pen," what emerges is that this is a family that makes discriminations between "better" and "worse" things, that is concerned with hierarchy, propriety, and order—the "rigidity which never intrudes," as we read a few lines further down—and that the narrator recalls registering a certain puzzlement about these things.

But these implications are never pressed or even clarified. Rather, new sentences are introduced that are as equivocal semantically as they are normal grammatically. "The plush must be worn away": there's a sentence anyone can construe. But what plush? From a stuffed animal? A sofa? And who is saying or thinking these things? Is the "she" who "stepped into people's gardens to pinch off cuttings from their geraniums and succulents" the girl herself or her mother or someone else? Here the *cause* is cited—the stepping into other people's gardens *so as* to pinch off cuttings—but note that the cause is separated both from the agent and from the result. For we never know whether the neighbors catch "her" taking their cuttings or even who "she" is. We only know that in this "Wool station" (elderly aunts knitting and "nodding, agreeably"), "the afternoon happens, crowded and therefore endless." Crowded with what? Well, as the preceding sentence tells us, "Long time lines trail behind every idea, object, person, pet, vehicle, event." Everything finally *matters* but how and to whom? "If only you could touch," says the narrator, "or, even, catch those gray great creatures"— a reference, perhaps, to the clouds above reflected in those puddles but also, quite possibly, to imaginary creatures read about in children's books or emerging from the narrator's "radio days."

Throughout *My Life*, secrets seem about to be revealed, enigmas about to be clarified, but the moment of revelation never comes. In the final sections of the expanded *My Life*, the familiar leitmotifs—"What is the meaning hung from that depend," "The obvious analogy is with music"—recur and almost cushion the reader's recognition that nothing has been or is going to be resolved. "I confess candidly," says the narrator, "that I was adequately happy until I was asked if I was," the question, evidently, having been put to her on a trip to the Soviet Union. But then, "happiness is worthless, my grandfather assured me when he was very old, he had never sought it for himself or for my father, it had nothing to do with whether or not a life is good. The fear of death is residue, its infinity overness, equivalence—an absolute." (ML 115). And the final sentence of the book is "Reluctance such that it can't be filled."

This reluctance, this deferral of meaning and denial of plenitude, is central to Hejinian's conception of writing. "Where once one sought a vocabulary for ideas," Hejinian remarked in an early essay, "now one seeks ideas for vocabularies."[49] *My morphemes mourned events* is one of the text's leitmotifs, and indeed Hejinian really does filter "events" through the morphemes of their articulation. Hers is autobiography that not only calls attention to the impossibility of charting the evolution of a coherent "self," the psychological motivation for continued action, but one that playfully deconstructs the packaged model crowding the bookstore shelves today—the autobiography, say, of Nancy Reagan or Shelley Winters, of Lee Iacocca or the Kennedys' chauffeur. In the popular imagination, after all, autobiography is the form in which you explain how you got where you are now. Ancestry and childhood invariably play a role as do, in most cases, schooling and the friction with one's childhood and teenage peers. In popular autobiography, these tentative forays toward separation invariably lead, sooner or later, to the Big Break followed by the Big Gamble and often by the Big Mistake(s).

Again, in popular or what we might call "informational" autobiography, language is largely and intentionally transparent, a vehicle used to convey facts, detail events, and produce, here and there, rhetorical flourishes that demand our attention. The emphasis remains on event and character—the shaping of a life according to social and cultural norms and constraints. It is this mode that *My Life* calls into question, refusing, as it does, to go for the Big Break, the Big Defeat, not even displaying the climactic moment of sex, of motherhood, of vocation. "Memory," says the narrator at one point, "is the money of my class." Which is to say, beware of the self-indulgence that "memory" brings, the endless dwelling on what happened or might have happened. The construction of "my life," for that matter, must compete with the constructions of others: "There were more storytellers than there were stories, so that everyone in the family had a version of history and it was impossible to get close to the original, or to know 'what really happened'" (ML 21).

No "characters," no "events," and finally, no "self," at least not in the usual sense of that word. It is difficult, reading *My Life*, to define the "I" of Lyn Hejinian, the particular person that she is, although of course the narrator's verbal habits and references do convey an identifiable voice and style. But compared to, say, Yeats's autobiography or Henry Adams's or even William Carlos Williams's, Hejinian's displays a studied refusal to engage in introspection, a steady suspicion of Romantic self-consciousness. As the narrator remarks wittily in 12, "Now that I was 'old enough to make my own decisions,' I dressed like everyone else" (ML 36).

What remains individual, however, is the construction of the artwork that "my life," any life, can prompt. For after all, even a phoneme can make a difference as when we come across such phrases as "seeming is believing" or "x plus you." Accordingly, the permutated phrases, many of them with quotes inside the quotes so as to signal the endless clichéing of language—*As for we "who love to be astonished," When one travels one might "hit" a storm, What memory is not a "gripping" thought*—work to create an intricate network, a highly wrought textuality that is enhanced by the strictness of the autobiograhy's number system: 45 × 45, each unit having its square white box containing the key phrase. *My Life* thus becomes, oddly, *My Art* or *My Writing*, the natural giving way to the artificial, the individual self to the body of words.

The pleasure of Hejinian's text—and here we come back to the larger issue of the rule-generated text in late twentieth-century writing—has less to do with what happens to her protagonist in the course of the "story" than with the reader's discovery that, however random and disjunctive the book's events, conversations, aphorisms, and commentaries seem to be at the level of microstructure, each unlisted number, when extracted, gives us a key to the behavior of "Lyn" at age x or y. Or does it? As in the case of Perec's *Life: A User's Manual, My Life* introduces a certain "bend" or clinamen into the carefully articulated mathematical structure. In 29, for example, the opening sentence with its reference to "brown and chirping trills of birds" could just as well be the opening sentence of number 3 or 4, and many other sentences and phrases—"The berries are kept in the brambles, on wires on reserve for birds," "The big trees catch all the moisture from what seems like a dry night"—defy the text's larger number system so that the "saturated structure" (ML 99) of *My Life* cannot be replicated.

The goal of such procedural writing may well be, as Michel Butor has put it, "to escape the poem that sticks to the poet like a suit of clothing (even if it is a 'splendid' one), so as to try to find, in a structure that is very confining and yet very rich in formal relations, a more profound poetic grammar." [50] "Mathematics," according to this way of thinking (see OU 93), "repairs the ruin of rules." It also repairs, we might add, the "ruin" of a "free verse" determined primarily by speech rhythm and "natural" pause—a speech rhythm used brilliantly by the Modernist poets and their heirs of the fifties and sixties but now increasingly problematic as "authentic voice" models and "natural speech" paradigms show increasing signs of strain. *A pause, a rose, something on paper:* something, perhaps, that takes us from the impasse of "free speech" rhythms to the "rhythm of cognition" (ML 92).

How It Means:
Making Poetic Sense in Media Society

Regard for the object rather than for communication is suspect in any expression: anything specific, not taken from pre-existent patterns, appears inconsiderate, a symptom of eccentricity, almost of confusion. . . . only the word coined by commerce, and really alienated, touches [people] as familiar.
—Theodor Adorno, *Minima Moralia*[1]

Each morning you have to break through the dead rubble afresh so as to reach the living warm seed.
—Ludwig Wittgenstein, *Culture and Value*[2]

In a recent appraisal of "the 'Language' school of American poetry" for *Textual Practice*, the British critic Rod Mengham cites a long extract from Charles Bernstein's "Fear of Flipping" and comments:

> [This poem] seeks refuge in the unsuspected, in a trial of wits with the reader for whom the experience of reading a poem is usually a preparation to *solve its difficulties*, to *formulate its meaning* and thus to *translate it into other words*. Clearly, this poem will not submit to any design except the need to delay that second stage of reading, the *reduction to sense*, and it derives nearly all its vitality from the need for evasive action. . . . "Fear of Flipping" . . . is so monotonous in register and has such a limited range of rhythms that the reader is only very faintly *instructed in the composition of ideas*.[3] (My italics)

What interests me here is that in a journal as sophisticated as *Textual Practice*, a journal produced, after all, under the sign of those theories (e.g., the Frankfurt school, Foucault, Althusser, Deleuze and Guittari, Derrida), whose common ground is that the "difficulties" of texts are not to be "solved," that their meanings are not to be "formulated," "reduce[d] to sense," or "translated into other words," and that a poem is not a vehicle for "instruct[ion] in the composition of ideas," we are witnessing, once again, a kind of pre–New Critical conception of literature as the verbal vehicle for a prior "subject matter." Indeed, the old battle that Cleanth Brooks was fighting in his famous essay of 1947, "The Heresy of Paraphrase," has by no means been won. In that essay, Brooks argued:

> The conventional terms [for reading poetry] are much worse than inadequate: they are positively misleading in their implication that the

> poem constitutes a "statement" of some sort, the statement being true or
> false, and expressed more or less clearly or eloquently or beautifully; for
> it is from this formula that most of the common heresies about poetry
> derive. The formula begins by introducing a dualism which thencefor-
> ward is rarely overcome. . . . it leaves the critic lodged upon one or the
> other of the horns of a dilemma: the critic is forced to judge the poem by
> its political or scientific or philosophical truth; or, he is forced to judge
> the poem by its form as conceived externally and detached from human
> experience. . . . [thus ignoring] the resistance which any good poem sets
> up against all attempts to paraphrase it.[4]

Brooks went on to define poetic structure as "a pattern of resolved
stresses," a "pattern of resolutions and balances and harmonizations,
developed through a temporal scheme" (WU 203). If these notions of
organic unity are now somewhat suspect, wary as we have become of
the vocabulary of "resolution," "balance," and "harmonious wholes,"
Brooks's emphasis on the structure rather than on formulated meaning is
a valuable antidote to a current discourse that is extremely sophisticated
in appraising and exposing the ideological currents behind particular
texts even as it assumes that "close reading" can be dispensed with.

Thus Rod Mengham quickly passes over the 22-line extract from the
Bernstein poem he himself cites, moving on to an interesting discussion
of the problems, in Language-writing theory, of relating transparent
language to commodity fetishism (RM 117). He does observe that the
"successive verb-forms relative to hurtling, racing, dodging, jumping,
and detouring are more concerted than anything else in the poem apart
from the hazards of this activity: getting hit, getting mangled, getting
cornered, snapping, all of which help to establish a code of reading
practice in which there are penalties for halting, predicting, or looking
back" (RM 116). But how those verbs might relate, say, to the "greeting
card list" in line 2, or to the references to Descartes and Freud later in
the passage seems not to be at issue.

Mengham's is by no means an isolated case; on the contrary, most
critiques of Bernstein's work, as of Language poetry in general, have
raised the issue of the work's nonreferentiality. Thus Eliot Weinberger
dismisses Language poetry as "an endless succession of depthless images
and empty sounds, each cancelling the previous one"; it is made up of
"words set free of any possible meanings, sentences that ignore or con-
tradict what has just been said, words whose effect is not meant to go
beyond the second in which they are uttered, words without history."[5]
Albert Gelpi concurs that most Language poetry is devoid of "perspec-
tive, attitude, response"; a "shapeless" poem like Bernstein's "Dys-
raphism," he argues, "has no teleology; it gets nowhere."[6] Gets nowhere

because, as Robert von Hallberg points out, when words, as is the case in Language poetry, are stripped of all context—of any plot, character, or argument, however tenuous—the construction of meaning becomes entirely the reader's responsibility, and given that "each reader's association with one word or another will be idiosyncratic," the very possibility of communication breaks down.[7] Indeed, as Charles Altieri puts it, "the reification of language *as such* is seriously limiting": after all, even in the radical avant-garde movements of the early century, movements that concentrated on "the medium rather than the message . . . the medium was rarely so rarefied, so confined to the properties of the physical."[8]

These objections, raised by some of the very best critics currently writing on twentieth-century poetry, must be taken seriously. At the same time, it should be noted that the critique of Language poetry, or, for that matter, of such related avant-garde poetries as those involving chance operations (John Cage, Jackson Mac Low), performance (Jerome Rothenberg, David Antin), and visual poetics (Steve McCaffery, Susan Howe, Johanna Drucker, bpNichol), draws heavily, as is usually the case when a movement is new, on the poets' own statements of intent, as culled from their many manifestos, essays, talks, and interviews.[9] When, for example, Bruce Andrews writes "Referentiality is diminished by organizing the language around other features or axes . . . [by] refusing to 'point,' or to be arranged according to a 'pointing system,'"[10] readers assume that Andrews is denying the very possibility of referentiality, even though the poet takes pains to contextualize the statement in question by embedding it in a set of aphorisms—"Words are the ghosts of regret," "Depth is a spiral . . . Not a tourniquet," and so on. Or again, when Lyn Hejinian suggests that "Probably all feelings are clichés . . . stunning only to the person feeling them at the time, and foolish (or boring) to everyone else," critics have jumped to the conclusion that Hejinian is undermining the expressive potential inherent in lyric poetry even though she herself concludes, "This is not to belittle feelings—anymore than one would belittle the lungs, or the intestines."[11]

But then what *do* the lungs and intestines have to do with poetry? And how does the poetry of Hejinian or Andrews convey emotion and meaning, or does it at all? In tackling these pressing questions, perhaps the first step is to stop referring all the aesthetic and ideological issues involved to a specific movement (the "Language school") or a specific kind of poetry ("Language-centered writing," "Language poetry"). Despite the publication in 1984 of *The L=A=N=G=U=A=G=E Book*, edited by Bruce Andrews and Charles Bernstein, and the subsequent publication of the two anthologies, *In the American Tree* and *Lan-*

guage Poetries, and the "language" periodicals *Tottel's, Jimmy and Lucy's House of K, Poetics Journal, Roof,* and *The Difficulties,*[12] the Language movement has always been an umbrella for very disparate practices; moreover, now that it is over a decade old, it has, like any other movement, displayed internal conflicts and ruptures. Thus Eliot Weinberger, attacking Language poetry in *Sulfur,* admits that he makes an exception of Clark Coolidge, Michael Palmer, and Susan Howe, on the grounds that these are not *really* Language poets,[13] even as others have criticized Ron Silliman's anthology *In the American Tree* (which includes Coolidge, Palmer, and Howe) for omitting a "real" Language poet like Steve McCaffery on the mere grounds of his Canadian (i.e., non-U.S.) citizenship. Such squabbles suggest, of course, that what we might call "criticism based on movement-affiliation" is bound, sooner or later, to give way to a historical and literary reshuffling of the deck. Beckett the "absurdist" becomes Beckett the Anglo-Irish heir to Yeats and Joyce. Frank O'Hara, the "New York school Abstract Expressionist poet" becomes O'Hara, the oppositional gay American poet in the line of Whitman, while another "New York poet" and close friend of O'Hara's, John Ashbery, is now often seen as a "belated" romantic and compared to Wordsworth and Keats. And so on.

Given this situation, it may be best to shift the focus from the overt poetics of this or that school (e.g., the West Coast branch of Language poetry, the Olsonian school still active in centers like Buffalo and San Francisco, second-generation New York school poetry, affiliated with St. Mark's in the Bowery, experimental women's poetry, as associated with Kathleen Fraser's journal *HOWever*) and look at some specific practices in their broader implications. Since Charles Bernstein's poetry is regularly singled out as an exemplar of meaninglessness, of "not saying anything," I want to submit a long Bernstein poem called "Safe Methods of Business" (1987)[14] to the sort of close reading Bernstein's detractors imply his work cannot tolerate.

"Safe Methods of Business" is, I think, most usefully construed, not as the prototypical "Language poem," but as one in a series of twentieth-century poems that explore the relationship of the individual to those elusive but ever-present structures of big businesss within which one negotiates one's daily life. An early exemplar is Hart Crane's "For the Marriage of Faustus and Helen" (a poem that may well have influenced Bernstein's); a later one is George Oppen's long sequence *Of Being Numerous,* a sequence, for that matter, prefigured by Oppen's little "Frigidaire" poem discussed in chapter 3. But perhaps the most immediate precursor of "Safe Methods of Business" is a poem published exactly a decade before Bernstein's: John Ashbery's "Business Personals." Indeed, taken in tandem, Ashbery's and Bernstein's "business poems" represent a kind of A and B of postmodern lyric practice. I begin, then, with the former.

II

Houseboat Days (1977), the volume in which "Business Personals" appeared,[15] contains numerous references to the "centers of communication" (HD 46) where business transactions take place: the titles alone—"Collective Dawns," "Bird's-Eye View of the Tool and Die Co.," "Unctuous Platitudes," "The Wrong Kind of Insurance"—are revelatory. "Business Personals": the invented oxymoron wittily invokes business persons, business mail, business cards, and so on, the irony being, of course, that these constructions were designed precisely to distinguish the business from the personal aspect. But—and this is the second irony—"business" products are now designed that simulate a "personal touch," so that the market now boasts series of goods we might designate as "business personals." I am thinking, for example, of a stationery line I came across not long ago, advertised in an elaborate pull-out section of the *American Way*, American Airlines's complimentary flight magazine, and titled EXECARDS. Here, I suggest, is an important intertext, both for Ashbery's poem and, as we shall see, for Bernstein's as well.

EXECARDS, designed "For Business Communication Solutions That Get through to the People You Want to Reach," are listed as supplying the following needs:

> Thanking
> Acknowledging
> Reminding
> Rewarding
> Prospecting
> Following Up
> Welcoming
> Inviting

This list itself tells us a great deal about the dynamics of "successful" business communication. Such social acts as "Welcoming" and "Inviting" are made parallel to the more overtly "business"-oriented duties of "Reminding" and "Following up," not to mention the slightly sinister "Prospecting"—a euphemism for going after or digging for potential clients. Subcategories are equally telling: the Ivory Embossed Line, based on the principle that "Nurturing personal contacts makes good business sense," provides a series of embossed cards ("There's something about raised, embossed lettering that says important, timeless, chiselled from stone") bearing messages designed "to keep in touch." Here an all-purpose "Congratulations" is followed by "Congratulations on Your Promotion" and "Congratulations on Your Retirement," the very real difference between the two (everyone wants to be promoted; not everyone wants to be retired) nicely obscured by the parallel syntax. Whatever happens, this parallel tells us, "People," in the words of a smiling Larry Munson, a partner of Munson & Dunn Corporate Development Service, "like to be acknowledged." And he explains: "I've found EXECARDS cover about 95% of my business needs." Which makes one wonder what those other 5%, for which there is evidently no appropriate EXECARD, could possibly be.

Whereas the Ivory Embossed Line still depends on verbal messages, the more upscale Custom Line features graphics, pictograms in which "archetypal images" are "blind embossed on the front of textured ivory stock," the message (optional) printed only on the inside (see fig. 6.1). "EXECARDS Custom Line," we read, "strongly expresses the power of the image." Indeed it does: such Imagist ideals as "direct treatment of the thing," the "primary pigment," and "constatation of fact" now coming into their own as the following examples testify:

1. Footprints (C10) = "Let's Meet."
2. A double door with rectangular moldings (C11) = "Open House" or "We Can Open Doors for You." If the door has "Greek" columns to the right and left rather than moldings (C19), it means "Welcome" (fig. 6.2). In both cases, we should note, the door is tightly *closed*.
3. A place setting (two forks, a knife, a spoon) = "Let's Meet for Lunch" (C15A) or "Thanks for Lunch" (C15B), a tribute to the idea that one can, so to speak, keep one's utensils clean even while having a business lunch.
4. A dollar sign = "Our Expertise Could Be Your Best Investment" or "Send Money" (C21A, B; fig. 6.3). At first, these might sound like contradictory messages but a moment's thought will tell us that, either way, the recipient pays. The $ does *not* announce a gift: in the world of EXECARDS, "warmth and thoughtfulness" don't go that far.

For those who want to get their "message across quickly and expressively," there are also EXECPOSTCARDS, the "ultimate in time-saving convenience" (see fig. 6.4). Think of the semiotic possibilities of a hand in outline. A plain hand means "Let's get together." Put a string on one finger and that jolly note of conviviality is replaced by the more severe "Just a Reminder." Put a bandaid on the palm of the hand and it means "Hope you're feeling better." Put a watch on the wrist and it means "Thanks for your time." Have one hand shake another and it means "Glad We're Doing Business Together." Or hold a glass, in which case the mes-

C17 Your Efforts Are
The Key To Our Success
C17NM *No message inside**

6.1 *EXECARD* advertising leaflet, the "Ivory Embossed Line," C17.

C19A Welcome

C19NM *No message inside**

6.2 *EXECARD* advertising leaflet, the "Ivory Embossed Line," C19.

C21A Our Expertise Could Be Your Best Investment
C21B Send Money
C21NM *No message inside* *

6.3 *EXECARD* advertising leaflet, the "Ivory Embossed Line," C21.

PC02 Let's talk soon

PC03 To Remind You of Our Meeting

PC11 Let's Celebrate

PC15 *no message ...just "OK" sign*

PC05 You be the judge...give us a try

PC09 Just to follow up

6.4 *EXECARD* advertising leaflet, "Execpostcards."

sage is "Let's Celebrate," whereas a gavel in the hand means "You be the judge . . . give us a try." The gavel looks, of course, like a hammer so that one feels a little bit uneasy about this "invitation" to be the judge. Will the hammer fall if we choose another company?

Throughout the EXECARD catalog, the emphasis is on *personalizing* business, on creating what Ashbery calls "Business Personals." The consumer can select imprint color and typeface; he or she can even "create" (here art comes in) a "custom message." "In business, as in life," we read, "good relationships are built on thoughtfulness. Nurturing personal contacts makes good business sense. Select from this wide assortment." The implication here is that since there is no "life" without "business," "business" might as well take on "life" values. What better way to nurture "personal contacts" than by selecting from such a "wide assortment of Ivory Embossed messages"?

For better or worse, "communication," as it exists in fin-de-siècle America, is increasingly dependent on EXECARD messages, whether real or metaphoric. Words like "congratulations" and "sympathy," "thank you" and "best wishes" become counters in an elaborate communication game whose real meanings are carefully displaced. Thus, once we put the EXECARD packet back into the seat pocket, we flight passengers (euphemistically addressed over the loudspeaker system as "Ladies and Gentlemen") can "sit back and relax" (wholly impossible given the proximity of seats) and "enjoy the flight." The flight attendants are, of course, about to tell us to put our tray tables "in their locked, upright positions" and to keep our "seat belts securely fastened"—"securely" and "locked" not being very conducive to enjoyment—but never mind. After we land, taxi interminably to the gate, and push and shove our way to the exit, the smiling flight attendants will surely tell us, yet again, to "Enjoy." Or, in a slightly more ambiguous version now in vogue, to "Have a good one."

But to whom does the voice that says "Have a good one," or "Thank you for flying American" belong? And to whom are the "personal" messages and pictograms printed on EXECARDS addressed? These are among the questions at the back of a poem like Ashbery's "Business Personals." The poem begins:

> The disquieting muses again: what are "leftovers"?
> Perhaps they have names for it all, who come bearing
> Worn signs of privilege whose authority
> Speaks out of the accumulation of age and faded colors
> To the center of today. Floating heart, why
> Wander on senselessly? The tall guardians
> Of yesterday are steep as cliff shadows;

> Whatever path you take abounds in their sense.
> All presently lead downward, to the harbor view.

The poem's rhythm seems to be deliberately ungainly:

> The disquíeting múses agáin: ‖ what áre "léftòvers"?

as if to say that neither the sonorities of Whitman's long line nor the conventions of blank verse (approximated in lines 3 and 7) are adequate to the poet's task, even as the traditional invocation to the muses is parodically inverted by the reference to Giorgio de Chirico's 1917 painting *The Disquieting Muses*, with its immobile columnar mannequins, faceless and featureless, towering over a pseudoclassical cityscape. Like de Chirico's, Ashbery's "disquieting muses" function as faintly absurd "leftovers," "Worn signs of privilege whose authority / Speaks out of the accumulation of age and faded colors / To the center of today." Confronted by these "tall guardians / Of yesterday [who] are "Floating heart, why / Wander on senselessly?" The question is merely rhetorical, given that no allowance is made for "wandering on" in this world whose paths "All presently lead downward, to the harbor view"— another cliché, this time from a travelogue or guidebook, in whose parlance seaport paths invariably lead the tourist to breathtaking views of the harbor.

In what has become a classic definition of postmodern practice, Fredric Jameson defines *pastiche* as "blank parody, parody that has lost its sense of humor." "Pastiche," he explains, "is, like parody, the imitation of a peculiar or unique style, the wearing of a stylistic mask, speech in a dead language: but it is a neutral practice of such mimicry, without . . . the satirical impulse, without laughter, without that still latent feeling that there exists something *normal* compared to which what is being imitated is rather comic." In late capitalist consumer culture, Jameson concludes, "all that is left is to imitate dead styles, to speak through the masks and with the voices of the styles in the imaginary museum." [16]

"Business Personals" may strike readers as just such a postmodern pastiche, wearing, as it does, the stylistic masks of Keats ("a pleasant half-heard melody climbs to its ceiling"; "In the beginning was only sedge, a field of water / Wrinkled by the wind"), of Rackham fairytale ("It's somewhere near / Cape Horn, despite all the efforts of Boreas to puff out / Those drooping sails"; "This giant will never let us out unless we blind him"), and of the Yellow Nineties ("Pale, pastel things exquisite in their frailness"; "the pale pink and blue handkerchiefs / That vanished centuries ago into the blue dome / That surrounds us")—all these presented with seeming neutrality, without reference to a particular norm.

But Ashbery's is hardly "parody that has lost its sense of humor." Its comic target is the self-delusion that comes from wanting to be unique and different, to tell one's own special story ("And that's how, one day, I got home. Don't be shocked . . ."), even as one's consciousness is everywhere manipulated and constructed—a consciousness not "personal" but only a "business personal." Consider, for example, this pitch for EXECARDS from Bernice Hardee, account assistant, Jeffrey/Scott Advertising, Inc.:

> Some of our agency's largest accounts are hospitals, and we've had them use EXECARDS repeatedly from Christmas cards to physicians' birthday cards. We find them to be ideal for our clients to send—the cards are distinguished-looking but also friendly and direct.

The hospital viewed from the business perspective as top account: it is a sobering thought. Similarly, in Ashbery's poem the unspecified "we" offer an equally unspecified "you" a good buy in sports equipment:

> Therefore do your knees need to be made strong, by running.
> We have places for the training and a special on equipment.
> Knee-pads, balancing poles and the rest. It works
> In the sense of aging: you come out always a little ahead
> And not so far as to lose a sense of the crowd
> Of disciples.

Here the advertising-speak of a Bernice Hardee is rendered wonderfully absurd, beginning with the convoluted "Therefore do your knees need to be made strong," to the implausible "balancing poles and the rest" (implausible because the language of sales must always be precise: one sells X and Y, knee-pads and balancing poles, not "the rest"), to the omission of a word like "slowing" or "preventing" in "It works / In the sense of [preventing] aging," and the cynical recognition that the "crowd" one doesn't want to "lose a sense of" is the "crowd / Of disciples."

Our everyday language, Ashbery suggests, is a tissue of just such clichés, sentimentalities, and slogans. Whether we wax archaic ("That were tyranny, / Outrage, hubris") or formulaic ("Not peace, but rest the doctor ordered"), we alternate between "memories" of a past that never existed ("Why can't everything be simple again, / Like the first words of the first song as they occurred / To one who, rapt, wrote them down and later sang them") and a "Tomorrow" that has "Already witnessed the events of which you write, / Tellingly, in your log." In between, there are "songs," climbing "out of the flames of the near campfires," songs that "decorate our notion of the world / And mark its limits, like a frieze of soap-bubbles." But these songs can only recycle a nature imagery that is always already mediated by echoes of romantic discourse, with its "harbor view," its "field of water / Wrinkled by the wind," its "slowly rising trees," "drooping sails," and "slow dripping [for strumming?] of a lute."

"Could one," the poet asks at a telling moment halfway through his narrative, "return / To the idea of nature summed up in these pastoral images?" The answer would seem to be no: when the poet-narrator finally comes up with an explanatory story line, pastoral fantasy gives way to the reality principle:

> And that's how, one day, I got home.
> Don't be shocked that the old walls
> Hang in rags now, that the rainbow has hardened
> Into a permanent late afternoon that elicits too-long
> Shadows and indiscretions from the bottom
> of the soul.

The "cliff shadows" of the first stanza are now internalized, but this is not to say that consciousness can evade external pressure. Indeed, the reference to the eliciting of "indiscretions from the bottom / of the soul" suggests that even the poet's epiphany, his moment of truth, as it were, slides back into the language of convention and cliché.

And that, perhaps, is why Ashbery's muses are so "disquieting." Given that "whatever path you take abounds in their sense" ("they" being "The tall guardians / Of yesterday") and that the poet's songs are addressed to "bleachers / Sparsely occupied by an audience which has / Already witnessed the events of which you write," it is tempting to follow the path of least resistance and engage in routine occupations like "scrimshaw" and "spinning tall tales." But the poet's elusive and fragmented narrative, his unspecified pronouns and referents, his movement in and out of citation, allusion, and burlesque—these constitute, not just a "blank parody" of romantic quest motifs, as a Jamesonian reading might suggest, but a comic and rueful recognition that in the "permanent late afternoon" which is ours, every message from the EXE-CARD to the remembered songs, "Pale, pastel things exquisite in their frailness," represents a case of what we might call the *déjà dit*.[17] No words, the poem implies, are the poet's own words, in which case every poem is in a sense a "found text." Indeed, the issue now is not whether a text is "original" or whether it is made up of citations, but how the poetic process of citationality takes place, how, in other words, an EXE-CARD is transformed into a poem called "Business Personals."

III

What makes Ashbery's poetry so puzzling is that he purposely confutes "real" citations with pseudo-ones, with phrases that sound familiar, that *are* familiar, even if they have no specific source in the literature of the past. "Worn signs of privilege," for example: is that a phrase taken from a Romantic poem, and if so, which one? And what about "Wrinkled by the wind"? Surely, we have heard that before, or is it Ashbery's own invention? Similar difficulties of reference occur in Charles Bernstein's lyric, but here the problem is compounded by a highly specialized, not to say eccentric diction, by the use of transferred epithets, the transformation of nouns into verbs, adjectives into nouns, and so on. Consider the opening of "Safe Methods of Business":

> The Sleepy impertinence of winsome actuarials
> Lambs me to accrue mixed beltings—or,
> Surreptitiously apodictic, impedes erstwhile.
> Pumice, for instance, has bowdlerized the steam
> As amulets of oddments cedar coatfins
> Or rake about shoals. (S 134)

Bernstein's oxymorons—"sleepy impertinence," "winsome actuarials," "surreptitiously apodictic"—are even less accessible than Ashbery's "business personals," relying, as they do, on words from specialized discourses like insurance ("actuarial"), or philosophy ("apodictic"), or on what are now almost archaisms like "winsome," an adjective that brings to mind Victorian novels and old songbooks. In line 2, the construction "lambs me" converts an ordinary noun into a very unusual verb form ("lamb" = "to bear or bring forth, to 'drop' a lamb" [*OED*], but also, in Australian usage, "lamb down" = "to induce [a person] to get rid of his money," to fleece), the pun on "lam" creating further complications. In line 3, "erstwhile" (adjective or adverb) is used oddly as the noun object of the verb "impedes"; in line 4 "bowdlerized," a verb applicable only to something written, is here applied to "steam"; and in line 5 "amulets of oddments" are said to "cedar" (can that be a verb?) "coat-fins"—a coinage perhaps on the analogy of "coat-feathers" (the "small or body feathers").

In all these instances, signification is obscure but by no means impossible. Take the verb "cedar" and recall the description in Keats's "Eve of St. Agnes" of Porphyro's feast for Madeline, with its "spiced dainties, every one, / From silken Samarcand to cedar'd Lebanon." James Russell Lowell used the phrase "Cedared solitudes" in his "Fireside Travels." By analogy to these past participles, Bernstein creates a transitive verb that, in the context, means that the "amulets" (magic charms to ward off evil) of "oddments" "cedar" (richly cover with trees, make fertile) "coatfins," which is to say, fertilize the small fins and dismembered parts of fish that make up shore debris.

Such arcane and specialized vocabulary seems to fly in the very face of midcentury American poetics with its emphasis on natural speech, direct emotional impact, and so on. The poet perhaps closest to Bernstein in this regard is Hart Crane:

> Then glozening decanters that reflect the street
> Wear me in crescents on their bellies. Slow
> Applause flows into liquid cynosures:
> —I am conscripted to their shadows' glow.
>   ("The Wine Menagerie") [18]

Or

> Often beneath the wave, wide from this ledge
> The dice of drowned men's bones he saw bequeath
> An embassy. Their numbers as he watched,
> Beat on the dusty shore and were obscured.
>   ("At Melville's Tomb," HC 34)

We recall Crane's famous letter of 1926 to Harriet Monroe, in which he explained, in response to her exasperated query, how it was possible for "dice" to "bequeath an embassy," and so on (HC 234–40). "In poetry," Crane insisted, "the *rationale* of metaphor belongs to another order of experience than science" (HC 237). Crane's plea for "another order," for a poetic artifice inherently different from ordinary speech and "natural language," was, as I have argued in chapter 2, by no means typical of modernism, but it points us toward what I have called the "radical artifice" in fin-de-siècle poetry like Ashbery's and Bernstein's.

That artifice must be understood in the context of postmodern information systems. Rod Mengham, we recall, complains of the "social deliquency of the language" in Bernstein's poetry, of "its refusal to give information about any state of affairs we might be familiar with or could take our bearings from"; this refusal, he posits, "is inspired by the conviction that reference in language is linked to commodity fetishism" (RM 117). The assumption here is that "reference" and "information" are the same thing. But, as has been noted in chapter 1, "information" refers to input, to a specific, quantifiable message that a sender transmits and which is not necessarily received intact, whereas "reference," involving, as it does, the receiver as well as the sender, is not primarily concerned with accuracy (is the received message identical to the one sent?) but with issues of connotation, nuance, context, and the like—indeed, all the factors that determine to what a given word or phrase is taken to refer. The meaning of a given message, in other words, includes not only information (the message actually sent) but whatever modifies that message, whatever references become relevant, in the course of its transmission. In information theory, the term for such modification is "noise." In William Paulson's words, "Noise may . . . be the interruption of a signal, the pure and simple suppression of elements of a message, or it may be the introduction of elements of an extraneous message . . . or it may be the introduction of elements that are purely random." [19] The poetic function, in this scheme of things, subordinates the informational axis (language used as a pure instrument of efficient communication) to what we might call the axis of redundancy, "meanings" now being created by all those elements of reference that go beyond the quantifiable communication of data from A to B.

Paulson's argument that literary, as opposed to ordinary, "communication *assumes* its noise as a constitutive factor of itself" (WP 83) is, of course, no more than a fancy and "scientific" version of Wittgenstein's theorem, cited in chapter 1, "Do not forget that a poem, even though it is composed in the language of information, is not used in the language-game of giving information." And this statement, in its turn, can be traced back to the famous statement in book 9 of Aristotle's *Poetics:* "The difference between a historian and a poet is not that one writes in prose and the other in verse. . . . The real difference is this, that one tells what happened and the other what might happen. For this reason poetry is something more scientific [*philosophoteron*] and serious [*spoudaioteron*] than history, because poetry tends to give general truths (*ta katholou*) while history gives particular facts (*kath ekaston*)" (1451b). [20]

General truths versus particular facts, meaning versus information: it may be that the urgency expressed in current debates on these issues is prompted by the recognition that poetry now functions in an environment that foregrounds precisely those information systems that suppress "redundancy" or "noise," particularly the digital environment of the computer. Even in the decade that has elapsed between the writing of "Business Personals" and "Safe Methods of Business," the computer network with its word-processing programs, its laser printers, modems, and FAX machines has come to create a semantic world that cannot help but influence the choices of the individual poet.

In a fascinating catalog essay for a show called "Hot Circuits: A Video Arcade," Charles Bernstein observes that "the experiential basis of the computer-as-medium" is "*prediction* and *control* of a limited set of variables."²¹ Not only are computers either ON or OFF, their "interaction" with the operator is characterized by "invariance, accuracy, and synchronicity" (HC 5), hardly "qualities that generally characterize human information processing." Invariance means that there are no surprises in computer processing: the same command will *always* produce the same response. And the reverse is also true: omit a single letter, space, or required punctuation mark, and the command becomes worthless. Call up, say, a file you have named "WILLIAMS.WCW" by just typing "WILLIAMS" and an error message will appear. This message will tell you, not that you need the author's Christian name or first initials as well as his or her surname; it simply responds to the command with the error message "File not found." You might as well have typed in JONES. And error messages of this sort—"Disk not ready," "Bad sector," "Invalid drive specification," "Format failure"—are inherent in word processing as are those eternal screen prompts: "Exit?" "Replace?" "Are you sure?" "Abort, Retry, Ignore?" and so on, prompts for which there are only two possible answers: Y (yes) or N (no).

Computer communication, I suggested in chapter 1, offers the reader enormous challenges with respect to reformatting and interacting with the text. But what about its effect on our human interactions? I think Bernstein is right when he observes that "the on-ness of the computer is alien to any sort of relation we have with people or things or nature, which are always and ever possibly present, but can't be toggled on and off in anything like this peculiar way" (HC 5). What Bernstein means is that computer processing seems to deny all temporality and variability: one either calls up a file or one doesn't, without going through a series of linear or temporal steps. "No searching on fast forward as in video, or waiting as in TV, or flipping pages as in a book: you specify and instantly access" (HC 5). The greatest fear, in this context, is the fear of mistakenly pressing the "delete" key or forgetting to "save." When it's gone, it's gone.

On/Off; Yes/No: No wonder there is now a disorder called "computer anxiety." For although, at one level, we are in total control over the computer (the right input invariably produces the right output), "the computer only simulates a small window of operator control. The real controller of the game is hidden from us, the inaccessible system core that goes under the name of Read Only Memory (ROM), that's neither hardware that you can touch nor software that you can change but 'firmware'. . . . We live in a computer age in which the systems that control the formats that determine the genres of our everyday life are inaccessible to us" (HC 6).

Such inaccessibility represents one side of the coin, whose other side is the extraordinary convenience of daily life in the late twentieth century. Banking by Readyteller, for example, is one of the great contemporary time-savers, but make one mistake on a deposit or withdrawal and chances are that a dozen phone calls and a few visits to the bank won't straighten it out. And the same holds true for tax forms, credit card renewals, driver's licenses, mortgage loan applications, mail order forms, real estate contracts, and so on.

What sort of "command," then, can "talk back" to the inaccessible system core that increasibly controls discourse? This is where artspace, poetry-space, comes in. For given the formulaic and synthetic rhetoric of EXECARDS ("For Ideas That Work, Give Us a Call," "We Can Open Doors for You"), whose composition is controlled by the equally formulaic On/Off, Yes/No, Save/Delete dialectic of computer-speak, poetic discourse defines itself as that which can violate the system, which refuses the formula and the binary opposition between 1 and 2. Instead of pressing, say, the Reveal Code key, the aim is to "reveal" that which falls, so to speak, between the control-key cracks. Given this perspective, no "methods of business" can be assumed to be "safe." And this recognition provides an entrance into Bernstein's "Safe Ways of Business."

IV

Now let us come back to those odd opening lines:

> The sleepy impertinence of winsome actuarials
> Lambs me to accrue mixed beltings—or,
> Surreptitiously apodictic, impedes erstwhile.

Here the verse form is itself parodic, a pop version of Jacobean blank verse. For although the syllable count per line is highly variable (15, 9, 13), the five-stresses-per-line rule is observed, and the heavy alliteration (e.g., "surre*pti*tiously a*p*odic*t*ic, im*p*edes") and predominance of polysyllables creates a tightly woven, highly formalized structure. The elaborately phrased oxymorons contribute to the same parodic effect. One doesn't usually think of "impertinence" as being "sleepy" or of "actuarials" (the reference is to the statistical tables used by insurance agents to calculate premiums, interest rates, life expectancies, and so on) as "winsome," but the language is, in fact, oddly exact: "safe methods of business" are those based on "winsome" (i.e., attractive, appealing) financial tables and yet the intrusions of these tables into our daily lives occurs with "sleepy" (e.g., quiet, low-key, turned off) "impertinence," "lambing" (fleecing? goading?) us to "accrue" (the word goes nicely with "actuarials") the "mixed beltings" ("trading was mixed,"

For choice is rivulets evidently refers to Whitman's opposition between the two "streams of Death and Life"—between "Object and Subject," "Real and Ideal," "Days and Nights." But Bernstein's "choice" is not between anything as grandiose as Life and Death, Day and Night; rather, "choice *is* rivulets," which is to say that we do have a choice, we can get beyond "the chase of / Carolinas" (again an allusion to Whitman, in this case the *Drum Taps* poems) [23] to a more fluid, meaningful sense of possibility.

The opening stanza of "Safe Methods of Business" thus presents a fallen world, specifically a fallen world of "safe" business methods, in which possibilities for change are perceived—but only dimly—through the daily din of overheard conversations, magazine headlines, billboards, traffic tickets, and garbled snatches of poetry, fairytale, and proverbial lore. As in Ashbery's "Business Personals," the "heard melodies" of Keats, and of Romantic poetry generally, reappear in what is a kind of Tin Pan Alley format. Indeed, Bernstein's muses are as "disquieting" as Ashbery's.

The second stanza reads:

> "They're starting to start up the cranes." & so
> For a long while Sophia bade her time
> A sorrowful adieu and sat in un-
> resplendent edginess near the wharves' waves.

Is this taken from a "real" Victorian novel? Like Ashbery's pseudo-citations, Bernstein's phrasing has a familiar ring without necessarily having a specific reference. There are any number of novels in which a young girl named Sophia bides "her time," but Bernstein turns this cliché into a transitive construction: "bade her time / A sorrowful adieu," and "un- / resplendent edginess" recalls *Mademoiselle* rather than nineteenth-century fiction. As for the "wharves' waves," the connection seems to have a phonemic rather than a descriptive value.

Such fragmentary story lines (the exotic tale of Balak and Suleiman on the next page is another instance) call up a distant past that might make sense of the confusing present. But not really. As in the case of Ashbery's references to giants and mysterious sea journeys around Cape Horn (HD 19), the past is endlessly amenable to recycling, reformatting, and *récriture*. "What are those exquisite lines?" asks Beckett's Winnie in *Happy Days*, the mound up to her neck. And then, after a futile attempt to call up a favorite poem ("Go forget me why should something o'er that something shadow fling . . ."), she remarks resignedly, "One loses one's classics." [24] Indeed, one does, especially in the

Manhattan of Bernstein's poem, with its endless jabbering away of news flashes, headlines, telephone ad campaigns, opinion polls, and information retrieval. "Statistical debates," says Michel de Certeau, "are our theological wars. The combatants no longer bear ideas as offensive or defensive arms. They move forward camouflaged as facts, data and events."[25]

One loses one's classics. Keats and Coleridge for instance, as in the following burlesque amalgam: "The dead, dull hours of summer's interminable days / On which no hope, nor shadow, sets to / Bring surcease of this blanched wildness." And also one's proverbs and slogans, which turn up in such constructions as "Always keeping / the Ball on the proverbial / 'Eye,'" "Narcotic of little care: wailing against / A wall," "Forsake the bow, embrace the Churl," "No rest for the wicked, less for the pure of heart," "You can swim / Or you can float," "Too many crooks spoil / the sidewalker," and so on. Postmodern consciousness, the poem suggests, is always already saturated with what we might call "culture bytes." No wonder Oliver Wendell Holmes's description of Boston as "the hub / of the solar system" (S 135) shades into a *National Enquirer* headline ("Why Women Admire Liberace").

Just as Ashbery's "Business Personals" plays on the format of EXE-CARDS, so "Safe Methods of Business" can be understood as a satiric version of video-scanning, of switching channels and catching unrelated bits that turn out to be very much related, being parts of the larger media culture cum business world, with its endless "how to" manuals, its "hot tips," its "personal" interactions, and clichéd explanations of behavior patterns. Interspersed with the alliterative blank verse passages, the burlesque allusions and quotations from literature, myth, and proverbial lore, we find snatches of "private" conversation:

> "Sometimes
> I think I hear
> a mosquito but it turns out to be the
> Refrigerator." "It's not so
> bad once you get used
> to it." (134)

Or

> "I
> told the man I would
> jerk sodas
> for him at his counter
> But

I would never prostitute
myself for that fee." (135)

Or

                              "I
don't think you should give
choice to a nine-
year-old. A thirteen-
year-old maybe." (135)

Or

"If you've got a wayward 17-year-old, its
going to be tough getting him or her to give you
a urine specimen," concedes Mr. Reuter, who
has tested his own five children. "But then,
if they won't give it to you, you know
you've got a problem." (138)

These "personal" conversations must be read against the public discourse with which Bernstein surrounds them. In each instance above, the nameless speakers, engaged in everyday talk, are animated by the conviction that they are *discriminating*, making judgments, choices. *For choice is rivulets.* The first example contains a conversation we have all had, at some time or other: X complains of Y; Z tells X that Y isn't so bad—which is, of course, just a manner of speaking. A refrigerator that buzzes like a mosquito—it could be pretty irritating. Similarly, the would-be soda jerk who won't "prostitute" himself for "that fee" is resorting to a verb hardly appropriate for the occasion. As for the wise words about the choice-making capacities of 9-year-olds versus 13-year-olds and the "problem" of getting a urine specimen from 17-year-olds: these are the folklore of a society that turns all "problems" into talk show or interview talk, where the subject's age (9, 13, 17?) is often presented as the only relevant fact about John X or Mary Y, real questions of history, motivation, and character remaining as inaccessible as the ROM system core inside the computer terminal.

To heighten this notion of inaccessibility, Bernstein inserts into his poem two letters contesting parking tickets received in Manhattan. The first letter follows an allusive seven-line stanza which juxtaposes a spoof of Red-baiting sloganeering ("The tide is red (just another Jewish American Peasant")), mock fairy-tale ("the beanstalk / Broods"), and holiday advertising ("a rocker for Syncopation / Day"), leading up to a pious reference to "the origin of *écriture* [scribbage]," where "scribbage" cleverly compounds "scribbling," "scrimmage" and "cribbage,"

to give a sense of *writing* as contest, as game, and also as "cribbing"—
the notion again that all writing is *récriture*.

At this point, Bernstein introduces the letter of complaint:

> The summons charges me with parking at a crosswalk on the northeast
> corner of 82nd street and Broadway on the evening of August 17, 1984.
> The space in question is east of the crosswalk on 82nd street as indicated
> by the yellow lines painted across the street. This space has been a legal
> parking space during the over ten years I have lived on the block. (S
> 137–38)

And so on for another twenty lines, the writer arguing with perfect
logic that (a) the space has been legal for at least ten years, that (b)
new crosswalk marking may well make it illegal, but that (c) since
these markings are new and not "clearly imprinted," "it is unjust to
ticket before new indications are fully in place and while the preceding
yellow lines are left intact."

Rational, logical, and perfectly sensible as is this response to a mis-
taken charge, the verbal "scribbage" in which it occurs guarantees its
underlying absurdity. For although this letter is, ironically enough, one
of the few "original" pieces of writing in Bernstein's poem, one of its few
messages to contain no allusions, citations, or borrowings from previ-
ous writings, its physical text is subject to penetration by a prolifera-
tion of intertexts that qualify its context and possibly negate it. Who
knows what will happen to the message addressed to the Traffic Court
by the time it makes its way through the bureaucratic mill? Who knows
what other messages will have crossed the path of this one, changing its
meaning? And suppose the office supervisor who reads Bernstein's letter
doesn't know the meaning of "override" in the phrase "override the
yellow lines" or of "indictions"?

In placing the letter of complaint, written in the clearest of "clear"
English prose, between the reference to "just another Jewish American /
Peasant" and the report of Mr. Reuter's views on teenagers and urine
samples, Bernstein implies that, given the "Blotter when / Blobbed" dis-
courses that permeate the daily scene, clarity of writing may no longer
be an uncontested virtue. One can designate time and place ("West
35th street just west of Seventh Avenue about 3:45 on Sunday afternoon
(9/2/84)"), white lines and yellow lines, just as one can follow com-
puter commands or receive accurate "information" on one's modem.
But what happens when one wants something outside the normal range
of operations? When, instead of simply paying the parking fine and
sending a check in the printed envelope, one tries to send a "personal"
letter to a traffic court?

"Safe" methods of business, the poem implies, do not allow for such deviations. In the "state of / subaltern lunacy" (S 140) in which we live, the stakes have changed:

> And so we returned to our basic question—
> How in heaven do you get an outside line?

So much for Prufrock's Overwhelming Question. So much, too, for the modernist longing (again via Prufrock) to make contact with "lonely men in shirt-sleeves, leaning out of windows." "Safe Methods" ends with the following 13-line stanza:

> One wants to be a stranger but retreats
> Into familiarity, into the face of a
> coin, a spearhead nickel. Bounding by
> two frames, a concept unhinged in
> its quiescent sag or sap, of whom
> is better to say "no glup, no
> pedimento". Too many crooks spoil
> the sidewalker, at least up to and
> excluding, four-and-one-eighth,
> $22.95. Merely myopic, queerly
> entokened. . . . the only true boats the ones
> that have never sailed, nor been wet
> by these kept oceans. (S142–43)

Here the first line (a perfect iambic pentameter) neatly sets the stage for the poem's inversion of the Romantic alienation theme. In the Manhattan of the eighties, one longs perversely not for community but for estrangement, for the possibility of distancing oneself from that "[re-treat] / Into familiarity" that belongs not to family or friendship or romantic love but to the arena of "business personals." Indeed, "familiarity" is equated with "the face of a / coin, a spearhead nickel," the "sag or sap" or "at least up to and / excluding, four-and-one-eighth, / $22.95." Stock quotations, price tags: again one is reminded of Hart Crane:

> Across the stacked partitions of the day—
> Across the memoranda, baseball scores,
> The stenographic smiles and stock quotations
> Smutty wings flash out equivocations.
>   ("For the Marriage of Faustus and Helen," HC 27)

In "Safe Methods" the "equivocations" take the form of bogus orders: "No glup, no pedimento," these nonwords speaking to the "merely myopic, queerly / entokened" who dwell on the shores of "kept oceans" (again one thinks of Hart Crane's "chained bay waters Liberty" in the

"Proem" to *The Bridge*), a place where "the only true boats [are] the ones / that have never sailed." Which brings us back to the poem's opening with its "bowdlerized . . . steam," its coatfin covered shoals and old men with wet mouths.

V

I have been explicating, somewhat tediously no doubt, the relation of specific words and phrases in Bernstein's poem in order to show that his is by no means the "socially delinquent" language that critics like Mengham have decried. On the contrary, what a close reading of this and related texts reveals is how charged with meaning and socially aware this poetry can be. The difficulty—a difficulty I don't want to minimize—even for readers accustomed to such modernist precursors of Bernstein's lyric satire as Crane's *Bridge* or Pound's *Cantos* is that whereas in, say, the *Pisan Cantos*, individual items (a citation from a letter, an historical narrative, a Latin quotation, a bit of Poundian slang) retain their identity, rather as do the items (a railroad ticket, a newspaper headline, a piece of ribbon) in a Schwitters collage, in Bernstein's poem, the pieces of the puzzle are always already contaminated, bearing, as they do, the traces of the media discourses (legalese, Wall Street–speak, *National Enquirer* gossip, and so on) in which they are embedded. When, for example, we read in Canto 81 the lines

> hot wind came from the marshes
> and death-chill from the mountains

we may not know to what landscape the poet is referring, but we certainly know that the reference is to nature and weather. When, on the other hand, we read in "Safe Methods of Business"

> Inconceivable in fact that waves
> in such
> proportion, that
> become a
> weathering (S 141)

we cannot tell whether the "waves" whose proportion is so "inconceivable" are ocean waves or air waves or waves on a graph, or indeed whether "waves" is a noun or verb, even as "weathering" can refer to "weathering a storm" or to wood that is "weathering," and so on. The collage piece, in this case, is the snatch of overheard conversation itself, the "serious" and businesslike words of someone who finds it "Inconceivable in fact that waves / in such / proportion" (whatever the waves are) would indicate X or Y. By the same token, "actuarials" and "mixed beltings" are presented in burlesque high style, discourse on "the origin of écriture" is reduced to "scribbage," and so on.

Poetry, that is to say, now functions in an arena where the simulacrum (say, the prime time TV melodrama) exerts increasing influence over the way business is actually done in the "real" world. A 1990 feature article for the *New York Times*, for instance, bears the headlines: "Ignorance of *L.A. Law* Is No Excuse for Lawyers"; "The popular series has become required viewing for many attorneys and has begun to affect their courtroom behavior."[26] What has happened, as the article's author David Margolick explains it, is that as jurors increasingly watch *L.A. Law*, they judge cases in the real courtroom according to their fictional counterparts:

> Over the years, *L.A. Law* has been credited with—or blamed for—increasing applications to law school, for dominating classroom discussions there and for disillusioning graduates once they discover how different the real world can be. Some lawyers say it has changed the way they dress themselves and address juries. It has been the subject of learned articles in such highfalutin publications as . . . the *Yale Law Journal*. . . . At the urging of Michael J. Kelly, the dean of the University of Maryland School of Law, Richard Dysart, who plays the avuncular, rather priggish McKenzie in the series, has made television spots encouraging lawyers to donate more time to public-interest activities. Even Susan Ruttan, the actress who plays Roxanne Melman, Arnie Becker's secretary, is on the road: this week she will be appearing at the Professional Secretary and Office Management Show at the Javits Center in Manhattan. (LL 27)

What does the actor Richard Dysart actually know about the law? And what advice can Susan Ruttan give to professional secretaries? One's first inclination is to dismiss these questions as utter nonsense. Dysart, after all, may never have read a brief; Ruttan may not know how to type. But the important thing, as Margolick points out, is that *L.A. Law* "creates expectations about how the law and lawyers operate—expectations that real-life lawyers . . . have come to realize they can no longer ignore." Indeed, the article reports that law professors use *L.A. Law* as a teaching tool, "one that can arouse even the most listless students to become interested in issues like client confidentiality, whistle-blowing and the traumas of representing heinous, abusive or guilty clients. As far removed as *L.A. Law* may be from the workaday world of practicing lawyers, most law schools are even more remote" (LL 29).

I find this last comment quite sobering. For even as we scoff at the notion that actors are now traveling around the country, addressing bar associations and law school groups on the fine points of jurisprudence, it is probably true that "real" trials and "real" cases are more influenced by the precedent established by this or that child custody or malpractice case, as presented on *L.A. Law*, than they are by the study of law in the library or classrooms.

Perhaps it won't be long before the *L.A. Law* actors really do try cases in court. Perhaps the physicians who treat us will soon be the actors who play doctors in *General Hospital*. To an extent, the line has already been crossed by talk show hosts like Oprah Winfrey, who, having no particular training or credentials in psychology, advise their guests on specific emotional problems. As for government service, Phil Donahue, himself a talk-show guest on the Sally-Jessy Raphael Show (21 June 1990), has declared that when his NBC contract is up in 1992, he may well decide to run for Congress. "What's your view on education?" asked Raphael, testing Donahue's ability to "speak to the issues." "Oh," said Donahue with a perfect sense of the occasion, "American education has declined so badly it's a security risk!" The audience applauded wildly.

Inevitably, such material is now providing metaphors for poetry; inevitably, our Waste Land is no longer Eliot's, no longer the "Fire Sermon," where Tiresias witnesses the fornication of typist and clerk as a debased reenactment of the great adulterous unions of Greek mythology, but a Waste Land where typist and clerk might make a videotape on "How to Create a Glamorous Setting for Romance in an Efficiency Apartment That Has No Washer/Dryer and Only a Small Kitchenette." As for Tiresias, he will no doubt continue to "walk among the lowest of the dead." But not in Hades, only up and down the studio aisles where Geraldo is now prophesying the future. The disquieting muses again . . .

cage: chance: change

Interviewer: "What is the place of Bertolt Brecht in [the Polish] theater?"
Jan Kott: "We do him when we want Fantasy. When we want Realism, we do
'Waiting for Godot.'"[1]

From its inception in the nineteenth century, the avant-garde has un-
dergone an assimilation process whereby works originally dismissed as
obscure and incomprehensible, works characterized even by their de-
fenders as fantastic, absurdist, or nonrepresentational, have gradually
been seen as quite "real," quite "true to life" after all.[2] Thus *Waiting for
Godot*, first produced in Paris in 1953, was regularly referred to as an
existentialist drama about the incomprehensibility of a universe in
which man waits for a sign that never comes. Only now that we have
put enough distance between ourselves and the French Occupation,
which is at the core of Beckett's drama, does *Godot* emerge as, after all,
an intensely *political* play, the circus clowning of Gogo and Didi and
the master-slave routines of Pozzo and Lucky representing, realistically
enough, the "waiting" that takes place in the face of a death threat that
is always already there.[3]

But the process of what we might call the "real-ization" of the avant-
garde—its gradual familiarization as "life" turns out to be curiously con-
sonant with the "fictions" of the theatre—is not necessarily equivalent
to that other move so regularly attributed to the avant-garde, namely,
its inevitable commodification and appropriation by the late capitalist
art market. For Peter Bürger and like-minded theorists, as I noted in
chapter 1, the failure of early twentieth-century avant-garde move-
ments (e.g., Futurism, Dada, Surrealism, Constructivism) to transform
the bourgeois institution of art itself, to create works that would effect
social and political as well as aesthetic change, produced a situation in
which the "shock of the new" has been reduced to more or less impo-
tent gesture. And furthermore, according to this argument, even when
the artwork in question is genuinely innovative (say, as in the case of
Jasper Johns), it is all too quickly absorbed into the commodity system,
an object whose exchange value no longer relates to its use. Hence the
much fabled "death of the avant-garde."

My own sense, as I have tried to make clear in the preceding chap-
ters, is that this "death" has been vastly exaggerated. True, the utopian
side of avant-gardism, its longing to change the world, to overcome the
bourgeois "dissocation [of art] from the praxis of life" (PB 49), has not

met with success, at least not directly. But if we take the term "avant-garde" more narrowly and literally as the advance guard of the army, that flank of artists who are in the forefront, and hence, as the cliché would have it, "ahead of their time," avant-garde art continues to be a reality. There is no reason to believe, in other words, that radical art practices will not continue to manifest themselves (often where and when least expected), even as their gradual assimilation into mainstream culture will not necessarily insure their commodification. Beckett, to take my original example, may well be performed and studied in countries around the globe, his manuscripts and first editions may well sell for enormous sums of money, and the photographic image of his gaunt face may well have become a familiar icon (especially in the year of his death). But the works themselves remain curiously impervious to the commodity system, as uncompromising in their demands on the audience as ever. Indeed, when in 1990 the Mark Taper Forum in Los Angeles produced *Happy Days*, even the unanimous critical acclaim for the production did not prevent a fair portion of the audience from leaving before or during intermission, complaining that the play had too little plot, too few characters (only Winnie and very occasionally Willie), and too much "meaningless" talk.[4]

To say that Beckett proved to be too "difficult" for the middle-class audience at the Mark Taper Theatre smacks, of course, of elitism. "The pedestal of high art and high culture," as Andreas Huyssen puts it, "no longer occupies the privileged space it used to, just as the cohesion of the class which erected its monuments on that pedestal is a thing of the past" (AGD 218–29). Indeed, nothing today raises a greater outcry, especially in academic circles, than the suggestion that there might be a distinction between "high art" and popular culture. Postmodernism, after all, is now most frequently defined as the challenge to what Huyssen has called "the Great Divide" that characterized modernism, and whose theorist par excellence was Adorno. Perhaps, Huyssen posits, Adorno's concept of a "presumably necessary and insurmountable barrier separating high art from popular culture in modern capitalist societies" was a "culturally and politically valid" project in its own time (the war years and their immediate aftermath), committed as it was to saving "the dignity and autonomy of the art work from the totalitarian pressures of fascist mass spectacles, socialist realism, and an ever more degraded commercial mass culture in the West" (AGD 9). But "this project has run its course and is being replaced by a new paradigm, the paradigm of the postmodern, which is itself as diverse and multifaceted as modernism had once been before it ossified into dogma" (AGD 9–10). And the case is put even more strongly by Russell A. Berman:

Adorno's modernist aesthetics have been robbed of much of their rele-
vance for the contemporary situation by a multifaceted transformation
of cultural organization: the denigration of technique, the accelerated
commodification of artistic production, the destabilization of the in-
stitutional discourse, and the loss of faith in the objectivity of the art-
work. High art has rapidly integrated culture-industrial forms in its
works (Lichtenstein, Warhol) as well as in its mechanisms of distribu-
tion (televised concerts, mass marketing of subscriptions).[5]

The argument against modernist elitism, as outlined by Huyssen,
Berman, and others,[6] is appealing, especially as a response to those lin-
gering Greenbergian notions of modern·art as an heroic struggle against
the encroachment of bad taste or kitsch, as the preservation of the pu-
rity of media, genre, and convention in the face of capitalist commer-
cialism.[7] One cannot help observing, however, that the argument for
the postmodernist erasure of the high-low dichotomy is almost always
presented at a generalizing theoretical level or from the point of view of
popular culture (e.g., a semiotic or cultural analysis of Elvis Presley or
MTV or *Twin Peaks*) rather than from the perspective of the experi-
mental and radical artworks which are supposedly in sync with that
culture. When we turn to praxis, in any case, we find that the happy
marriage between "high art" and mass culture is at best shaky. For
when Winnie (the heroine of *Happy Days*) is actually compared to an
equally middle-aged wife like Mary Williams in *The Young and the
Restless*, the differences, at least between Beckett and daytime serial,
are hard to explain away. A convincing case for textual identity or even
similarity between, say, the experimental fiction of Burroughs and the
formulaic narrative of the prime time whodunit, at any rate, has yet to
be made.

On the other hand, studies like *After the Great Divide* do suggest,
even if they don't quite make the case themselves, that, given our media
culture, the pretense that this mass culture does not exist, that life goes
on as it always has for the sensitive individual—a series of sunsets and
love affairs and social disappointments—just will not work. To put it
another way: the culture always intervenes, the great love poems of
Goethe and Heine, for example, responding to a particular cultural
situation in the preurban, heavily traditional, and autocratic German
states in the French Revolutionary period.

If American poets today are unlikely to write passionate love poems
or odes to skylarks or to the Pacific Ocean, it is not because people don't
fall in love or go birdwatching or because the view of the Pacific from,
say, Big Sur doesn't continue to be breathtaking, but because the elec-

tronic network that governs communication provides us with the sense
that others—too many others—are feeling the same way. The desire to
have a child, for instance, surely one of the most personal and private of
emotions, can hardly seem an appropriate "subject" for poetry, when
the front page of the *New York Times* carries Connie Chung's announce-
ment that, since she is almost forty-four, she is going to cancel her fall
news show in order to "try aggressively to have a baby."

Given such media "events" (we can all now play the "will she, won't
she" watching game), the poet turns, not surprisingly, to a form of *ar-
tifice* that is bound to strike certain readers as hermetic and elitist. The
felt need, as the poet Joan Retallack puts it, is "to explore a different
focal range, e.g., the multiple intersecting perspectives we are now
'privy' to, rather than the single point perspective of the deeply sensing
'I.'"[8] Accordingly, in the radical little magazines currently published in
the United States and Canada—a short alphabetical list would include
*Abacus, Aerial, Avec, Big Allis, Acts, Avec, Caliban, Central Park,
Conjunctions, Contact II, The Difficulties, How(ever), Line, Notus,
O.Ars, O.blek, Ottotole, Paper Air, Raddle Moon, Rampike, Screens
and Tasted Parallels, Sulfur, Talisman, Temblor, Writing*—we are likely
to come across poetic writing that looks like this:

> I like to watch the patties melt—suck the testicles
> propeller-like paintbrush
> decorative jello wrestling photo orgy, to people who don't—
> public humidity. How impertinent your pets can be—plus
> sight-seeing tours of colony.
>> (Bruce Andrews, "I Like to Watch the Patties Melt," *Aerial* 5 [1989]: 11)

Or this:

> Struck with this word implies a relation
> most do, *cousin* being the site and in that
> sadness two more little ones next to the sea.
>
> Wrong end of a funnel's disappearing act.
> The acrostic stripe pins all
> possible urgencies incline to a thunderstorm.
>> (Karen Mac Cormack, "One No Trump,"
>> *Screens and Tasted Parallels* 1 [1989]: 21)

Or

> Wasn't it done then undone, by
> us and to us, enveloped, sid-

erated in a starship, listing
with liquids, helpless letters—
what else—pouring from that box,
little gaps, rattles and slants
(Michael Palmer, "Letters from Zanzotto," *Avec* 3 [1990]: 24)

Or

---

et iam Iunonia and turning the page space becomes time
FAMILY RE-UnIon Appetizers Cheese Spreads and Dips (Top
cream cheese with capers or chutney. Liquid Smoke, wine or
beer pep up yellow cheese.) when the cliché becomes real panic
sets in *laeva parte Samos* not goodbye forever or a suicide note
WHATEVER HAS HAPPENED BETWEEN YOU AND ME on
every wall on every scrap of paper on every matchbox: ALFA-
BETIZACION ES LIBERACION Mug Shot #1 Father Fig. #2 Is
this the correct way to address these matters? (*fuer ant Delosque
Parosque relictae*) you always remember the person who taught
you to eat an artichoke fondly no matter what has hap

(Joan Retallack, "Icarus Ffffalling,"
O.blek 7 [Spring 1990]: 180)

In each of these otherwise quite different texts, one hears conflicting
discourses that penetrate and interrupt one another; in each, everyday
items, whether melting hamburger patties or "listless liquids" or "cream
cheese with capers or chutney," or the relation of "sadness" to "sea" in
the dictionary, provide a kernel of "reality" with which language can
play. More important: impenetrable as these texts may seem on a first
reading, they turn out to be surprisingly mimetic. Retallack's columnar
text, for example, is not "about" the fall of Icarus; rather, it imitates
what it feels like to read that myth in Ovid, even as the reader's mind
wanders to thoughts of a pending family reunion, to the appetizers she
plans to prepare for it, to magazine headlines and matchbox slogans, to
family photographs (to be shown at the reunion?), to questions of pro-
tocol, all these responding, in one form or another, to the idea that
"when the cliché becomes real panic sets in." The technique is not so
much *collagiste* as one of layering: "WHATEVER HAS HAPPENED BETWEEN
YOU AND ME," for example, may be a snatch from something read, but,
given the context, it may also refer to family relationships that are
about to be activated. But then Icarus too was part of a family: the "Fa-
ther" of "Fig. #2" might be Daedalus. And so on.

Is writing of this sort elitist? My own experience has been that the fewer the preconceptions the reader has—and this is the case with younger audiences—the greater the willingness to "go with it," to be amused by Bruce Andrews's exasperated "how impertinent your pets can be" (following hard on a "meal" where melting patties give way to "sucking testicles" and then "decorative jello"), or Karen Mac Cormack's wry observation that "Struck with this word implies a relation / most do," and to participate in the delicate dialectic of "done then undone," and "by us and to us," in Michael Palmer's verse letter to the postmodern Italian poet Zanzotto. Then, too, these are elaborately sounded poems, appealing in their music. Note, for example, the complex weave of alliterating *p*'s in Andrews's text and the very delicate vocalic play ("sid- / erated in a starship, listing / with liquids, helpless letters— / what else . . .") in Palmer's lyric. As for the "impenetrable" imagery, often the appeal is to plain common sense: acrostics (see Mac Cormack's "One No Trump") really do produce a "stripe" of letters down the left margin. And if a funnel is turned upside-down, its "wrong end" does do a "disappearing act." Thus, when what Charles Bernstein has called "official verse culture" declares that such images are murky and incomprehensible, it is not because meaning won't reveal itself to a receptive reader, but because the culture has preconceptions of how images should be articulated and connected. The stumbling block, that is to say, is not so much obscurity as convention.

The poets' repeated denial of "normal" word order or syntactic integrity, their introduction of arcane vocabulary and difficult, indeed confusing reference, functions, I think, to mime the coming to awareness of the mind in the face of the endless information glut that surrounds us. We can see this especially clearly in the recent work of John Cage, with which I shall conclude, thus coming back to my beginning with his *Lecture on the Weather*. My text is *I–VI*, the six Charles Eliot Norton Lectures given at Harvard University during the 1988/89 academic year, and published in 1990.

II

On the face of it, nothing could seem more unCagean than this elaborately produced volume with its thick, acid-free paper, its illustrations of fifteen different chance-determined prints (made from a single negative by Robert Mahon of the first autograph page of Cage's *Sixteen Dances* [1951]), and its two sixty-minute audiocassettes, one of Cage reading Lecture IV, the other a selection from the question-and-answer sessions Cage held in conjunction with the Norton Lectures. The inclusion of the cassettes, packed in plastic wrap and attached to the cardboard promotional panel at the back of the book, seems especially odd, since Cage has consistently declared that he dislikes recordings "because they turn music into an object, and music is actually a process that's never the same twice."[9] The whole "package," with its elegant wrapping (a color reproduction from Cage's Crown Point Press series of etchings *11 Stones* [1989] on the front, a full-page black-and-white photograph of Cage on the back), looks and feels like a coffee-table item: it weighs in at about four pounds and sells for $34.95.

Is this, then, the commodification of the late avant-garde? In his *New Republic* essay, to which I have already referred in chapter 5, Edward Rothstein suggests that indeed it is:

> Cage's distinguished musical predecessors in the [Norton] lectures included Igor Stravinsky, Roger Sessions, and Charles Rosen. But for the 1988–89 season at Harvard the heritage of theoretical and critical rigor was put aside. After all, modernism has fallen on hard times, contemporary musical culture has long since subsided into sullen regularity, and many universities have become weary of disinterested scholarship. So Harvard turned its attention to the only remaining sign of life—the sometime avant-garde.

"The result," adds Rothstein, "is a random collection of atoms bumping into each other, creating a Brownian motion of clichés. Cage tries to have it all, hovering above his text like some Dadaist clown." In the end, "His career—and these lectures—are best seen as symptoms of our era's poverty."[10] Many members of the Harvard audience presumably felt the same way. The *New York Times* reported that during the first lecture, "over a third of the audience walked out in the middle, and one local professor emeritus who preferred anonymity remarked that 'it was a testimony to the disastrous state of American education that anybody stayed and listened.'"[11] Others, however, responded differently. According to the *Times*, "a respected young composer, Rodney Lister, called the lecture 'the most direct and moving political piece of music I have ever heard,'" thus setting in motion a month-long debate "between the enchanted, the outraged, and the befuddled." Those who stayed for the whole series, at any rate, tended to pronounce Cage's performance "hypnotic," the transformation, in John Rockwell's words, of "didactic prose into elusive poetry."[12]

One of Cage's distinguished predecessors in the Charles Eliot Norton lectureship was T. S. Eliot, whose topic for 1932/33 was *The Use of Poetry and the Use of Criticism*. The point of departure of this famous text comes in the Introduction:

criticism [can never] arrive at any final appraisal of poetry. But there are these two theoretical limits of criticism: at one of which we attempt to answer the question "what is poetry?" and at the other "is this a good poem?" [13]

And Eliot proceeds to take up and primarily to question earlier theories of poetry from Sidney to Arnold and I. A. Richards.

Cage has regularly paid homage to his favorite modernists, James Joyce and Gertrude Stein, and even Ezra Pound's *Cantos* has become the source of a mesostic text, but Eliot seems never to have figured in Cage's work: there are no "writings through" the *Four Quartets*, no citations from Eliot's critical prose to match the citations from Thoreau or Marcel Duchamp or Buckminster Fuller. All the more curious, therefore, that *I–VI* does contain some buried Eliot allusions. Under "Method," the first of the source texts at the back of the book, for example, we find "HURRY UP PLEASE IT'S TIME," here cited as "from T. S. Eliot's *The Waste Land*, cited in [Marshall] McLuhan, *Through the Vanishing Point*." In the text itself, this source yields phrases like "Its / time" (*I–VI* 123), followed some twenty lines further on by the passage:

> we go ' Beyond
> his <u>murder in the cathedraL</u>
> convincEd are not (*I–VI* 123–24)

This reference to Eliot is again mediated by Marshall McLuhan: it appears in the source text "Imitation" as part of an entry from *Understanding Media* on film technique: "T. S. Eliot reported how, in the making of the film of his *Murder in the Cathedral*, it was not only necessary to have costumes of the period, but—so great is the precision and tyranny of the camera eye—these costumes had to be woven by the same techniques as those used in the twelfth century" (*I–VI* 436). Note that the McLuhan source is much more respectful of Eliot than is Cage's spliced version, where emphasis shifts to going "Beyond" Eliot's tragedy as well as "not" being "convincEd" by it.

The notion of Eliot citations appearing in Cage's text only in the form of secondary citations from McLuhan will undoubtedly strike many readers as outrageous, an example of Cage's arrogance and Dada clowning. But it may also provide us with an entrance into the strange lecture world of *I–VI*, whose every word is cited, the whole (if we can speak of wholes in a case like this one) therefore constituting a found text.

The full title of *I–VI* is

**MethodStructureIntentionDisciplineNotationIndeterminacy
InterpenetrationImitationDevotionCircumstancesVariableStructure
NonunderstandingContingencyInconsistencyPerformance**

These fifteen terms provide Cage with his "mesostic strings,"[14] each term, beginning with "Method," being used a number of times in succession in each "lecture." For the six Norton Lectures, Cage chose 487 quotations which were put in fifteen files corresponding to the terms above, although—and this is a typically Cagean attitude—the placement of a given entry in a given file had "nothing to do with the file names as subjects, unless by coincidence" (*I–VI* 3). The sources for the quotations (and each source text at the back of the book arranges its sources in the same order) come from Cage himself (57 taken from his earlier *Composition in Retrospect*, and 15 from *Theme and Variations*), Wittgenstein (93), Thoreau (49), Emerson (only 5 because Cage discovered that he "couldn't stomach Emerson"), Marshall McLuhan (91), Buckminster Fuller (64), and the rest from newspaper (*New York Times, Wall Street Journal*, and *Christian Science Monitor*) accounts of international events and from L. C. Beckett's *Neti Neti* (*Not this Not this*), a mystical book "of which my life," says Cage, "could be described as an illustration" (*I–VI* 3).

The computer program Mesolist devised by Jim Rosenberg, which is Cage's electronic version of the *I Ching*, was used to select the mesostic words, and chance operations (also on the computer) were used to reduce the volume of source material to a manageable length. Once the mesostic words were chosen, Cage's method was to add "all the wing words from the source text" and then "take out the words I don't want." "The situation," says Cage, "is not linear. It is as though I am in a forest hunting for ideas" (*I–VI* 2).

A further complication is introduced by juxtaposing the mesostics themselves, which are centered on the page horizontally, with the transcription, in small print at the foot of the page, of the six "seminars" or question-and-answer sessions that followed each lecture at a one-week interval. The resultant text, which is continuous from beginning to end, ignoring the breaks between respective lectures, is meant to serve "as a counterpoint throughout the book to the mesostics above them" (*I–VI* 6). The questions are in italics, Cage's responses in roman, the variation in typefaces corresponding to visual layout of the mesostics above, where "a space followed by an apostrophe indicates a new breath. Syllables that would not normally be accented but should be are printed in bold type" (*I–VI* 5). (See the sample page in fig. 7.1.)

What is the point of this elaborate schematization? To begin with, the running commentary of the "seminars" may be said to supply the work's reality principle. The transcription is absolutely faithful so that a question (the askers are anonymous) will appear in conversational

and mosT
villagE freedom from '
kiNds of
The '
the correspondIng
nOr about
Not
possIble '
we **caN**
meTabolics '
monEy is obsolete because it stores work '
a kiNd of peep show and inside we now move '
sTop
Is
sOmewhere
by aN
to success **mIght yet**
caN oc**cur** for
once we knew whaT mankind had and what
succEss
the grouNd '
iT was a case of
Is '
seven five seven fOur eight six six '
wastes usiNg algae chlorella and others for food '
It's
a patterN
effecTs on
consciousnEss ' to see that it is
as maNy people as possible
only To say that **for** '
four seven fIve seven
extending the central nervOus system '
experimeNt '
set all well afloat ' thoreau ' yes and no are IIes ' **the**
is this oNly
acTions and
chlorElla
withiN him or
To
agrIculture '
gO about
dazzliNg me as
dIplomats
laNguage
opened fire on youThs

playing so that we made a kind of performance out of it and his way was to have this large stack of xeroxed
copies of the piece and to throw them the room was just full of scattered paper *we've been talking in rather
theoretical and abstract terms so i have a rather practical question to ask many years ago i was teaching
the usual liberal arts course in music appreciation to a class and we talked early in the term about classical*

85

7.1 John Cage, *I–VI*, page 85.

rhythm, even as it was actually asked. The range is from short staccato phrases like

> *how do you feel what decisions do you make does it surprise you please you how* (*I–VI* 201)

to long repetitive polemics of a sort we've all heard at conferences and seminars, for example:

> *i've been puzzling through the idea of chance operations and intentional work and intentionless work and i have a cluster of questions about that it seems that there's some combination of chance and choice in your and you take out the words you don't like and so on it seems that it's not possible to do anything but by a chance operation if somebody had given the most formal lecture on musicology in the world that would still be a chance operation because that person would have had very contingent experiences and influences and tastes and values and so on everything seems to be a chance operation you seem to think that what you're doing is a chance operation in a different way you say i'm doing it by chance operation as if there's something else and you also seem to be doing it intentionally which raises another paradox you're intentionally doing something by chance if you're intentionally doing it it seems to be a choice so it's not by chance and you have a very elaborate structure to construct your lectures and some of your music so it seems on the one hand that it can't fail to be by chance and on the other hand it can't succeed because when people come to hear you they come to hear john cage when did you decide to become john cage or whatever people come and they say i'm going to hear john cage i'm going to hear something you know way out or avant garde or this that and the other things so it's not by chance . . .*

and it goes on in the same vein for another ten lines ending with the exasperated question, "*why not read a phone book or why not invite someone else from the audience to get up and say whatever they like i mean how do you go about deciding what*" (*I–VI* 141–51). To which Cage responds quietly that he simply has to carry on his work "*in the direction that seems to me necessary*" (153).

The exasperated question (which is, of course, not a question at all but a comment) so to speak deconstructs itself in the process of utterance, the "questioner" declaring that (1) everything is chance operation, but—change of mind—(2) everything is intention, so that (3) everything is both chance and intention, and since this boxes the speaker into a corner, he or she abruptly shifts ground and declares that (4) anyway, people only come because John Cage is famous, a "persona," and he might just as well read from the phone book!

The transcription of such questioning, it seems to me, has a central function in the larger system of the book. For one thing, it illustrates what happens when discipline (the discipline, in this case, of the mesostic system that controls the lectures) is absent. The "natural," Cage implies, is sloppy and self-indulgent; art uses the natural but does things with it, which is to say that, as Cage put it as early as *Silence* (1961), "poetry is not prose simply because poetry is in one way or another formalized."[15] Thus poetry differs from the small-print commentary at the bottom of the page which represents, as I said above, the reality principle, specifically the information world, where "meaningful" messages keep coming through the conduit but where what is received is not equivalent to what is sent out, the hearer's (or reader's) mind being so overwhelmed by repetition (*chance operation* or *chance* appears eleven times in the twenty lines above) that finally almost nothing is heard.

At one point in the question-and-answer text, someone comments,

> *I find that during your lectures especially the longer ones I have a real hard time paying attention through a lot of it little things will catch my ear and i'll be able to concentrate on certain parts of it but then before i know it i'll be looking at the chandelier or counting the stacks of chairs or something and missing yeah i wonder if you think that changes the result of the performance or do you think it's of just as much value to me i don't understand i mean to be speaking in a monotone . . . makes it really tough to pay attention (I–VI 313–15)*

To which Cage responds,

> *many people don't see anything until they're struck over the head you have the opportunity with these lectures to discover how to pay attention to something that isn't interesting (I–VI 316)*

And that may well be the key to Cage's Norton Lectures. In the "authentic" text that runs like a ticker-tape along the bottom edge of the page, people ask questions *about* the problem of paying attention; the audience is so to speak "hit over the head" with "real" subject matter, with specific topics, Yes/No, Either/Or. But in the "lectures," these information components are replaced by a set of verbal constructs that give the audience very little help on how to respond, that refuse to "hit you over the head." Ironically, then, Cage does follow Eliot in presenting his own poetics but whereas Eliot juxtaposed the Theory Question ("What is poetry?") to the Practical Criticism Question ("Is this a good poem?"), the second being unanswerable without some kind of formulation of the first, even as the first requires exemplification, Cage relegates these "two theoretical limits" to the *practicum* of the small-print text and produces lectures that are really poems, the implication being that to talk about poems is to write them. Interestingly, the twin audio-cassettes (one a mesostic lecture, the other, the talk session) mirror this pattern, Cage's distrust of recordings matching the skepticism expressed in the "seminars" sessions.

But—and this is perhaps the most ingenious feature of *I–VI*—the "Source Text" at the back of the book provides, to use Cage's own terms, the **"Interpenetration"** between the **"DisciplineNotationIndeterminacy"** of the mesostics and the **"NonunderstandingContingencyIn-**

consistency" of the running commentary. For although, as I said above, *I–VI* is a found text, its *finding* takes a very strange turn. Beginning with **"VariableStructure"**—and the Introduction is, perhaps intentionally, quite misleading in this regard—Cage introduces series of "sources" written by himself in April 1988, which is to say evidently at the same time or shortly before he was composing the Norton Lectures themselves. Thus, whereas earlier mesostic texts like *Empty Words* and *Roaratorio* were entirely dependent on preexistent source texts, *I–VI* juxtaposes actual sources to those invented solely for the purpose of being fragmented and cut into the poetic text. These "sources" (there are 25 entries in all, found at the beginning of each of the last five sections), moreover, themselves become increasingly "poetic." The final section **"Performance,"** for example, opens as follows (p. 450):

> Practicality, action is action. The metal ones won't burn, wooden statues of the Buddha, winter fire. Quick o quick, a word of truth. One arm holding the cat, the other the knife. Quick, or I slit the cat's throat. (John Cage, April 1988)

Clearly, this elusive plan of action (what, who is going to be thrown into the fire?) has a very different status from, say, the *Wall Street Journal.* The mode of Cage's self-citation recalls the elliptical prose entries of Williams's *Kora in Hell,* with their lyric urgency and decontextualized reference. In its conversational quality ("Quick, or I slit the cat's throat"), Cage's entry is closer to the seminar text at the bottom of the page than to the lectures. Yet the "source" is of course also recycled into the mesostics. For example (*I–VI* 46):

A particular
use ' his kNowledge with
Costs
holding thE cat
deal with collective mankind'S needs the bare maximum was what

Here "holding thE cat" is emptied of its emotional freight, its position in a narrative that leads to the potential slitting of the cat's throat, and is instead embedded in an economic discourse that gives the phrase a much more abstract sense, for example, letting the cat out of the bag. Thus "Performance" can be seen as the "Interpenetation" of "Intention" (after all, the source text is Cage's own, invented for the purpose) and "Contingency": the use of computer operations precludes the poet's advance knowledge of just where in the text a phrase like "holding thE cat" will appear.

Perhaps this is what Cage means when he says, in answer to a question (*I–VI* 16), that in his lectures, "ideas" are "brushed" by "source material." Such "brushing" may produce boredom, as Cage is the first to admit. But, as those who attended the performances have frequently reported, and as Cage has often suggested with reference to Zen meditation, such boredom can be productive. Consider the "borEdom" at the opening of Lecture *I*, the mesostic string being "Method":

Much of **our** '

of borEdom

Toward talks in

it misled Him '

diplOmatic skill to

place to place ' but Does it look

at present **Most** '

fivE iranian fishermen '

cuTbacks would not

wHat i have ' but

pOssibilities

i frequently haD to look up at the opening between

the rule ' **My**

thE

iT '

migHt

lOng time **what** '

of metal Driven '

the rule My

thE '

cuTbacks would not

it misled Him '

lOng time **what** '

place to place ' but Does it look

Here the units are so short and the sources so multiple that one doesn't, as in the case of *Roaratorio*, go back to the source and try to see how Cage has adapted it. The only phrase that stands out sharply is "five iranian fishermen," taken from a *Christian Science Monitor*, August 9, 1988, account of a rescue operation during flooding in Burma (see "Structure," *I–VI* 424). The other phrases, for example "Much of **our**'" and "of borEdom," could come from a variety of the source texts—in this case, from Cage himself or Wittgenstein, from Thoreau or McLuhan— the sources being, I think, deliberately neutralized so as to create what looks and sounds like a seamless structure.

In part, this seamlessness derives from the odd consensus of Cage's sources, odd because of course Wittgenstein isn't the least bit like the

Wall Street Journal or McLuhan like the *Christian Science Monitor*. As culled and condensed, however, the Cage world of ideas—Cage / Fuller / McLuhan / Wittgenstein / Thoreau / L. C. Beckett / only a tiny bit of Emerson—presented in the context of ongoing international events (military actions, fires, raids, bombings) as reported in the newspapers is remarkably self-consistent. All extraneous items, which is to say most of the items contained in written discourse, whether descriptive or narrative or expository (e.g., description of place, personal anecdote, love story, argument for this or that position)—these are by definition absent. In this sense, then, no phrase calls excessive attention to itself and everything coheres.

Again, the lectures' seamlessness results from the use of what Cage calls "empty words." "The have-nots of language," he says, "what the Chinese call empty words, particles, connectives, etc., have a position equal to that of the full words" (*I–VI* 5). Thus, in the passage cited above, the first four words are "Much of **our** ' / of," four short breath units plus a fifth designated by the apostrophe, and a rest indicated by the bold face of **our** and the line break. One takes these "empty words" in very slowly, waiting for something to happen that will help us to construe a syntactic unit that "says" something. But when we come to such a word, it is only "borEdom," and as we continue down the page, "boredom" gives way to enigma. We learn that something is moving "Toward talks in," but never find out where or what the "it" is that "misled Him." A bit later, we learn of "pOssibilities," in which "i frequently haD to look up at the opening between," and the next line has only three one-styllable words:

the rule ' **My**

All of us have had moments when we "frequently haD to look up at the opening between"; and the relationship of this enormously suggestive phrase to "the rule '" (what rule?) is governed by any number of "pOssibilities." As for "**My**"—is this a possessive or an expletive ("My, my!")? The single-word lines "thE," "**iT**," and "migHt" don't help much, and by the time, after "lOng time **what** ' / of metal Driven," that "the rule My" (this time without stress on "My") comes back, we know even less about the possessive construction. Indeed, the fourth or refrain stanza, in which every line repeats an earlier one (i.e., line 20 repeats line 14, 21 = 9, 22 = 4, 23 = 17, 25 = 6), creates even greater prominence for the text's "empty words," decontextualizing and recontextualizing its "lOng time **what** '" so that "it misled Him '" becomes at once emphatic and elusive.

The irony, as far as the source texts are concerned, is that, once used, they no longer matter, at least not in the way we might think, judging from Cage's Introduction. Does it really matter whether a "thE" is taken from Wittgenstein or from McLuhan? Whether "lOng time **what**'" comes from Thoreau or the *Wall Street Journal?* And, by implication, isn't Cage saying that the media, whether radio or TV or the print media, should not be regarded as sources of "hard" information? That a lecture series cannot really impart A's "knowledge" to B, there being too many distracting factors and contextual circumstances for B to "take in" everything A says and absorb it? Handle carefully, this elegant volume seems to say, otherwise you will remain at the level of "i oNly has meaning" (*I–VI* 13).

At the structural level, then, *I–VI* is extraordinarily complex. Open the book at random and study the repetitions, and Cage's numerological and formal patterning reveals more and more intricacy. Yet—and this may seem paradoxical—an adjective Cage's Harvard performances repeatedly evoked, so the *New York Times* tells us (p. 27), was "relaxing." Relaxing, perhaps because the lectures don't impose preconstructed ideas upon the audience, preferring to let us participate in the process whereby unfinished news items and bits of information ("killing a po-licE officer," "a rumanian Citizen," "washington to use," "mexiCan opposition leaders") can be absorbed into the rhythms of individual consciousness; they remain discrete entities that we restructure according to our own predilections. So layered are the "information arEas they were constructing" (*I–VI* 109) that we inevitably respond to some particular thing we hear or see rather than attempting to take in everything. To put it another way: saturation creates difference.

But difference should not be confused with detachment. One of the common complaints about Cage's poetry, as about his music, is that it rejects emotion, that it is not sufficiently expressive. But, as Cage has frequently remarked in conversation, it is precisely because emotions are so central to life that one must learn to discipline them: "Heroism doesn't consist in brilliantly combatting someone else. It is not a question, as Nixon undoubtedly believed, of winning battles . . . What is heroic is *to accept the situation in which you find yourself.* Yes!" [16] In poetic terms, this means that one can only use what is given: in *I–VI*, that given consists of source texts, title words, mesostic rules, and the hour-long frame of the individual lecture. The "combat" is thus a struggle with letters, words, and numbers, a struggle animated by the passion—and it is a passion—to get it right. As such, the text challenges the audience to recreate the process whereby it was actually created, to "lay bare," as the Russian Formalists would have it, the devices of its own making.

Ironically, then, *I–VI* is, as its detractors claim, an *unreadable* book. But its "unreadability," far from being the consequence of what Rothstein calls "a random collection of atoms bumping into each other," is of course intentional, a carefully plotted overdetermination designed to overcome our conventional reading habits. Thus the elegant format and oversize numbered pages raise expectations that the text purposely deconstructs, engaging us as it does in a "relaxing" reading process that involves *making* rather than *taking:* open any place you like and follow whichever path interests you. That path may be aural (tracing the phonemic repetitions and variations) or visual (tracing mesostic capitals versus the "wing" word groups) or dialectic (reading the A text [mesostic] against B [commentary] and both against C [source]) or semantic (inspecting the recurrent "news" items and relating them to the abstract speculations that surround them), or, for that matter, literary, in that we can discover Cage's poetic lineage in studying his recreations of found texts. *The Use of Poetry and the Use of Criticism:* like Eliot, Cage is preoccupied with these ultimately political topics. As the final stanza of *I–VI* puts it (the mesostic word here is "PERFORMANCE"):

comPosition **is**

is askEd

foRth through us

Filled with

right tO one

my pictuRe isn't vivid enough for

teMpo only

A '

suggestiNg a vast and undeveloped nature '

Communist

it usEs

•

Notes

Chapter 1

1. Ludwig Wittgenstein, *Lectures and Conversations on Aesthetics, Psychology, and Religious Belief*, compiled by Yorick Smythies, Rush Rhees, and James Taylor, ed. Cyril Barrett (Berkeley and Los Angeles: University of California Press, 1938), p. 1.

2. *CompuServe Magazine*, October 1990, p. 22.

3. John Donne, *Devotions upon Emergent Occasions*, no. 17, in *The Complete Poetry and Collected Prose*, ed. Charles M. Coffin (New York: Random House, Modern Library, 1952), p. 441.

4. See "Professional Notes and Comment," *PMLA* 105 (October 1990): 1176. The first issue of ⟨*Postmodern Culture*⟩, Fall 1990, includes fiction as well as critical writing by Kathy Acker, John Beverley, Bell Hooks, Laura Kipnis, Neil Larsen, and Andrew Ross.

5. See Richard A. Lanham, "The Electronic Word: Literary Study and the Digital Revolution," *New Literary History* 20 (Winter 1989): 265–90. I take up Lanham's argument below.

6. It may seem ironic that a movement wedded to tradition, to what is, so to speak, "Making It Old," should call itself the *New* Formalism, *New* Narrative Poetry, etc. But what such epithets signify is that even such "traditional" poets cannot escape the contemporary market pressure to claim novelty, originality, difference. In this scheme of things, the "old" is never good enough: it must become the "new old."

7. *Expansive Poetry: Essays on the New Narrative and the new Formalism*, ed. Frederick Feirstein, Introduction with Frederick Turner (Santa Cruz, CA: Story Line Press, 1989), pp. vii–xv. Subsequently cited in the text as FF.

8. See on this point Wyatt Prunty, "Emaciated Poetry," FF 176–94, esp. 183.

9. Peter Bürger, *Theory of the Avant-Garde*, trans. Michael Shaw, Foreword by Jochen Schulte-Sasse (Minneapolis: University of Minnesota Press, 1984), p. 49. Subsequently cited in the text as PB; Schulte-Sasse's important Foreword, to which I shall also refer, is cited as SS.

10. Here Bürger takes issue with the Frankfurt school's still prevalent theory of modernity. Adorno, for example, held that in a society in which exchange value had come to dominate, the "authentic" artwork must actively "resist" society, negating its practices and cleansing itself from all practical concerns. Modernist art, in this sense, stands opposed to the culture industry with its kitsch and commodification. For an interesting critique of Adorno's distinction between "art" and "kitsch," see SS, pp. xvi–xxvi; M. Jimenez, "Théorie critique et théorie de l'art," in *Revue d'ésthetique* 1–2 (1975): 139–62.

11. In his Foreword, Jochen Schulte-Sasse writes, "In its accurate and historically reflected definition of the avant-garde, Peter Bürger's *Theory* can hardly be overestimated" (SS xlvi).

In *Au Nom de l'art: Pour une archéologie de la modernité* (Paris: Les Editions de Minuit, 1989), Thierry de Duve provides a fascinating account of how Duchamp's readymades like *Fountain* force us to redefine the word "art." But although de Duve does not share Bürger's ideological perspective, he too takes as a given that Duchamp's urinal is in itself an arbitrarily chosen and wholly ordinary object. In *The Philosophical Disenfranchisement of Art* (New York: Columbia University Press, 1986), Arthur C. Danto similarly writes: "Duchamp's *Fountain* is, as everyone knows, to all outward appearances a urinal—it was a urinal until it became a work of art and acquired such further properties as works of art possess in excess of those possessed by mere real things like urinals. . . . But then what is the conceptual fulcrum of this still controversial work? My view is that it lies in the question it poses, namely why—referring to itself—should this be an artwork when something else exactly *like* this, namely *that*—referring now to the class of unredeemed urinals—are just pieces of industrial plumbing?" (pp. 14–15).

12. The porcelain urinal came from the J. L. Mott Iron Works in Philadelphia. Duchamp later explained that he changed "Mott" to "Mutt"

> after the daily strip cartoon "Mutt and Jeff," which appeared at the time, and with which everyone was familiar. Thus, from the start there was an interplay of Mutt: a fat little funny man, and Jeff: a tall thin man. . . . And I added Richard [French slang for money bags]. That's not a bad name for a "pissotière."
>
> Get it? The opposite of poverty. But not even that much, just R. MUTT.

This comment, originally cited by Otto Hahn ("Passport No. G 255300," *Art and Artists* 1, no. 4 [July 1966]: 10), is reprinted, with a wealth of other information about *Fountain*, in William A. Camfield's excellent *Marcel Duchamp Fountain* (Houston: The Menil Collection, 1989); see esp. 21–60. Camfield also notes (p. 23, n. 21) that "Mutt" is a mirror reversal of *Tu'M*, Duchamp's painting of 1918, which includes shadows of readymades. Subsequently cited as WAC.

13. Camfield also notes a further irony in that *Fountain* "was changed from a receptacle for waste fluid to a dispenser, a fountain of life-giving water" (WAC 53).

14. Hal Foster, "Between Modernism and the Media," *Recordings: Art, Spectacle, Cultural Politics* (Port Townsend, WA: Bay Press, 1985), p. 35. Subsequently cited as REC.

15. Fredric Jameson, "Postmodernism and Consumer Society," in *The Anti-Aesthetic*, ed. Hal Foster (Port Townsend, WA: Bay Press, 1983), p. 115. Subsequently cited as AA. In the revised version of this essay called "Postmodernism, Or, The Cultural Logic of Late Capitalism," *New Left Review*, 146 (July–August 1984): 59–92, which is, in turn, reprinted in *Postmodernism, Or, The Cultural Logic of Late Capitalism* (Durham, N.C.: Duke University Press, 1991), the wording is slightly different: "With the collapse of the high-modernist ideology of style—what is as unique and unmistakable as your own fingerprints . . . the producers of culture have nowhere to turn but to the past: the imitation of

dead styles, speech through all the masks and voices stored up in the imaginary museum of a now global culture" (pp. 17–18). This text is subsequently cited as CLLC.

16. Andreas Huyssen, *After the Great Divide: Modernism, Mass Culture, Postmodernism* (Bloomington and Indianapolis: Indiana University Press, 1986), p. 170. Subsequently cited in the text as AGD.

17. Fredric Jameson, "Reification and Utopia in Mass Culture," *Social Text* 1 (Winter 1979): 140.

18. James Clifford, *The Predicament of Culture: Twentieth-Century Ethnography, Literature, and Art* (Cambridge and London: Harvard University Press, 1988), pp. 1–12. Subsequently cited in the text as PC.

For the larger argument, see especially Clifford's chapter "On Ethnographic Authority" (PC 21–54), which contains a trenchant critique of the attempt, on the part of early twentieth-century anthropologists like Mead and Malinowski, to "enter" the alien culture that was taken to be the object of study.

19. Arthur Kroker and David Cook, *The Postmodern Scene: Excremental Culture and Hyper-Aesthetics* (New York: St. Martin's, 1986), p. 8.

20. Marcel Broodthaers, *Art Actuel* (Brussels: Galerie MTL, 1970); cited in Michael Compton, "In Praise of the Subject," *Marcel Broodthaers* (Minneapolis: Walker Art Center; New York: Rizzoli, 1989), p. 49.

21. Charles Bernstein, "Centering the Postmodern," *Socialist Review* 19 (1989): 48.

22. See, on this point, George Hartley, *Textual Politics and the Language Poets* (Bloomington: Indiana University Press, 1989), esp. chap. 3: "Jameson's Perelman: Reification and the Material Signifier," in which Hartley, also writing from a Marxist perspective, argues that Jameson's reading of Bob Perelman's poem "China" as an instance of schizophrenic language misses the real force of the poem.

23. "Centering the Postmodern," 52–53. My own favorite example of this sort of comparison is that, frequently made, between Joseph Conrad's *Heart of Darkness* and Francis Coppola's film *Apocalypse Now*, which was overtly based on Conrad's novel. But such overt debts mean little: Coppola's commercial venture has much less in common with the deep structure of *Heart of Darkness* than do such intertexts as Burroughs's *Naked Lunch*, Beckett's *The Lost Ones*, or Steve McCaffery's *Panopticon*.

24. Michel Serres, *Hermes ou la communication* (Paris: Éditions de Minuit, 1968), p. 40. I cite the translation, published as *Hermes*, ed. Josue V. Harari and David F. Bell, trans. Harari, Bell, et al. (Baltimore: Johns Hopkins University Press, 1982), p. 66. Subsequently cited in the text as H.

25. See, on this point, William R. Paulson, *The Noise of Culture* (Ithaca, NY: Cornell University Press, 1988), p. 83.

26. Richard A. Lanham, "The Electronic Word," *New Literary History*, p. 265, subsequently cited in the text as RL. See also, Lanham, "The Extraordinary Convergence: Democracy, Technology, Theory, and the University Curriculum," *South Atlantic Quarterly* 89, no. 1 (Winter 1990): 27–50.

27. The phrase is Beatrice Warde's in *The Crystal Goblet: Sixteen Essays on Typography* (Cleveland: World Publishing, 1956), p. 11, as cited in Lanham, "Extraordinary Convergence," 31, 50.

28. Charles Bernstein, "The Academy in Peril: William Carlos Williams Meets the MLA," *Content's Dream: Essays, 1975–1984* (Los Angeles: Sun & Moon Press, 1986), pp. 244–51. Subsequently cited in the text as CD.

29. Jed Rasula, "Literary Effects in the Wad: Handling the Fiction, Nursing the Wounds," *Sulfur* 24 (Spring 1989): 77. Subsequently cited in the text as JR.

30. James Wright, *Collected Poems* (Middleton, CT: Wesleyan University Press, 1971), pp. 127–28. "From a Bus Window . . ." first appeared in *The Branch Will Not Break* (1963).

31. Robert Lowell, "Epilogue," *Day by Day* (New York: Farrar, Straus & Giroux, 1977), p. 127.

32. John Cage, "Preface to *Lecture on the Weather*," *Empty Words: Writings '73–'78* (Middleton, CT: Wesleyan University Press, 1979), pp. 3–5, subsequently cited as LW. Individual performances of *Lecture on the Weather* have been videotaped but at this writing none are available for sale or rent.

33. Cage's references, here and elsewhere, to "*I Ching* chance operations" have often been misunderstood. He first came across the *I Ching, Book of Changes,* when the Bollingen edition, translated from the Chinese by Cary Baynes, was published in 1950. Using the *I Ching* method of throwing coins or marked sticks that, like the throw of dice, provided him with particular numbers, Cage then located the numbers in question on a complicated system of charts in the book itself. The charts, in turn, provided specific answers: in the case of the Thoreau text, for example, they would tell him with which letter or word to begin, and so on. But the *I Ching* (now transferred to various computer programs, designed for Cage by his assistants) constitutes no more than a starting point, the composition itself depending on rules that Cage himself invents and which are discussed below.

The typescript of the performance directions and the twelve collage-texts used in *Lecture on the Weather* have been made available to me by Marilyn Boyd de Reggi, the organizer of the John Cage Symposium at the Strathmore Hall Arts Center in Rockville, Maryland, on 5–6 May 1989, at which *Lecture on the Weather* was performed. I also have a copy of the videotape of that performance, of which more will be said below.

34. See James Gleick, *Chaos: Making a New Science* (New York: Viking Penguin, 1987), pp. 132–35. The analogy between Cage's structure and a "strange attractor" was suggested to me by Joan Retallack, unpublished manuscript contained in a letter to me, 15 April 1990, cited by permission of the author as JR. Joan Retallack attended the Strathmore Hall performance of *Lecture on the Weather* (which I have only seen on videotape) and I am further indebted to her for providing a detailed account of it.

35. For example, while Reciter 1 reads, "I have found repeatedly, of late years, that I cannot fish without falling a little in self-respect, I have tried it again and again" (*Journal*), Reciter 2 reads, "If a man who has no property

refuses but once to earn nine shillings for the state, he is put in prison for a period unlimited by any law that I know. . . ." (*Civil Disobedience*), and so on.

36. This is a point Cage made in the question period following the Strathmore Hall performance.

37. Cage's directions read: "The film should be framed slightly larger than the screen so that some of the drawings could project outside of it. This gives the film of lightning a more environmental dimension."

38. John Cage, *Silence* (Middleton, CT: Wesleyan University Press, 1962), p. 12.

Chapter 2

1. W. B. Yeats, *Letters on Poetry from W. B. Yeats to Dorothy Wellesley* (London: Oxford, 1964), p. 56. Subsequently cited in the text as LDW.

2. Ezra Pound, "A Retrospect," *Literary Essays of Ezra Pound*, ed. with an Introduction by T. S. Eliot (New York: New Directions, 1954), p. 5. Subsequently cited in the text as LE.

3. Charles Bernstein, "Stray Straws and Straw Men," *Content's Dream: Essays 1975–1984* (Los Angeles: Sun & Moon Press, 1986), p. 40. This book is subsequently cited in the text as CD.

4. T. S. Eliot, *On Poetry and Poets* (New York: Noonday Press, 1961), p. 21. Subsequently cited in the text as OPP.

5. William Wordsworth, "Preface to *Lyrical Ballads*, with Pastoral and Other Poems" (1802), *The Poems*, ed. John O. Hayden, vol. 1 (New Haven and London: Yale University Press, 1977), p. 877. Subsequently cited in the text as WWP.

6. T. S. Eliot, *The Use of Poetry and the Use of Criticism. Studies in the Relation of Criticism to Poetry in England* (1933; Cambridge, MA: Harvard University Press, 1964), p. 63. Subsequently cited as UPUC. Wordsworth's emphasis on rustic life, says Eliot, has to do with the particular social conditions of his time, when rural life was increasingly destroyed by rapid industrialization: "It is Wordsworth's social interest that inspires his own novelty of form in verse, and backs up his explicit remarks upon poetic diction," p. 65.

7. I purposely say poetics, not poetry: in practice, of course, "natural speech" was itself a carefully crafted simulation, especially for Yeats whose syntactic and verbal artifices are legendary. But what interests me is that, with notable exceptions like Gertrude Stein and Hart Crane, the major Anglo-American modernists regarded the speech model as normative. Indeed, the "artifice" of Crane's style was held against him in his own day; only in the later twentieth century has this style come in for revaluation and, as I suggest in chapter 6, we are now witnessing a Crane influence, for instance in the case of Charles Bernstein. On the artifices of Stein's poetry (again now exerting a strong influence on the poetry of Lyn Hejinian, Rae Armantrout, Bruce Andrews, and others), see my *Poetic License: Essays in Modernist and Postmodernist Lyric* (Evanston: Northwestern University Press, 1990), pp. 145–59.

this poet's extreme artifice—an artifice that became acceptable only in the past decade or so. *The Double Dream of Spring* (1970), *Three Poems* (1972)— these were written against the grain of sixties "authenticity."

29. Robert Grenier, "On Speech," in *In the American Tree*, ed. Ron Silliman (Orono, ME: National Poetry Foundation, 1986), p. 496.

30. Jacques Derrida, *Of Grammatology*, trans. Gayatri Chakravorty Spivak (Baltimore and London: Johns Hopkins University Press, 1976), p. 8.

31. Michel De Certeau, "The Jabbering of Social Life," in Marshall Blonsky, ed., *On Signs* (Baltimore and London: Johns Hopkins University Press, 1985), pp. 151–52.

32. See Donal Carbaugh, *Talking American: Cultural Discourses on "DONAHUE"* (Norwood, NJ: Ablex Publishing Co., 1988), p. 3. According to Carbaugh, the show "airs in more than 200 markets, including Alaska, Hawaii, and Puerto Rico" and has won several awards including Emmys for "best show," "best host," and "outstanding achievement for a creative technical craft."

33. Jean Baudrillard, *Simulations*, trans. Paul Foss et al. (New York: Semiotext(e), 1983), p. 2. Subsequently cited in the text as SIM.

34. Jean Baudrillard, "Requiem for the Media" (1972), *For a Critique of the Political Economy of the Sign*, trans. Charles Levin (St. Louis, MO: Telos Press, 1981), p. 169; rpt. in *Video Culture: A Critical Investigation* (Rochester, NY: Gibbs M. Smith, and Peregrine Smith Books, 1987), p. 129. I cite the essay in the latter text as RM.

35. Steve McCaffery, *North of Intention: Critical Writings, 1973–1986* (New York: Roof Books,1986), pp. 40–41. Subsequently cited in the text as NI.

36. Louis Simpson, "The Character of the Poet," in Hank Lazer, ed., *What Is a Poet? Essays from the Eleventh Alabama Symposium on English and American Literature* (Tuscaloosa and London: University of Alabama Press, 1987), p. 15.

37. Robert Lowell, "An Interview with Frederick Seidel" (1961), *Collected Poems*, ed. Robert Giroux (New York: Farrar Straus Giroux, 1987), p. 266.

38. Robert Lowell, *Life Studies* (New York: Farrar, Straus & Giroux, 1959), pp. 59, 79; *For the Union Dead* (New York: Farrar, Straus & Giroux, 1964), p. 19. The phrase "the grace of accuracy" comes from "Epilogue," *Day by Day* (New York: Farrar, Straus & Giroux, 1977), p. 127.

39. I discuss the art of Lowell's "confessionalism" in *The Poetic Art of Robert Lowell* (Ithaca: Cornell University Press, 1973), esp. in chapter 3 passim.

40. Charles Altieri, *Enlarging the Temple: New Directions in American Poetry during the 1960s* (Lewisburg, PA: Bucknell University Press, 1979), p. 72.

41. John Berryman, "Tea," *Love and Fame* (New York: Farrar, Straus & Giroux, 1970), p. 50.

42. Philip Levine, *Don't Ask*, Poets on Poetry, ed. Donald Hall (Ann Arbor: University of Michigan Press, 1981), p. 101; ellipses are Levine's as recorded by the interviewer, Calvin Bedient. This text is subsequently cited as DA.

43. Philip Levine, *One for the Rose* (New York: Atheneum, 1981), pp. 60–61; rpt. in DA 135–36.

44. For a typical view, see Robert S. Miola, "Philip Levine," in James Vin-

refuses but once to earn nine shillings for the state, he is put in prison for a period unlimited by any law that I know. . . ." (*Civil Disobedience*), and so on.

36. This is a point Cage made in the question period following the Strathmore Hall performance.

37. Cage's directions read: "The film should be framed slightly larger than the screen so that some of the drawings could project outside of it. This gives the film of lightning a more environmental dimension."

38. John Cage, *Silence* (Middleton, CT: Wesleyan University Press, 1962), p. 12.

Chapter 2

1. W. B. Yeats, *Letters on Poetry from W. B. Yeats to Dorothy Wellesley* (London: Oxford, 1964), p. 56. Subsequently cited in the text as LDW.

2. Ezra Pound, "A Retrospect," *Literary Essays of Ezra Pound*, ed. with an Introduction by T. S. Eliot (New York: New Directions, 1954), p. 5. Subsequently cited in the text as LE.

3. Charles Bernstein, "Stray Straws and Straw Men," *Content's Dream: Essays 1975–1984* (Los Angeles: Sun & Moon Press, 1986), p. 40. This book is subsequently cited in the text as CD.

4. T. S. Eliot, *On Poetry and Poets* (New York: Noonday Press, 1961), p. 21. Subsequently cited in the text as OPP.

5. William Wordsworth, "Preface to *Lyrical Ballads*, with Pastoral and Other Poems" (1802), *The Poems*, ed. John O. Hayden, vol. 1 (New Haven and London: Yale University Press, 1977), p. 877. Subsequently cited in the text as WWP.

6. T. S. Eliot, *The Use of Poetry and the Use of Criticism. Studies in the Relation of Criticism to Poetry in England* (1933; Cambridge, MA: Harvard University Press, 1964), p. 63. Subsequently cited as UPUC. Wordsworth's emphasis on rustic life, says Eliot, has to do with the particular social conditions of his time, when rural life was increasingly destroyed by rapid industrialization: "It is Wordsworth's social interest that inspires his own novelty of form in verse, and backs up his explicit remarks upon poetic diction," p. 65.

7. I purposely say poetics, not poetry: in practice, of course, "natural speech" was itself a carefully crafted simulation, especially for Yeats whose syntactic and verbal artifices are legendary. But what interests me is that, with notable exceptions like Gertrude Stein and Hart Crane, the major Anglo-American modernists regarded the speech model as normative. Indeed, the "artifice" of Crane's style was held against him in his own day; only in the later twentieth century has this style come in for revaluation and, as I suggest in chapter 6, we are now witnessing a Crane influence, for instance in the case of Charles Bernstein. On the artifices of Stein's poetry (again now exerting a strong influence on the poetry of Lyn Hejinian, Rae Armantrout, Bruce Andrews, and others), see my *Poetic License: Essays in Modernist and Postmodernist Lyric* (Evanston: Northwestern University Press, 1990), pp. 145–59.

8. *The Letters of W. B. Yeats*, ed. Allan Wade (London: Ropert Hart-Davis, 1954), p. 583. Unlike Eliot, Yeats took seriously Wordsworth's concern for the "common man." A few years before his death, he told Dorothy Wellesley that the correct formula for poetry was to "think like a wise man, yet express our selves like the common people" (LDW 58). Like many of Yeats's aphorisms this one has more rhetorical force than practical substance: nowhere did Yeats ever simulate the actual speech of common people.

9. Ezra Pound, *Selected Letters, 1907–1941*, ed. D. D. Paige (New York: New Directions, 1971), pp. 48–49. Cf. Pound's review of Robert Frost's *North of Boston*, in LE, p. 384: "Mr. Frost has dared to write, and for the most part with success, in the natural speech of New England; in natural spoken speech."

10. David Antin, "Modernism and Postmodernism: Approaching the Present in American Poetry," *boundary 2*, 1, no. 1 (Fall 1972): 131.

11. Eliot, "Introduction," *Paul Valéry: The Art of Poetry* (New York: Vintage, 1961), p. xvii. Subsequently cited in the text as PV.

12. W. B. Yeats, *Autobiographies* (London: Macmillan, 1966), p. 48. Subsequently cited in the text as Auto.

13. T. S. Eliot, *Selected Essays* (London: Faber & Faber, 1953), p. 326. Subsequently cited in the text as ESE.

14. Samuel Taylor Coleridge, *Biographia Literaria*, ed. James Engell and W. Jackson Bate (Princeton: Princeton University Press, Bollingen Series, 1983), p. 52. On the large question of Wordsworth and "rustic language," see Engell and Bate's "Editors' Introduction," pp. civ–cxiv; Karl Kroeber, "William Wordsworth," in *The English Romantic Poets: A Review of Research*, 4th ed., ed. Frank Jordan (New York: Modern Language Association of America, 1985), pp. 329–39.

It is interesting that Eliot cites "a remarkable letter of Wordsworth's in 1801 which he wrote to Charles James Fox [a "fashionable politician"] in sending him a copy of the *Ballads*." In this letter, Wordsworth speaks of the "spreading of manufactures," the "heavy taxes upon postage," the "workhouses, houses of industry, and the invention of soup shops," as well as the "increasing disproportion between the price of labour and that of the necessities of life" as eroding "the bonds of domestic feeling among the poor." Eliot concludes that Wordsworth's predilection for humble life as poetic subject is thus motivated by social concern (UPUC 64–65).

15. Charles Bernstein, *The Sophist* (Los Angeles: Sun & Moon Press, 1987), p. 44. Subsequently cited in the text as S.

16. Eliot's strongest position statement on the subject was the declaration in the Preface to *For Lancelot Andrewes* (London: Faber & Faber, 1928) that he was "classicist in literature, royalist in politics, and anglo-catholic in religion" (p. ix).

17. T. S. Eliot, *Collected Poems, 1909–1962* (New York: Harcourt, Brace & World, 1970), p. 121. Subsequently cited in the text as ECP.

18. T. S. Eliot, *The Waste Land: A Facsimile and Transcript of the Original Drafts including the Annotations of Ezra Pound*, ed. Valerie Eliot (London: Faber & Faber 1971), p. 127.

19. Donald Allen, ed., *The New American Poetry* (New York: Grove Press, 1960), p. xi.

20. Stephen Berg and Robert Mezey, eds., *Naked Poetry: Recent American Poetry in Open Forms* (Indianapolis and New York: Bobbs-Merrill Co., 1969), p. xi.

21. The two best treatments of the "opening of the field," the former primarily theoretical, the second primarily historical, are Charles Altieri's *Enlarging the Temple: New Directions in American Poetry during the 1960s* (Lewisburg, PA: Bucknell University Press, 1979), and James E. B. Breslin's *From Modern to Contemporary: American Poetry, 1945–65* (Chicago and London: University of Chicago Press, 1984).

As in the case of high modernism (see note 7 above), I don't want to claim that in practice, Black Mountain poets and Projectivists adhered to a speech-based poetics; certainly Robert Duncan himself did not, his verbal patterns being closer to the late romantics and pre-Raphaelites than to Eliot or Pound. What allies Duncan to the "natural speech" advocates, however, is his refusal of meter, traditional stanzaic structure, and what the New Critics called "key design" or "integral" metaphoric structure—a refusal on the grounds that such poetic features are too contrived, that they inhibit natural inspiration.

22. Charles Olson, "Projective Verse," *Human Universe and Other Essays*, ed. Donald Allen (New York: Grove Press, 1967), pp. 51–56.

23. Allen Ginsberg, "Notes for *Howl and Other Poems*" (1959), in *The Poetics of the New American Poetry*, ed. Donald Allen and Warren Tallman (New York: Grove Press, 1973), p. 319. This collection is subsequently cited in the text as PNAP.

24. Allen Ginsberg, "When the Mode of the Music Changes the Walls of the City Shake" (1961), in *Esthetics Contemporary*, ed. Richard Kostelanetz (Buffalo, NY: Prometheus Books, 1978), p. 335.

25. Gary Snyder, "Poetry and the Primitive: Notes on Poetry as an Ecological Survival Technique" (1967), in PNAP, 401–2.

26. Arthur Kroker and David Cook, *The Postmodern Scene: Excremental Culture and Hyper-Aesthetics* (New York: St. Martin's Press, 1986), p. 269.

27. Denise Levertov, "Some Notes on Organic Form," *The Poet in the World* (New York: New Directions, 1973), pp. 7–8.

28. I am referring to the dominant poetic mode of the sixties. There were, of course, notable exceptions, which will be taken up in later chapters. To give just one example, consider the opening of John Ashbery's "Clepsydra," which appears in *Rivers and Mountains* (1966; rpt. New York: Ecco Press, 1977), p. 27:

> Hasn't the sky? Returned from moving the other
> Authority recently dropped, wrested as much of
> That severe sunshine as you need now on the way
> You go.

This is hardly a representation of "one person talking to another." Indeed, the relative neglect of Ashbery's poetry until the late seventies, when he published *Self-Portrait in a Convex Mirror*, may well have something to do with this poet's extreme artifice—an artifice that became acceptable only in the past decade or so. *The Double Dream of Spring* (1970), *Three Poems* (1972)— these were written against the grain of sixties "authenticity."

29. Robert Grenier, "On Speech," in *In the American Tree*, ed. Ron Silliman (Orono, ME: National Poetry Foundation, 1986), p. 496.

30. Jacques Derrida, *Of Grammatology*, trans. Gayatri Chakravorty Spivak (Baltimore and London: Johns Hopkins University Press, 1976), p. 8.

31. Michel De Certeau, "The Jabbering of Social Life," in Marshall Blonsky, ed., *On Signs* (Baltimore and London: Johns Hopkins University Press, 1985), pp. 151–52.

32. See Donal Carbaugh, *Talking American: Cultural Discourses on "DONAHUE"* (Norwood, NJ: Ablex Publishing Co., 1988), p. 3. According to Carbaugh, the show "airs in more than 200 markets, including Alaska, Hawaii, and Puerto Rico" and has won several awards including Emmys for "best show," "best host," and "outstanding achievement for a creative technical craft."

33. Jean Baudrillard, *Simulations*, trans. Paul Foss et al. (New York: Semiotext(e), 1983), p. 2. Subsequently cited in the text as SIM.

34. Jean Baudrillard, "Requiem for the Media" (1972), *For a Critique of the Political Economy of the Sign*, trans. Charles Levin (St. Louis, MO: Telos Press, 1981), p. 169; rpt. in *Video Culture: A Critical Investigation* (Rochester, NY: Gibbs M. Smith, and Peregrine Smith Books, 1987), p. 129. I cite the essay in the latter text as RM.

35. Steve McCaffery, *North of Intention: Critical Writings, 1973–1986* (New York: Roof Books,1986), pp. 40–41. Subsequently cited in the text as NI.

36. Louis Simpson, "The Character of the Poet," in Hank Lazer, ed., *What Is a Poet? Essays from the Eleventh Alabama Symposium on English and American Literature* (Tuscaloosa and London: University of Alabama Press, 1987), p. 15.

37. Robert Lowell, "An Interview with Frederick Seidel" (1961), *Collected Poems*, ed. Robert Giroux (New York: Farrar Straus Giroux, 1987), p. 266.

38. Robert Lowell, *Life Studies* (New York: Farrar, Straus & Giroux, 1959), pp. 59, 79; *For the Union Dead* (New York: Farrar, Straus & Giroux, 1964), p. 19. The phrase "the grace of accuracy" comes from "Epilogue," *Day by Day* (New York: Farrar, Straus & Giroux, 1977), p. 127.

39. I discuss the art of Lowell's "confessionalism" in *The Poetic Art of Robert Lowell* (Ithaca: Cornell University Press, 1973), esp. in chapter 3 passim.

40. Charles Altieri, *Enlarging the Temple: New Directions in American Poetry during the 1960s* (Lewisburg, PA: Bucknell University Press, 1979), p. 72.

41. John Berryman, "Tea," *Love and Fame* (New York: Farrar, Straus & Giroux, 1970), p. 50.

42. Philip Levine, *Don't Ask*, Poets on Poetry, ed. Donald Hall (Ann Arbor: University of Michigan Press, 1981), p. 101; ellipses are Levine's as recorded by the interviewer, Calvin Bedient. This text is subsequently cited as DA.

43. Philip Levine, *One for the Rose* (New York: Atheneum, 1981), pp. 60–61; rpt. in DA 135–36.

44. For a typical view, see Robert S. Miola, "Philip Levine," in James Vin-

cago: University of Chicago Press, 1984), pp. 176–86. The more sophisticated version of Bly's credo is, as Breslin argues, James Wright's; see Breslin, chapter 7, passim.

15. The major work on the subject was done in the 1950s, perhaps not coincidentally at the time when the Image was beginning to lose its status: see Frank Kermode, *Romantic Image* (1957; rpt. New York: Vintage Books, 1964); Northrop Frye, *Anatomy of Criticism* (Princeton: Princeton University Press, 1957); Meyer Abrams, *The Mirror and the Lamp* (New York: Oxford University Press, 1953). During the next decade, the study of poetic imagery became more complex and theoretical; see J. Hillis Miller, *Poets of Reality: Six Twentieth-Century Writers* (1965; rpt. New York: Atheneum, 1968); Harold Bloom, *The Anxiety of Influence: A Theory of Poetry* (New York: Oxford University Press, 1973), and *A Map of Misreading* (New York: Oxford University Press, 1975). Interestingly, poststructuralist criticism has largely carried on these concerns, even if the concept of the image itself has radically changed; see, for example, J. Hillis Miller, *The Linguistic Moment: From Wordsworth to Stevens* (Princeton: Princeton University Press, 1985).

Interestingly, as early as the 1920s, the Russian Formalists had argued that, in the words of Viktor Zirmunskij, "The material of poetry is neither images nor emotions, but words. . . . Poetry is a verbal art"; and Roman Jakobson suggested that poetry could, in fact, dispense with "images" completely, using sound or syntax as the poetry differentium; see Victor Erlich, *Russian Formalism: History-Doctrine*, 4th ed. (The Hague, Paris, and New York: Mouton, 1980), pp. 174–76, 230–32.

For a superb recent treatment of theories of the image and of representation, both in the verbal and the visual arts and with respect to ideology, see W. J. T. Mitchell, *Iconology: Image, Text, Ideology.*

16. *The Collected Poems of William Carlos Williams* (2 vols.), vol. 1, 1909–39, ed. A. Walton Litz and Christopher MacGowan (New York: New Directions, 1986); vol. 2, 1939–62, ed. Christopher McGowan (New York: New Directions, 1988), 1:372. Subsequently cited in the text as WCWCP.

17. "A 1 Pound Stein" (1934), *Selected Essays of Williams Carlos Williams* (New York: New Directions, 1954), p. 163. Subsequently cited in the text as SE.

18. Paul Mariani is representative of the many Williams scholars who consider "Asphodel" the culmination of Williams's work, the elegiac confession in which "time and death" are finally "annihilated 'by grace of the imagination'" (*Williams Carlos Williams: A New World Naked* [New York: McGraw-Hill, 1981], p. 677). J. Hillis Miller calls "Asphodel" "the extraordinary love poem of Williams' old age" and writes of its "quiet mastery of supreme attainment." "Each object," says Miller, "could be substituted for any of the others, for all say the same thing, do that one thing which all poetic speech does—perpetuate the dance" (*Poets of Reality*, p. 356).

Others like James E. B. Breslin are more cautious: see his *William Carlos Williams: An American Artist*, rev. ed. (Chicago: University of Chicago Press, 1985), chapter 7, passim, esp. p. 222. For my own assessment, see "William Carlos Williams," in *Voices and Visions*, ed. Helen Vendler (New York: Random

House, 1987), pp. 201–3. I would now add that, from a feminist perspective, the treatment of the poem's "you" (Floss Williams) is irritatingly condescending. Throughout the poem, the conflict is Williams's, the difficulty is Williams's, whereas Floss appears as, so to speak, the Woman Without Qualities, the unmovable object rather than the worthy antagonist of the poem's speaker. "Listen," he tells her, "while I talk on / against time," and his wife has no choice but to do so, to learn that "Love / to which you too shall bow / along with me . . . shall be our trust / and not because / we are too feeble to do otherwise / but because / at the height of my power / I risked what I had to do" (WCWCP 2:317–18). And the poem's final image is of Floss the bride, "a girl so pale / and ready to faint / that I pitied / and wanted to protect you," a "sweet-scented flower . . . poised [that] for me did open" (WCWCP 2:336).

19. Robert Lowell, "Williams Carlos Williams," in *William Carlos Williams: Twentieth-Century Views* (Englewood Cliffs, NJ: Prentice-Hall, 1966), p. 159. Williams's own response to the Wellesley audience is recorded in *I Wanted to Write a Poem: The Autobiography of the Works of a Poet*, reported and edited by Edith Heal (Boston: Beacon Press, 1958), pp. 94–95. "They were so adorable," he recalls, "I could have raped them all"—a sentiment that supports my reading in note 18.

20. See, for example, Virginia Kelley, et al., "Television: A New Season," *Look*, 9 October 1962, pp. 76–100.

21. Robert Bly, "Driving toward the Lac Qui Parle River," in *Silence in the Snowy Fields* (Middletown, CT: Wesleyan University Press, 1962), p. 20. Cited and discussed by Robert Pinsky in *The Situation of Poetry: Contemporary Poetry and Its Traditions* (Princeton: Princeton University Press, 1976), p. 77.

22. Bill Moyers, "The Poet Speaks: A Conversation with Robert Bly," in *Transmission: Theory and Practice for a New Television Aesthetics* (New York: Tanam Press, 1985), p. 235. Subsequently cited in the text as CRB.

23. This tripartite division is by no means hard and fast; I merely want to suggest possible emphases. Charles Bernstein, for example, could also be included in the first group; see chapter 6, where I so group him with Ashbery. And McCaffery could just as well be in the third group, his experiments with syntax being among the key examples of this mode. And, since my focus here is on image, I say nothing of the prosodic innovations which are the subject of chapter 5.

24. See, for example, Tom Mandel, "Appendix to Poetry and Politics: A Conversation with George Oppen," in *George Oppen: Man and Poet*, ed. Burton Hatlen (Orono, ME: National Poetry Foundation, 1981), pp. 49–50; and, in the same collection, Burton Hatlen, "'Not Altogether Lone in a Lone Universe': George Oppen's *The Materials*," pp. 325–58, esp. pp. 325–26. This collection is subsequently cited as GOMP.

25. *This in Which* (1965) has an epigraph from Heidegger, " . . . the arduous path of appearance." Oppen has commented on the importance of Heidegger, and particularly of *Being and Time*, in various interviews: see L. S. Dembo, "George Oppen: An Interview," *Contemporary Literature* 10 (Spring 1969): 168, subsequently cited as LSD; and Burton Hatlen and Tom Mandel,

"Conversation with George Oppen," GOMP 34–35. For an excellent discussion of the Heidegger-Oppen relationship, see Randolph Chilton, "The Place of Being in the Poetry of George Oppen," GOMP 89–112.

The influence of Kierkegaard and Maritain on Oppen has also been noted, and in recent years we have become more aware of the interesting relationship to Wittgenstein. See, for example, David McAleavey, "Clarity and Process: Oppen's *Of Being Numerous*," GOMP 392–93; Burton Hatlen, "Zukofsky, Wittgenstein, and the Poetics of Absence," *Sagetrieb* 1 (Spring 1982): 63–93. Although, as the title indicates, this essay deals with Zukofsky rather than Oppen, the discussion of the Wittgensteinian refusal to relate words to things applies neatly to Oppen as well.

26. Charles Bernstein, *Content's Dream: Essays, 1975–1984* (Los Angeles: Sun & Moon Press, 1986), p. 90.

27. See the following: *Ironwood* (ed. Michael Cuddihy, Tucson, Arizona) has had three special Oppen issues: 5 (1975), 24 (1984), and 26 (1985). *Paideuma* (ed. Carroll F. Terrell, Orono, Maine) had a special Oppen issue: 10, no. 1 (Spring 198); this was followed by Burton Hatlen's *George Oppen: Man and Poet* (1981), which includes only a few of the *Paideuma* contributors and has extensive notes and annotated bibliography. The *Ironwood* issues are subsequently cited as IR; *Paideuma* is cited as P.

28. In "The New Political Economy," *Poetry* 44 (1934): 220–25; rpt. in GOMP 267–70, Williams praises the technical excellence of Oppen's poems in *Discrete Series* and comments on the poet's "plain words" and his "metric . . . taken from speech" (pp. 269–70). But the tone of the review, which sidetracks into a general attack on those who judge poetry according to its subject matter, suggests a certain perplexity on Williams's part, as if he wanted very much to praise the younger poet but didn't quite see what he was getting at. See, on this point, my *Dance of the Intellect* (Cambridge and New York: Cambridge University Press, 1985), pp. 119–34.

29. George Oppen, *The Collected Poems* (New York: New Directions, 1975), p. 4. This text is subsequently cited as GOCP.

30. Roland Marchand, *Advertising the American Dream: Making Way for Modernity, 1920–1940* (Berkeley and Los Angeles: University of California Press, 1985), pp. 270–72.

31. Harold Schimmel, "(On) *Discrete Series*," GOMP 293–321, esp. p. 301.

32. "An Adequate Vision: A George Oppen Daybook," ed. Michael Davidson, in IR 26:5–31, esp. 29. This text is subsequently cited in the text as DBK.

33. "As for Imagisme" (1915), in SPR 374–75. In "George Oppen, *Discrete Series*, 1929–1934," GOMP 271–92, Tom Sharp cites this passage as evidence that Oppen's is best understood as the second or objective image (see pp. 272–73).

34. The first version of this poem (January 1959), recently published in "The Circumstances: A Selection from George Oppen's Uncollected Writing," ed. Rachel Blau duPlessis, *Sulfur* 25 (Fall 1989): 23–24, is called "The Town":

> There can be a brick in a brick wall
> The eye picks

> So empty on a Sunday.
> The silent signs.
>
> Quiet Sunday
> On the flatof the table
> The match box, there asmuch as anything.
>
> Handling baggage in leather gloves,
> A few years out of high school,
> A young man furious. The new wine.

Note that Oppen revises in the direction of ellipsis, abstraction, less figurative language and that "Mary-Anne" does not appear in the more imagistic early version at all.

35. See, on this point, the interesting discussion in Burton Hatlen, "Opening Up the Text: George Oppen's 'Of Being Numerous,'" IR 85:274–75.

36. H. D., "The Helmsman," *Collected Poems, 1912–1944*, ed. Louis L. Martz (New York: New Directions, 1983), p. 6.

37. See LSD 163. In the poem "Psalm," which Oppen cites in this passage, we find the lines "The small nouns / Crying faith / In this in which the wild deer / Startle, and stare out"; see CP 78. This poem is frequently cited as evidence of Oppen's faith in the "small nouns," but the fact is, that as Oppen remarks in a number of places, nouns, like verbs, pose a problem for him. See, for example, Oppen, DBK 13: "Not sure I can count further on the nouns in an open voyage." And on the same page, we read: "the verbs, which I have never been able to hand," "the verb, the *ACT* of things—even as I say it, it seems to me that that necessarily involves failure."

38. Ludwig Wittgenstein, *Philosophical Investigations*, 3d ed., trans. G. E. M. Anscombe (New York: Macmillan, 1968), section 108. The numbers refer not to page but to section. Subsequently cited as PI.

39. Rae Armantrout, "Double," *Precedence* (Providence, RI: Burning Deck Press, 1985), p. 11.

Chapter 4

1. Walter Benjamin, "Zentralpark," *Gesammelte Schriften* (Frankfurt: Suhrkamp, 1977), vol. 1, p. 568. I cite the translation by Benjamin H. D. Buchloch in "Open Letters, Industrial Poems," *Broodthaers: Writings, Interviews, Photographs*, ed. Benjamin H. D. Buchloch, special issue of *October* 42 (Fall 1987): 74. Buchloch's essay is subsequently cited in the text as BHDB and the issue itself as OCT.

2. Robert Venturi, Denise Scott-Brown, and Steven Izenour, *Learning from Las Vegas* (Cambridge and London: MIT Press, 1972), p. 10. Since it is too cumbersome to cite all three authors each time, I refer collectively to "the Venturis." The book is subsequently cited in the text as LL.

3. Ironically, when the Venturis make analogies to the other arts, for instance poetry, they invariably cite writers committed to "high art." Thus they

write: "Perhaps a fitting requiem for the irrelevant works of Art that are today's descendants of a once meaningful Modern architecture are Eliot's lines in 'East Coker':

> That was a way of putting it—
> not very satisfactory
> A periphrastic study in a worn-
> out poetical fashion,
> Leaving one still with the
> intolerable wrestle
> With words and meanings.
> The poetry does not matter." (LL 58, 60)

Eliot would, I think, have been very surprised to find his "intolerable wrestle / with words" applied to the Las Vegas strip.

4. Marcel Broodthaers, "Ten Thousand Francs Reward," in OCT: 41–42. Subsequently cited in the text as TTF.

5. See Michael Compton, "In Praise of the Subject," in *Marcel Broodthaers*, catalog for the exhibition at the Walker Art Center, Minneapolis, organized by Marge Goldwater and Michael Compton (Minneapolis: Walker Art Center; New York: Rizzoli, 1989), pp. 42–43, and see plates 44, 45, 136, 137. This catalog is subsequently cited in the text as MB.

6. John Ashbery, *Three Poems* (New York: Viking Press, 1972), p. 3.

7. Steve McCaffery, *The Black Debt* (Toronto: Nightwood Editions, 1989).

8. Samuel Johnson, cited by James Boswell in the *Life of Johnson* (London and New York: Oxford University Press, 1961), p. 443 (December 1770; *Aetat* 61). The phrase *lucidus ordo* (clearness of order) comes from Horace, *Ars Poetica*, line 41.

9. Ludwig Wittgenstein, *Philosophical Investigations*, 3d ed., trans. G. E. M. Anscombe (New York: Macmillan, 1968), no. 13 (p. 7e). Subsequently cited in the text as PI.

10. *Evoba: The Investigation Meditations, 1976–78* (Toronto: Coach House Press, 1987). *Evoba* functions as a kind of parallel response to Wittgenstein's *Philosophical Investigations*, an application, so to speak, of Wittgenstein on Wittgenstein.

11. The imagery here recalls John Ashbery's "'They Dream Only of America,'" *The Tennis Court Oath* (Middletown, CT: Wesleyan University Press, 1962), p. 13:

> And hiding from darkness in barns
> They can be grownups now
> And the murderer's ash tray is more easily—
> The lake a lilac cube.

Ashbery's narrative alludes to a murky conversation about a key, a slow move into the bedroom, a falling against a living room table. These elements, in radically fragmented form turn up here too.

12. The relationship of McCaffery's work (together with that of other Cana-

dian poets like bill bissett and bpNichol) to Concretism is discussed in Caroline Bayard's recent *New Poetics in Canada and Quebec: From Concretism to Post-Modernism* (Toronto and London: University of Toronto Press, 1989). See esp. pp. 59–68. Subsequently cited in the text as CB.

13. bpNichol, "The Annotated, Anecdoted, Beginnings of a Critical Checklist of the Published Works of Steve McCaffery," in *Open Letter*, Sixth Series, no. 9 (Fall 1987): 72–73. McCaffery's description is in response to Nichol's question about how "the idea of page manifests itself in the work" and how "masking works as a compositional tool." Subsequently cited as BPN.

14. Preliminary Notes for Panel Two, "Carnival," unpublished typescript, courtesy of the author.

15. Mary Ellen Solt, *Concrete Poetry: A World View* (Bloomington and London: University of Indiana Press, 1971), pp. 44–45 and figure 106 (p. 207), with the accompanying note on p. 296. Subsequently cited in the text as MES.

16. Caroline Bayard writes, "The concrete texts published in Europe and both Americas in the 1950s and 1960s were replaced in the later part of the second decade by productions which showed anagrammatic dispersion and affirmed only the de-centring of all systems, the rejection of truth, origin, nostalgia and guilt" (CB 53). The relation of this later "deconstructivist" (or "dirty" in McCaffery's words) mode to the theoretical writings of Derrida, Baudrillard, and others, is discussed in Bayard's third chapter.

17. Rosmarie Waldrop, "A Basis of Concrete Poetry," *Bucknell Review* 22 (Fall 1976): 141–51, esp. pp. 141–42. Subsequently cited in the text as RW.

Concrete poetry has been subjected to an enormous body of criticism, perhaps because it presented itself as a coherent international movement with clearcut theories and practices and hence lends itself especially well to scholarly investigation. Among the key works are the following:

Mary Ellen Solt, "Introduction," *Concrete Poetry: A World View* (see note 15), pp. 1–66. Solt also includes a good selection of concrete manifestos and her notes and bibliographies are invaluable. Herself a very talented Concrete poet, Solt gives us an inside view; there is no critique of Concrete poetry or questioning of Concrete theorems.

Liselotte Gumpel, *Concrete Poetry from East and West Germany* (New Haven and London: Yale University Press, 1976).

Richard Kostelanetz, *Visual Literature Criticism: A New Collection*, ed. Richard Kostelanetz (Carbondale and Edwardsville: Southern Illinois University Press, 1979).

Claus Clüver, "Languages of the Concrete Poem," *Transformations of Literary Language in Latin American Literature*, ed. K. David Jackson (Austin, TX: Abaporu Press, 1987), pp. 32–42, subsequently cited in the text as CCL; and Clüver, "From Imagism to Concrete Poetry: Breakthrough or Blind Alley?" in *Amerikanische Lyrik: Perspektiven und Interpretationen*, ed. Rudolf Haas (Berlin: Erich Schmidt Verlag, 1987), pp. 113–30, subsequently cited as CCF; Clüver, "Reflections on Verbivocovisual Ideograms," *Poetics Today*: Special Issue, *Poetics of the Avant-Garde*, ed. Richard Kostelanetz, 3, no. 3 (Summer 1982): 137–48. This issue is subsequently cited as PAG.

Jon M. Tolman, "The Context of a Vanguard: Towards a Definition of Concrete Poetry," PAG 149–66.

Wendy Steiner, *"Res Poetica"*: The Problematics of the Concrete Program," *New Literary History* 12, no. 3 (Spring 1981): 529–45.

R. F. Draper, "Concrete Poetry," *New Literary History* 2 (Winter 1971): 329–40.

Some of the key texts by the leading Concretists are gathered in the following:

Eugen Gomringer, *Zur Sache der Konkreten* (2 vols.; St. Gallen: Erker, 1988), vol. 1: *Konkrete Poesie;* vol. 2: *Konkrete Kunst.*

Augusto de Campos, Decio Pignatari, Haroldo de Campos, *Teoria de Poesia Concreta: Textos Criticos e Manifestos 1950–1960* (São Paulo: Editora brasiliense, 1987).

For translations of the Brazilian manifestos, see MES 70–72; Augusto de Campos, "The Concrete Coin of Speech," PAG 167–76; Haroldo de Campos, "The Informational Temperature of the Text," PAG 177–88; Decio Pignatari, "Concrete Poetry: A Brief Structuro-Historical Guideline," PAG 189–95.

An invaluable bibliographical resource is *The Ruth and Marvin Sackner Archive of Concrete and Visual Poetry* (Miami Beach, Florida, 1984).

18. In an interview with Julio Ortego, Haroldo de Campos recalls that for the Noigandres group, "the high point of our experience [was the creation of] the poem reduced to its common multiple minimum—anonymous and collective. . . . It comes from Mallarmé's idea of the disappearance of the 'I' as speaker in poetry." See "Concrete Poetry and Beyond," *Latin American Literature and Arts* (New York: Center for Inter-American Relations, 1986), p. 36. Compare CCF 115: "The Concrete text . . . tends to refuse service as a vehicle for subjective experience and as a carrier of messages, to abolish the lyrical 'I' and the narrative voice, to strive for impersonality."

19. See on this point Augusto de Campos, Decio Pignatari, Haroldo de Campos, "Pilot Plan for Concrete Poetry" (1958) MES 71–72.

20. In "Languages of the Concrete Poem" (p. 35), Claus Clüver writes of *silencio:* "The greater the reader's store of association with 'silence,' the richer will the text appear, and it may ultimately be read as the perfect emblem for the Romantic-Symbolist concern with the ineffable, for the idea that at the core of each poem there is silence. It can also be read as a banal travesty of the idea. But by offering itself as the source for the construction of a possibly endless chain of interpretants, it will draw our attention more and more to the process of signification itself. Such a text tends to be first and foremost a metasign."

But the fact is that metasigns have no absolute status; they function historically and intertextually. Once we have seen a constellation like *silencio* a few times, once we are accustomed to similar "metasigns" in advertising, etc., it is doubtful that such a text does in fact "draw our attention more and more to the process of signification itself."

21. In his *Theory of Semiotics* (Bloomington and London: Indiana University Press, 1979), p. 191, Umberto Eco uses the term "iconic fallacy" to desig-

nate the confusion between a sign and its object. The plane surface bearing the visual constellation "silenzio" does not, in fact, have the same properties as the term *silence*. Similarly, Wendy Steiner notes that "Semiotically . . . concrete art is a contradiction in terms. Paintings and poems by definition are signs rather than things, except in the sense that ultimately a sign is a thing; a poem that is literally a tree or a rose is not a poem but that tree or rose." All that visual poetry can really do, Steiner argues, is to maximize "iconic properties at the expense of symbolic ones," "*Res Poetica*," pp. 529–31.

22. *Codigo* is reproduced in Augusto de Campos's beautifully produced *Poesia 1949–1979* (São Paulo: Editora brasiliense, 1986), unpaginated, in the section *Enigmagens*.

23. Chris Dawson, "The Iconography of the Mundane," in Derek Walker, guest ed., *Los Angeles* (New York: St. Martin's/Academy Editions, 1981), p. 128.

24. In his early manifesto "From Line to Constellation" (1954), Eugen Gomringer writes, "Restriction in the best sense—concentration and simplification—is the very essence of poetry" (MES 67). In "The Poem as a Functional Object" (1960), he explains this theorem as follows: "The purpose of reduced language is not the reduction of language itself but the achievement of greater flexibility and freedom of communication (with its inherent need for rules and regulations). The resulting poems should be, if possible, as easily understood as signs in airports and traffic signs" (MES 69–70).

Note that this formula for "reduced language" is by no means comparable to the "simple" rebuses of Broodthaers with their pastiche of signboards, schoolbooks, learning devices, and so on. For in Concrete poetry, the emphasis is still on *structure*, on the use of letters, numbers, formal figures to make a beautiful art construct.

25. McCaffery's "concretist" experiments are extremely varied; see esp. *Ow's Waif and other poems* (Toronto: Coach House Press, 1975) and *Panopticon* (Toronto: Blew Ointment Press, 1984).

26. Johanna Drucker, "Close Reading: A Billboard," *Poetics Journal* 2 (September 1982): 82.

27. Johanna Drucker, *The Word Made Flesh* (Cambridge, MA: Druckwerk, 1989). "Druckwerk" is the name Drucker has chosen for her own press. The colophon reads: "This book was printed by Johanna Drucker between December 1988 and January 1989 in the sometimes torrid, frequently frigid, basement of Adams House at the Bow and Arrow Press. . . . The paper is Mohawk Superfine and the type is some of everything linear." The edition had 55 copies.

In Drucker's earlier *Through Light and the Alphabet* (Berkeley: Druckwerk, 1986), printed in an edition of 50 copies, the "normal" printface of the opening page evolves, as soon as the first page is turned into something else: double-sized boldface letters start to jump out from the words and form their own words, and as the "story" continues, alternate words are introduced along with extra lines (in miniature print), italics, and so on. On the last page, typography brings together "the possession of the site," "experience," and "response," in a provocative and challenging semiotic structure.

For Drucker's earlier work, see *Twenty-Six '76 Let Her's* (Chased Press,

1976); *From A to Z* (Chased Press, 1977), *'S Crap 'S Ample* (Chased Press, 1980), *Against Fiction* (Druckwerk, 1985), and *Through Light and the Alphabet* (Druckwerk, 1986).

28. Johanna Drucker, "Hypergraphy: A Note on Maurice Lemaître's Roman Hypergraphique," *Poetics Journal* 6 (1986): 115.

29. I owe this insight to the author (letter to me, 4 May 1990), in which she writes, "The title of the red text . . . is 'The Flesh Made Word'. . . . The idea was partly conceived as a way to critique (humorously) the possibility of transcendence—here the referent is also material, thus, materiality is both the resistant form and the referent, returning one to the stuff on the page."

30. Steve McCaffery, *North of Intention: Critical Writings, 1973–86* (New York: Roof Books, 1986), p. 105.

31. Frederick Garber, "Re Positioning: The Syntaxes of Barbara Kruger," *University of Hartford Studies in Literature* 21 (1989): 4, subsequently cited in the text as FG. See also Craig Owens, "The Medusa Effect, or The Spectacular Ruse," in *We Won't Play Nature to Your Culture*, catalog of an exhibition of photographic montages by Barbara Kruger (London: Institute of Contemporary Arts, 1983); and Owens, "The Discourse of Others: Feminists and Postmodernism," in *The Anti-Aesthetic: Essays on Postmodern Culture*, ed. Hal Foster (Port Townsend, WA: Bay Press, 1983), pp. 75–77; Kate Linker, "Representation and Sexuality," *Art after Modernism: Rethinking Representation*, ed. Brian Wallis (Boston: David Godine, 1984), p. 414; Henry M. Sayre, *The Object of Performance: The American Avant Garde Since 1970* (Chicago and London: University of Chicago Press, 1989), pp. 192–201. Sayre writes enthusiastically of Kruger and Jenny Holzer, whose work raises similar issues, although it seems to me much more successful than Kruger's, a comparison I can't develop fully here. On Holzer's 1990 Guggenheim show, featuring electronic billboards, see Mark Stevens, "Jenny Takes a Ride," *New Republic*, 26 March 1990, pp. 30–33.

Chapter 5

1. Denise Levertov, "Some Notes on Organic Form" (1965), in *The Poet in the World* (New York: New Directions, 1973), p. 11.

2. Jacques Roubaud, "Mathematics in the Method of Raymond Queneau," in *Oulipo: A Primer of Potential Literature*, ed. and trans. Warren F. Motte, Jr. (Lincoln and London: University of Nebraska Press, 1986), p. 93. Subsequently cited in the text as OU.

3. Marcel Bénabou, "La Règle et le contrainte," *Pratiques* 39 (1983); rpt. in OU, p. 41.

4. Charles Olson, "Projective Verse," *Selected Writings*, ed. Robert Creeley (New York: New Directions, 1966), p. 19.

5. Allen Ginsberg, "'When the Mode of the Music Changes the Walls of the City Shake,'" in *The Poetics of the New American Poetry*, ed. Donald M. Allen and Warren Tallman (New York: Grove Press, 1973), pp. 324–25.

6. Frederick Seidel, "An Interview with Robert Lowell," *Paris Review* 25 (Winter-Spring 1961); rpt. Michael London and Robert Boyers, eds., *Robert*

Lowell: A Portrait of the Artist in His Time (New York: David Lewis, 1970), p. 270. For a typical later formulation of this view, cf. Stanley Plumly, "Chapter and Verse," *American Poetry Review* 7, no. 1 (January-February 1978): 23: "Free verse is really flexible verse. . . . [it] makes for a poetry at once more responsive and potentially irresponsible, as if each event, each experience had its own free verse equivalent in form."

7. Anthony Easthope, *Poetry as Discourse* (London and New York: Methuen, 1983), pp. 152–53. Subsequently cited in the text as AE. The Pound citation is from "A Retrospect," *The Literary Essays of Ezra Pound* (London: Faber & Faber, 1963), p. 9.

8. D. H. Lawrence, "Poetry of the Present" (Preface to the American Edition of *New Poems* [1918])," in *The Completed Poems of D. H. Lawrence*, ed. Vivian de Sola Pinto and F. Warren Roberts (New York: Viking Press, 1971), pp. 184–85.

9. Marjorie Perloff, "Lawrence's Lyric Theatre: *Birds, Beasts and Flowers*," in *D. H. Lawrence: A Centenary Consideration*, ed. Peter Balbert and Phillip Marcus (Ithaca: Cornell University Press, 1985), pp. 108–29; rpt. in *Poetic License: Studies in Modernist and Postmodernist Lyric* (Evanston: Northwestern University Press, 1990), pp. 99–117.

10. Robert Hass, "One Body: Some Notes on Form," *Twentieth-Century Pleasures: Prose on Poetry* (New York: Ecco Press, 1984), p. 70. Cf. Ron Silliman, "Interview with Tom Beckett," *The Difficulties: Ron Silliman Issue* 2, no. 2 (1985): "The closed forms of the Academics (so-called) admitted their self-constructedness, but were non-generative, capable only of the repetition of the past in the face of the present. The open forms of the New Americans (so-called) concealed their 'madeness,' but for a time offered a more fully generative response to daily life. Once, however, the creative euphoria of sketching out what the false model of a (non-constructed because 'natural') speech-imitating poetics would look like was complete, the same limiting claustrophobia set it" (p. 34). This issue of *The Difficulties* is subsequently cited as DRS.

11. The single exception is James Stone's translation of Sappho, rendered in four-line Sapphic stanzas.

12. See, for example, Charles O. Hartman in *Free Verse: An Essay on Prosody* (Princeton: Princeton University Press, 1980), p. 11: "*Verse is language in lines.* . . . This is not a really satisfying distinction, as it stands, but it is the only one that works absolutely. The fact that we can tell verse from prose on sight, with very few errors . . . indicates that the basic perceptual difference must be very simple."

13. Brad Leithauser, "Symposium," *Crosscurrents* 8, no. 2 (1989); reprinted in *Expansionist Poetry: The New Formalism and the New Narrative*, pp. 91–92. Subsequently cited in the text as CC.

14. Timothy Steele, "Symposium," CC 101. Steele's more recent book-length study *Missing Measures: Modern Poetry and the Revolt against Meter* (Fayetteville and London: University of Arkansas Press, 1990), subsequently cited as MM, is ostensibly a history of the rise, in the early twentieth century, of the

free verse aesthetic and its subsequent hegemony, but the book is more properly understood as a disguised New Formalist manifesto pleading for a return to meter. Steele's critique of the free-verse model is often on target, but his argument is vitiated, at least for me, by his either/or model (a model he claims to derive from classical precedent but which explains away Aristotle's crucial distinction between *verse* and *poetry* [pp. 112–31, 166–70]), which regards poetry as written *either* in "meter" *or* in "free verse," ignoring the complex shadings of the two. Thus Steele criticizes Eliot's discrimination between "poetry" and "verse" on the grounds that "the discrimination deprives metrical composition not only of its claims to 'poetry,' but makes it share its claim to 'verse' with free verse" (p. 285), thus ignoring Eliot's actual practice, which honors traditional prosodic precedent even as it abjures standard meters: see note 17 below.

15. Henri Meschonnic, *Critique du rythme: Anthropologie historique du langage* (Paris: Editions Verdier, 1982), esp. chap. 9, pp. 395–436. Meschonnic takes up, one by one, all the possible explanations of verse structure, demonstrating how relativistic such explanations are.

16. See Jacques Roubaud, *La vieillesse d'Alexandre. Essay sur quelques états récents du vers français* (Paris: Maspéro, 1978).

17. In "Reflections on Vers Libre" (1917), Eliot makes his own position very clear: "the most interesting verse which has yet been written in our language has been done either by taking a very simple form, like the iambic pentameter, and constantly withdrawing from it, or taking no form at all, and constantly approximating to a very simple one. It is this contrast between fixity and flux, this unperceived evasion of monotony, which is the very life of verse." And a few pages later in the same essay: "the ghost of some simple metre should lurk behind the arras in even the 'freest' verse; to advance menacingly as we doze, and withdraw as we rouse"; *To Criticize the Critic* (New York: Farrar, Straus & Giroux, 1965), pp. 185, 187.

Eliot's own poetry fulfills these mandates: in "Prufrock" and "Portrait of a Lady," for example, the verse can be seen to "constantly withdraw" from the iambic pentameter; *The Waste Land* and *Four Quartets* are written essentially in the alliterative four-stress line, with iambic pentameter insertions and occasional longer measures. But, as Eliot himself says, there is nothing "free" about this verse.

18. Easthope himself approvingly cites Derrida's argument against logocentrism ("the view that speech is the original source of meaning and the location of its full presence") and his emphasis on the "graphematic structure of every 'communication'" (AE 13–15).

19. This is the assumption behind New Formalist practice. Timothy Steele, for example, declares that "What is most essential to human life and to its continuance remains a love of nature, an enthusiasm for justice, a readiness of good humor, a spontaneous susceptibility to beauty and joy, an interest in our past, a hope for our future, and, above all, a desire that others should have the opportunity and encouragement to share these qualities. An art of measured speech nourishes these qualities in a way no other pursuit can" (MM 294). And Steele cites Robert Frost's "The Aim Was Song" as his Exhibit A.

Notice that Steele takes for granted the poetry = speech equation even as he assumes that "nature" is somehow beyond cultural contamination, a universal to be "loved."

20. Jacques Derrida, *Of Grammatology*, trans. Gayatri Chakravorty Spivak (Baltimore and London: Johns Hopkins University Press, 1976), pp. 8–9, 70–71.

21. John Ashbery, "The Songs We Know Best," *A Wave* (New York: Viking Press, 1984), p. 3.

22. In "History of the Lipogram" (OU 97–108), Perec traces the form back to Lasus of Hermione (sixth century B.C.), noting that "according to [Ernst] Curtius, [it is] the most ancient systematic artifice of Western literature" (p. 100). An interesting ancient example is Nestor of Laranda's rewriting of the *Iliad*, denying himself the alpha in the first canto, the beta in the second, the gamma in the third, and so on (OU 100–101). Perec cites many German and Spanish examples from medieval and Renaissance writings.

23. The "S + 7 method," says Raymond Queneau, "consists in taking a text and replacing each substantive with the seventh following it in a given dictionary. The result obviously depends on the dictionary one chooses. Naturally, the number seven is arbitrary. Of course, if one takes, for example, a 2,000-word dictionary and uses the S + 2000 Method, one ends up with the original text" ("Potential Literature," OU 61).

24. Meschonnic (HM 576) cites Michel Butor, "La prosodie de Villon," *Critique*, no. 310 (March 1973), p. 284: Roubaud "a voulu fuir le poème qui colle au poète comme un vêtement (même 'splendid') pour chercher dans une structure à la fois très contraignant et très riche en relations formelles, un approfondissement de la grammaire du poème."

25. Cited by Gabriel Josipovici, "Georges Perec's Homage to Joyce and Tradition," *Yearbook of English Studies*, ed. C. J. Rawson and Jenny Mezciems (London: Modern Humanities Research Association, 1985), p. 181. Subsequently cited in the text as GJ.

26. Georges Perec, *La Vie mode d'emploi* (Paris: Gallimard, 1978). The diagram of the apartment building appears on p. 603. For the English translation, see *Life: A User's Manual*, trans. David Bellos (Boston: David Godine, 1987); the diagram is on p. 501. Subsequently cited in the text as LUM.

27. The pages of the Preamble are unnumbered. But this particular discussion of jigsaw puzzles is repeated verbatim in chapter 44 ("Winckler," 2), pp. 189–91. Perhaps Perec wanted to remind us of the puzzle metaphor; perhaps he wanted us to relate puzzling to Winckler rather than to a generalized narrative voice.

28. David Bellos, "Georges Perec's Puzzling Style," *Scripsi* 5, no. 1 (1988): 63–78, esp. p. 66. Subsequently cited in the text as DB.

29. *80 Flowers*, published in a very limited and expensive edition (80 copies) by the Stinehour Press, New York, in 1978, has only recently been reprinted in Louis Zukofsky, *Complete Short Poetry* (Baltimore and London: Johns Hopkins University Press, 1991), pp. 325–51. Subsequently cited in the text as CSP. The entire text is cited in the poem-by-poem analysis made by Michele J. Leggott in her important recent study *Reading Zukofsky's 80 Flowers*

(Baltimore and London: Johns Hopkins University Press, 1989), to which I am heavily indebted in what follows. The notebook entries cited are reproduced by Leggott on pp. 12–14. The book is subsequently cited in the text as RZ.

30. Like Perec, Zukofsky puts a slight bend in his system: there are in fact 81, not 80, poems in *80 Flowers* (the first being an epigraph) and certain other variations are introduced (see RZ 74–90).

31. For careful analysis of the poem's etymologies, sources (Chaucer, Theophrastus, Dante, Rossetti), and word play, see RZ 90–103.

32. David Lévi-Strauss, "Approaching *80 Flowers*," in *Code of Signals: Recent Writings in Poetics*, ed. Michael Palmer (Berkeley: North Atlantic Books, 1983), pp. 86–87. Subsequently cited in the text as DLS.

33. Rosalind E. Krauss, "Grids," *The Originality of the Avant-Garde and Other Modernist Myths* (Cambridge and London: MIT Press, 1985), p. 9.

34. IRCAM is the acronym for Institut de recherche et de coordination acoustique/musique. *Roaratorio* has gone through many incarnations, having become, notably, a dance piece for the Merce Cunningham company as well; in this guise, it was first performed by Cage and Cunningham at the Brooklyn Academy of Music in 1986.

35. The full title is *I–VI* (**MethodStructureIntentionDisciplineNotationIndeterminacyInterpenetrationImitationDevotionCircumstancesVariableStructureNonunderstandingConsistencyInconsistencyPerformance**) (Cambridge: Harvard University Press, 1990).

36. Edward Rothstein, "Cage's Cage," *New Republic*, 28 May 1990, pp. 26–27. My italics.

37. John Cage, "_____, _____ _____ Circus on _____," in *Roaratorio: An Irish Circus on Finnegans Wake*, Sound and Text, ed. Klaus Schoening (Koeningstein: Atheneum Verlag, 1982), p. 173. This text is subsequently cited as R. My italics.

38. Cf. Henri Meschonnic: "Un paradoxe de la combinatoire est que, tout en étant à l'exact opposé de l'aléatoire, elle en partage le déni du sens comme historicité des sujets. Elle en partage le ludique, même si elle joue autrement" (HM 576).

39. See John Cage, interview with Paul Hersch, Santa Cruz, CA, 1982; rpt. in Richard Kostelanetz, ed., *Conversing with Cage* (New York: Limelight Editions, 1988), p. 151. This text is subsequently cited as CC.

In the standard Viking Press edition (1972), the text opens on p. 3 and the final page is 628, i.e., 626 pages in all. Subsequently cited as FW.

40. See R 144–45 for a complete listing of the participating musicians, the musical pieces played by each one, and their time of entry.

41. Cage explains: "I removed the punctuation too. And then sent it through chance-operations back on the page. So that each page is illustrated by its punctuation rather than clarified by its punctuation" (R 85). Thus commas, exclamation points, parentheses and the like are scattered around the page, becoming part of its visual design.

42. W. B. Yeats, "Stream and Sun at Glendalough," *The Poems* (revised), ed. Richard J. Finneran (New York: Macmillan, 1988), p. 255.

43. Richard A. Lanham, "The Extraordinary Convergence," *South Atlantic Quarterly* 89, no. 1 (Winter 1990): 31. Subsequently cited as RLEC.

44. See James Gleick, *Chaos: Making a New Science* (New York: Penguin Books, 1987), p. 102.

45. Ron Silliman, *Tjanting* (Berkeley: Figures, 1981), pp. 11–13.

46. See Charles Bernstein, "Narrating Narration: The Shapes of Ron Silliman's Work," DRS 94–95; reprinted in *Content's Dream*, pp. 309–12.

47. Lyn Hejinian, *My Life* (Providence, RI: Burning Deck Press, 1980).

48. Lyn Hejinian, *My Life* (Los Angeles: Sun & Moon Press, 1987). All subsequent references are to this edition, designated as ML.

49. Lyn Hejinian, "If Written Is Writing," in Bruce Andrews and Charles Bernstein, eds., *The L=A=N=G=U=A=G=E Book* (Carbondale and Edwardsville: Southern Illinois University Press, 1984), p. 29.

50. Cited in HM 576. The translation is mine.

Chapter 6

1. Theodor Adorno, *Minima Moralia: Reflections from Damaged Life*, trans. from the German by E. F. N. Jephcott (1951; London: Verso, 1974), p. 101.

2. Ludwig Wittgenstein, *Culture and Value*, ed. G. H. von Wright, trans. Peter Winch (Chicago: University of Chicago Press, 1980), p. 2e (1929).

3. Rod Mengham, review essay on recent "Language writing" books (Charles Bernstein, Bruce Andrews, Barrett Watten, Steve McCaffery, Clark Coolidge), *Textual Practice* 3, no. 1 (Spring 1989): 114–23, p. 116. Subsequently cited as RM.

4. Cleanth Brooks, *The Well Wrought Urn* (New York: Harcourt Brace, 1947), p. 196. Subsequently cited as WU.

5. Eliot Weinberger, "A Note on *Montemora*, America and the World," *Sulfur* 20 (Fall 1987): 197. This polemic essay, written by a poet-translator himself strongly committed to avant-garde writing, generated equally polemic response; see the debate between Michael Davidson and Weinberger in *Sulfur* 22 (Spring 1988): 177–88, and cf. the further letters by Rachel Blau du Plessis and Clayton Eshleman as well as Weinberger's rather ominously titled "Final Response," pp. 188–202.

6. Albert Gelpi, "The Genealogy of Postmodernism: Contemporary American Poetry," *Southern Review* 26 (Summer 1990): 532.

7. Robert von Hallberg, "American Poetry, 1945–1990," forthcoming in *Cambridge History of American Literature*, ed. Sacvan Bercovitch, Vol. 5 (1993).

8. Charles Altieri, "Without Consequences Is No Politics: A Response to Jerome McGann," *Critical Inquiry* 13 (Spring 1987); rpt. in *Politics and Poetic Value*, ed. Robert von Hallberg (Chicago and London: University of Chicago Press, 1987), p. 304. The essay to which Altieri is responding, "Contemporary Poetry, Alternate Routes," appears in the same issue of *Critical Inquiry* and then *Politics and Poetic Value*, subsequently cited as PPV.

The argument against the reification of language is also made by Rod Mengham in the *Textual Practice* essay, pp. 117–20.

9. In the case of self-declared avant-garde movements, the first stage of

criticism is almost inevitably one of exposition and advocacy: the poets' theories are cited, explained, and clarified for a readership not yet familiar with them. When, for example, F. O. Matthiessen wrote on T. S. Eliot in the mid-thirties, he gave an "inside" view of the "objective correlative," explaining, as clearly as possible, what Eliot himself meant by the term; by the late fifties, however, the "objective correlative" was being reassessed as a later version of the romantic symbol; see, for example, Frank Kermode, *Romantic Image* (1957; New York: Vintage, 1964), chaps. 7 and 8. Again, Black Mountain, which seemed to early commentators as a cohesive movement of like-minded poets, now strikes us as a fairly dubious category, a "Black Mountain poet" like Denise Levertov having little in common with Charles Olson.

In the same vein, examination of "language poetry" and its cognates began largely as clarification and defense of a new and difficult poetics: see my own "The Word as Such: L=A=N=G=U=A=G=E Poetry in the Eighties," *The Dance of the Intellect: Studies in the Poetry of the Pound Tradition* (Cambridge and New York: Cambridge University Press, 1985), pp. 215–38; Jerome J. McGann's "Contemporary Poetry, Alternate Routes," PPV, cited in the preceding note; and George Hartley's very interesting *Textual Politics and the Language Poets* (Bloomington and Indianapolis: Indiana University Press, 1989).

Inevitably, the exposition-advocacy model also leads to detraction, not of the poetry as such, which continues to be accorded second place, but of the theory of language poetry. See, for example, Andrew Lawson, "The Short Revolution: Reassessing Language Writing," *Fragmente* 2 (Autumn 1990): 73–79.

10. Bruce Andrews, "Text and Context," in *The L=A=N=G=U=A=G=E Book*, ed. Bruce Andrews and Charles Bernstein (Carbondale and Edwardsville: Southern Illinois University Press, 1984), p. 35. This volume is subsequently cited as LB.

11. Lyn Hejinian, "Variations: A Return of Words," *In the American Tree*, ed. Ron Silliman (Orono, ME: National Poetry Foundation, 1986), p. 507. Subsequently cited as IAT.

12. See Ron Silliman, ed., *In the American Tree* (Orono, ME: National Poetry Foundation, 1986); Douglas Messerli, ed., *Language Poetries: An Anthology* (New York: New Directions, 1986).

More recent proto-Language journals like *O.blek*, *Writing*, *Raddle Moon*, *Paper Air*, and *Talisman*, as well as *Sulfur* itself and *Temblor*, whose ten issues, edited by Lee Hickman, constitute one of the most important forums for the new work, have always taken pains to maintain a broader base than "language poetry."

13. See *Sulfur* 22:180. Weinberger makes further exceptions of "Jackson Mac Low (whose inclusion in the Messerli anthology is rather like the Red Brigades bestowing honorary membership on Jean-Paul Sartre), Bernadette Mayer (whose presence in the Silliman book I can't understand), and the two writers of crystalline narrative prose, Robert Gluck and Lydia Davis, whose appearance in the 'language' poetry canon is the greatest mystery of all" (p. 181). Which is to say that seven of the so-called Language poets aren't Language

poets—a disclaimer that certainly qualifies Weinberger's assertions about the movement's failures.

14. Charles Bernstein, "Safe Methods of Business," *The Sophist* (Los Angeles: Sun & Moon Press, 1987), pp. 134–43. Subsequently cited in the text as S.

15. John Ashbery, "Business Personals," *Houseboat Days* (New York: Viking Press, 1977), pp. 18–20. This volume is subsequently cited in the text as HD.

16. Fredric Jameson, "Postmodernism and Consumer Society," in *The Anti-Aesthetic: Essays on Postmodern Culture*, ed. Hal Foster (Port Townsend, WA: Bay Press, 1983), pp. 114–15. In the longer version of this essay in Jameson, *Postmodernism, Or, The Cultural Logic of Late Capitalism* (Durham, N.C.: Duke University Press, 1991), the wording is slightly different; see pp. 16–19.

17. The phrase is Antoine Compagnon's: "Ce livre pose une question de principe: comment se débrouiller dans les broussailles du *déjà dit?* Problème de la quadrature du cercle ou du mouvement perpétuel." See Compagnon, *La seconde main, ou le travail de la citation* (Paris: Editions du Seuil, 1979), p. 9, and Sequence I passim. One of Compagnon's arguments in this seminal study is that the still common view of citation as, at best, "just a copy," and, at worst, plagiarism, has to do with nineteenth- and early twentieth-century notions of private property, ownership, and copyright, notions that are being eroded in a more collectivist age like ours.

18. Hart Crane, *The Complete Poems and Selected Letters and Prose*, ed. Brom Weber (New York: Doubleday Anchor, 1966), p. 23. Subsequently cited as HC.

19. William Paulson, *The Noise of Culture: Literary Texts in a World of Information* (Ithaca, NY: Cornell University Press, 1988), p. 67. Subsequently cited as WP.

20. The translation is that of W. Hamilton Fyfe for the Loeb Classics, Aristotle, *The Poetics*, "Longinus," *On the Sublime*, Demetrius, *On Style* (Cambridge, MA: Harvard University Press, 1960), p. 43.

21. Charles Bernstein, "Hot Circuits: A Video Arcade," *American Museum of the Moving Image*, 14 June–26 November 1989, p. 4. Subsequently cited as HC.

22. See Sculley Bradley and Harold W. Blodgett, Introduction, Walt Whitman, *Leaves of Grass*, A Norton Critical Edition (New York: W. W. Norton & Co., 1973), pp. xxxii–xxxiii. Subsequently cited as WW.

23. See, for example, the reference to "hot Carolina" in "Over the Carnage Rose Prophetic a Voice," WW 315–16.

24. Samuel Beckett, *Happy Days* (New York: Grove Press, 1961), p. 57. The poem Winnie is trying to remember is by the minor part Charles Wolfe, hardly a "classic," although throughout *Happy Days*, Winnie does use garbled quotes from *Hamlet*, *Twelfth Night*, *Romeo and Juliet*, *Paradise Lost*, and so on.

25. Michel de Certeau, "The Jabbering of Social Life," in *On Signs*, ed. Marshall Blonsky (Baltimore: Johns Hopkins University Press, 1985), p. 151.

26. David Margolick, "Ignorance of *L.A. Law* Is No Excuse for Lawyers," *New York Times*, 6 May 1990, pp. 27, 29. Subsequently cited as LL.

Chapter 7

1. Reported by Eric Bentley, "Postscript 1967," review of *Waiting for Godot*, in *New Republic*, 14 May 1956, in *Samuel Beckett: The Critical Heritage*, ed. Lawrence Graver and Raymond Federman (London and Boston: Routledge & Kegan Paul, 1979), p. 110.
The title of this chapter comes from Augusto de Campos's fascinating paracritical book *o anticritico* (São Paulo: Companhia das Letras, Editora Schwarcz Ltda., 1986), pp. 211–27. The title *cage: chance: change* introduces a critical text in the form of a poem that both explains and applies the Cagean aesthetic.

2. Or the other way around, which is, of course, an instance of the same thing. The purportedly "realistic" social and political awareness of Brecht, for example, is, as Jan Kott slyly implies above, qualified by a stylization, a parabolic figuration and ambiguity, that places Brecht in the tradition of the fantastic rather than in the line of nineteenth-century naturalism.

3. Kott's prescience in this regard is no doubt related to his own experience in wartime Poland, an experience that surely made it impossible *not* to notice the political dimension of Beckett's play.

4. *Happy Days*, starring Charlotte Raye and directed by Carey Perloff, played between March and May 1990. As the director's mother, I attended a number of performances and had a chance to observe audience reaction both in and out of the ladies' room. Reaction was about evenly divided between those who were captivated by Beckett's painful text and those who dismissed it as "not being *about* anything," and therefore "boring."

5. Russell A. Berman, *Modern Culture and Critical Theory: Art, Politics, and the Legacy of the Frankfurt School* (Madison: University of Wisconsin Press, 1989), p. 89.

6. For a particularly reductive version, see Jim Collins, *Uncommon Cultures: Popular Culture and Post-Modernism* (New York and London: Routledge, 1989). Unlike Berman and, to some extent, Huyssen, both of whom recognize the difficulties in postmodernism, Collins regards the demise of the modernist view of "culture," which he takes to be a kind of "Grand Hotel," a "totalizable system that somehow orchestrates all cultural production and reception according to one master system" (p. xiii), as a step forward. Indeed, Collins's straw-man modernism, which reduces the extraordinarily varied art practices of the early twentieth century to so much "centered," "mastersystem" pulp, is presented as so objectionable that its opposite, the nonelitist postmodernism that presumably makes no distinction between "high" and "low" or "avant-garde" and "popular culture," is welcomed as the demise of anything so elitist as "high" art.

7. See, on this point, Matei Calinescu, *Five Faces of Modernity: Modernism, Avant-Garde, Decadence, Kitsch, Postmodernism* (Durham: Duke University Press, 1987), pp. 288–96. Hilton Kramer's *New Criterion* remains committed to Clement Greenberg's "high art" notions.

8. Joan Retallack, letter to the author, 29 November 1990.

9. See John Darter, interview with Cage, *Keyboard* (September 1982), re-

produced in Richard Kostelanetz, *Conversing with Cage* (New York: Limelight Editions, 1988), p. 237. Cage elaborates this point by telling an amusing anecdote: "I was present when Stravinsky conducted one of his early pieces for orchestra, one of the ballets, and after it was finished, [a] child turned to his father—they were sitting in front of me—and he said, 'That isn't the way it goes.'" "Record listeners," in other words, "are not really prepared for listening to live music" (p. 237). Or, as Cage told Jeff Goldberg in 1974, "All [hi-fi records do] is move toward a faithful reproduction of something that's already happened" (Kostelanetz, pp. 237–38 and cf. p. 116).

10. Edward Rothstein, *New Republic*, 28 May 1990, pp. 25–28.

11. Anthony Tommasini, "The Zest of the Uninteresting," *New York Times*, 23 April 1989, p. 27. Tommasini's feature article is an unusually fine piece of reporting.

12. See Mark Swed, "John Cage: A Rebel Sets Up Shop in Ivied Halls," *Los Angeles Times: Calendar* (13 November 1988), pp. 69–70; John Rockwell, "A Man Inspired by Chance," *New York Times Book Review*, 13 May 1990, p. 10.

13. T. S. Eliot, *The Use of Poetry and the Use of Criticism: Studies in the Relation of Criticism to Poetry in England* (1933; Cambridge, MA: Harvard University Press, 1964), p. 6.

14. For a discussion of the "mesostic" mode of *Roaratorio*, see chap. 5. In the Introduction to *I–VI* (p. 1), Cage gives this definition: A mesostic "is a string which spells a word or name, not necessarily connected with what is being written, though it may be. This vertical rule is lettristic and in my practice the letters are capitalized. Between two capitals in a perfect or 100% mesostic neither letter may appear in lower case. In an imperfect or 50% mesostic the first letter may reappear but the second is not permitted until its appearance on the second line as a capital in the string."

15. John Cage, *Silence* (1961; Middletown, CT: Wesleyan University Press, 1976), p. x.

16. John Cage, *For the Birds: John Cage in Conversation with Daniel Charles* (Boston and London: Marion Boyers, 1981), p. 56.

Index